CONTENTS

CW00751254

INTRODUCTION

The so-called Battle of the Atlantic was actually the longest naval campaign of World War II. Fought between the Allies and the Germans, it was the most important and best-known naval campaign in the European theatre. Because of its expanse, complexity and duration, this account has been broken into several parts. This volume is the first of three that will examine the struggle between Allied naval and air forces and the German U-boat force in the Atlantic. This is something of an artificial division since the Germans were fighting a 'tonnage' war with the goal of sinking as many Allied merchant ships as possible using a variety of forces, not just U-boats, and in many areas besides the Atlantic. Focusing on the Atlantic will preclude detailed treatment of U-boat operations in other ocean areas. Other volumes will examine the German Navy's attempts to use large surface combatants as commerce raiders and its efforts to employ disguised surface raiders against Allied shipping.

ORIGINS OF THE CAMPAIGN

Before World War I, the Germans spent enormous resources on a battle fleet built around state-of-the-art dreadnoughts to challenge the power of the Royal Navy (RN). The German battle fleet proved of little use during the war, being bottled up in the North Sea. Meanwhile, the RN instituted a stifling blockade of German ports, which had the long-term aim of strangling Germany and its war effort. Given the inability of the German fleet to threaten British control of key sea areas or to attack British commerce, the U-boat (*Unterseeboot* shortened to *U-Boot*) became the German Navy's primary striking force.

The Germans first used U-boats to attack British shipping in October 1914. By an agreed convention among the maritime powers, these attacks were to be conducted under 'prize regulations', which required the U-boat to surface in order to remove the crew and passengers and move them to 'a place of safety' (for which lifeboats did not usually qualify) before sinking the ship. Such a procedure left the U-boat in an extremely vulnerable position and eliminated all the strengths of a submarine. In practice, German U-boat commanders did not always adhere to prize regulations, even early in the war. Making the use of prize regulations even more problematic was the British tactic of deploying Q-ships, which were merchant ships equipped with hidden guns used to lure the unsuspecting U-boats to their demise.

CAMPAIGN 408

BATTLE OF THE ATLANTIC (1)

The U-Boat Campaign against Britain, 1939–41

MARK STILLE   ILLUSTRATED BY JIM LAURIER

OSPREY PUBLISHING
Bloomsbury Publishing Plc
Kemp House, Chawley Park, Cumnor Hill, Oxford OX2 9PH, UK
29 Earlsfort Terrace, Dublin 2, Ireland
1385 Broadway, 5th Floor, New York, NY 10018, USA
E-mail: info@ospreypublishing.com
www.ospreypublishing.com

OSPREY is a trademark of Osprey Publishing Ltd

First published in Great Britain in 2024

A catalogue record for this book is available from the British Library.

ISBN: PB 9781472861368; eBook 9781472861337; ePDF 9781472861344;
XML 9781472861351

24 25 26 27 28   10 9 8 7 6 5 4 3 2 1

Maps by Bounford.com
3D BEVs by Paul Kime
Index by Alan Rutter
Typeset by PDQ Digital Media Solutions, Bungay, UK
Printed by Repro India Ltd.

Osprey Publishing supports the Woodland Trust, the UK's leading woodland
conservation charity.

To find out more about our authors and books visit
www.ospreypublishing.com. Here you will find extracts, author
interviews, details of forthcoming events and the option to sign up for
our newsletter.

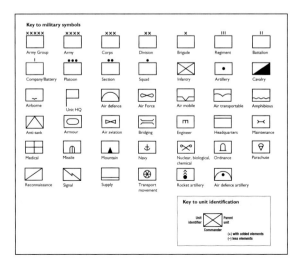

Front Cover Main Illustration: U-boat attack on HX 72 on
21/22 September 1940. (Jim Laurier)
Title page image: All 24 Type VIIB boats were completed by early 1940,
making them a mainstay in the opening phases of the Atlantic campaign.
(Naval History and Heritage Command)

In an all too familiar sight from World War I, British steamship SS *City of Glasgow* sinks after being torpedoed in the Irish Sea on 1 September 1918. Note the ship is painted in dazzle camouflage, a tactic that was not as widely repeated in World War II. During the first Atlantic campaign of World War I, U-boats sank some 12.5 million Gross Register Tons (GRT) of Allied and neutral shipping, almost bringing the Allied war effort to collapse. (Naval History and Heritage Command)

Under prize regulations restrictions, it was impossible for the Germans to achieve decisive results against British shipping. In an attempt to starve Britain before the British blockade defeated Germany, on 4 February 1915 the Germans declared a blockade zone around Britain to pursue unrestricted submarine warfare. Merchant ships would be sunk without warning in this area. During this period, British counter-measures were immature and ineffective – there were no means to attack or even detect submerged U-boats. Despite good results in terms of ships (370) and tonnage (750,000) sunk, the Germans were forced to abandon their unrestricted submarine warfare campaign on 1 September 1915 after the loss of American ships and lives threatened to bring the United States into the war. The Germans simply lacked the means to inflict decisive sustained losses on British shipping with only 37 submarines available at the start of the unrestricted warfare campaign.

After trying unsuccessfully to use their battle fleet more aggressively in 1916 and the failure of another restricted submarine warfare campaign under the prize regulations beginning in October of that year, the Germans decided to resume unrestricted submarine warfare on 1 February 1917. There was no other choice. The efforts of the U-boats from 1914 to 1916 were ineffective. By the end of 1916, Britain's Merchant Navy was still 94 per cent of the size it was at the start of the war. Now the Germans assessed that if they could sink 600,000 GRT of shipping per month for five months, Britain would be forced to negotiate for peace by August.

At the start of the new campaign, the Germans had 105 U-boats. Even though not all of these were available or suited to operations in the Atlantic, this gave the Germans hopes for success. The U-boat force reached a peak of 129 boats on 1 June 1917. Early results were encouraging. In February, 414,000 GRT were sunk in the waters around Britain, with the total tonnage sunk in all areas coming to 540,412. In the following month, losses around Britain rose to 500,000 GRT of the total of 564,497 GRT lost. In April, losses reached crisis proportions of 860,334 GRT lost overall, with 600,000 GRT sunk in British waters. Only nine U-boats were lost in the first three months of the campaign, and in April, the exchange rate was 167 merchants sunk for every U-boat lost. Had losses continued at this pace, the British would have been compelled to make peace by November. However, this early success came at a price when the US entered the war on 6 April. This was

One of the measures undertaken by the Allies during World War I was to establish a mine barrier to prevent U-boats from exiting the North Sea. In this view from 1918, American minelayer USS *Shawmut* lays mines under cover of a RN destroyer. German control of Norway in World War II prevented a repeat performance by the Allies in the second Atlantic campaign. German possession of bases in France made the U-boat threat much more significant in World War II. (Naval History and Heritage Command)

not unexpected, but the Germans made the calculation that they could defeat the Allies before the US could mobilize and send a significant number of troops to Europe.

The British responded slowly to the U-boat peril. In particular, the RN resisted the call for instituting convoys. There were many reasons, primarily based on the supposed lack of escorts and the vulnerability of the convoys to detection and attack. Probably the biggest argument rested on the RN's reluctance to assume a 'defensive' stance by resorting to convoys. In fact, convoys offered a greater chance to attack U-boats. It reduced the number of targets available to the U-boats, and when convoys were detected, it made the U-boats attack the most heavily defended spots in the ocean. So deep was the reluctance to adopt convoys, that in December 1917 with losses mounting, the First Lord of the Admiralty was forced to dismiss Admiral John Jellicoe from his post as First Sea Lord in part for his opposition to the institution of the practice.

In spite of this resistance, desperation forced the introduction of convoys beginning in May. It took many months to organize all shipping into convoys, but losses began to fall almost immediately. Within the first three months of convoying, just 27 ships of the 8,894 in convoy were lost. However, not all ships were organized this way – in the same period 365 ships were lost as they proceeded independently.

Beginning in May 1917, the British instituted transatlantic convoys. Until the end of the war, just over 1 per cent of ships in convoy headed to England were sunk (104 out of 9,250); for outbound convoys, the losses were even lower (0.68 per cent) with 50 out of 7,289 ships being lost. These figures include 36 ships that failed to keep up with their convoy (becoming stragglers) and another 16 lost to weather. More than any other factor, convoys defeated the U-boats in World War I. Losses for the remainder of 1917 went down from a high of 696,725 GRT in June to a low of 302,599 GRT in November.

As losses in the Atlantic decreased, the Germans concentrated on attacking shipping in the Mediterranean in order to reach their 600,000 GRT per month goal. Because use of convoys was less prevalent in the Mediterranean, shipping losses there remained high and, in 1918, accounted for nearly a third of all shipping losses. After the Allies introduced convoys to the Mediterranean on a widespread basis, the Germans once again switched tactics by concentrating on attacking shipping in British coastal waters after convoys dispersed and the ships headed to their individual ports. Eventually, enough escorts were found to create coastal convoys and by the end of the war almost all shipping was convoyed. In coastal areas, the use of aircraft proved extremely useful. Their presence near a convoy was sufficient to force a U-boat to submerge, greatly reducing its effectiveness.

In addition to convoys and Q-ships, many other measures were introduced to neutralize the U-boat threat. Direction-finding stations were used to locate U-boats when they communicated so that convoys could be steered away from them. Late in the war, sonar (an underwater locating device that uses sound waves) and depth charges (an explosive charge dropped into the water and set to explode at a pre-determined depth) were introduced. Mines also proved to be a formidable weapon. A mine barrier was laid across the Strait of Dover to close the English Channel as a transit route to the key South-West Approaches to Britain. By February 1918, the barrier had destroyed enough U-boats to force all but the small U-boats based in Belgium to transit around Scotland instead of using the English Channel. In 1918, the Allies, led by the United States Navy (USN), attempted to establish a mine barrier across the southern Norwegian Sea to block U-boat access to the Atlantic via the northern route. The North Sea Mine Barrage was not completed before the end of the war, but six U-boats were sunk as a result.

Owing to all these measures, in 1918, the U-boat threat was largely contained. In the Atlantic, losses in January amounted to 98 ships of just 170,000 GRT with total U-boat losses reaching 295,558 GRT. After a rise in losses in February and March, shipping losses did not surpass 300,000 GRT for the remainder of the year. Germany's collapse in late 1918, in large measure due to the Allied naval blockade, meant an end to the U-boat war. On 20 October, the unrestricted submarine warfare campaign was ended; on 11 November, Germany surrendered.

Germany's submarine offensive against Britain's merchant and military fleets ultimately failed, but the cost had been very high. In total, some 12.5 million GRT of Axis and Allied shipping was sunk during World War I, over 8 million GRT in the Atlantic. The scale of these losses was enormous, but it failed to bring victory to the Germans. In return, the Germans lost 178 U-boats during the war, 153 of these in the Atlantic. Following the Treaty of Versailles in 1919, the German Navy was not allowed to design, build or possess submarines and was limited to a small force of obsolescent surface ships.

When Germany and the Allies headed into another war in 1939, Britain's North Atlantic lifelines again became a target. Using essentially the same types of submarines, the new German Navy again attempted to defeat Britain by attacking its vulnerable shipping. The Allies were confident that they had the means to defeat a renewed U-boat assault in the Atlantic. The second Battle of the Atlantic was ready to begin.

At the conclusion of World War I, the Germans were forced to surrender 122 U-boats; another 14 were scuttled. Enemy action accounted for another 178. This is a group of surrendered German submarines at Harwich after the war. (Naval History and Heritage Command)

CHRONOLOGY

1939

19–23 August   16 U-boats deploy to the North Atlantic.

3 September   Great Britain and France declare war on Germany.

Germany begin the campaign with 57 U-boats of all types.

Though U-boats are under orders to operate under prize regulations, *U-30* attacks and sinks passenger liner *Athenia* without warning, opening the Atlantic campaign.

6 September   RN institutes a convoy system.

17 September   *U-29* sinks carrier *Courageous*.

30 September   German submarines account for 41 merchant ships of 153,879 Gross Register Tons (GRT)[1] during the month.

14 October   *U-47* sinks battleship *Royal Oak* in Scapa Flow.

31 October   German submarines account for 27 merchant ships of 134,807 GRT during the month.

30 November   German submarines account for 21 merchant ships of 51,589 GRT during the month.

31 December   German submarines account for 25 merchant ships of 80,881 GRT during the month.

1940

31 January   German submarines account for 40 merchant ships of 111,263 GRT during the month.

28 February   German submarines account for 45 merchant ships of 169,566 GRT during the month.

31 March   German submarines account for 23 merchant ships of 62,781 GRT during the month.

9 April   Germany invades Denmark and Norway; most of the U-boat force is pulled from the North Atlantic to support the invasion.

30 April   German submarines account for seven merchant ships of 32,467 GRT during the month.

May   *Rösing* pack sinks 27 merchant ships.

31 May   German submarines account for 13 merchant ships of 55,580 GRT during the month.

June   First U-boat deployment to the South Atlantic.

8 June   Allies evacuate their last forces from Norway; U-boats have free access to Norwegian bases.

---

1   Tonnage for merchant ships is measured in Gross Register Tons (GRT), which is calculated by measuring all the enclosed spaces of a ship and allocating 100 cubic feet for one ton. When tonnage losses are provided in this book, they represent GRTs.

22 June	French seek armistice with Germany.
30 June	German submarines account for 58 merchant ships of 284,113 GRT during the month.
7 July	First U-boat arrives in Lorient, France; use of French bases gives U-boat force direct access to the Atlantic.
31 July	Axis submarines account for 38 merchant ships of 195,825 GRT during the month.
August	US 'loans' 50 old destroyers to Britain for use at British bases in the Western Hemisphere.
31 August	Axis submarines account for 56 merchant ships of 267,618 GRT during the month.
4 September	First Italian submarines arrive at Bordeaux, France, to assist in the Atlantic campaign.
6–8 September	Convoy SC 2 loses five ships to pack attack.
20–21 September	Convoy HX 71 loses 12 ships to pack attack.
30 September	Axis submarines account for 59 merchant ships of 295,335 GRT during the month.
16–19 October	Convoy SC 7 loses 16 ships to pack attack.
19–20 October	Convoy HX 79 loses 12 ships to pack attack.
31 October	U-boats reach their peak effectiveness during the 'Happy Time' in July–October; Axis submarines account for 63 merchant ships of 352,407 GRT during the month.
30 November	Axis submarines account for 32 merchant ships of 146,613 GRT during the month.
31 December	Axis submarines account for 37 merchant ships of 212,590 GRT during the month; for all of 1940, merchant losses to submarines total 471 ships of 2,186,158 GRT.
	At the end of the year, the German U-boat force grows to 89 boats of which 22 are operational with the remainder devoted to training or on trials.

1941

31 January	Axis submarines account for 21 merchant ships of 126,782 GRT during the month.
9–10 February	In the only operation of its kind during the campaign, German air, surface and submarine forces combine to sink 9 of 16 merchants in Convoy HG 53.
26 February	Fw 200 Condors sink seven merchant ships from Convoy OB 290, the highest daily total of the entire campaign.
28 February	Axis submarines account for 39 merchant ships of 196,783 GRT during the month.
March	US extends Lend-Lease to Britain allowing British to receive aid and pay for it later.
7 March	U-boat ace Günther Prien is killed.

16 March	Convoy HX 112 escorts under Donald Macintyre capture U-boat ace Otto Kretschmer and kill ace Joachim Schepke.
31 March	Axis submarines account for 41 merchant ships of 243,020 GRT during the month.
30 April	Axis submarines account for 43 merchant ships of 249,375 GRT during the month.
May	RN establishes first eight escort groups and creates Newfoundland Escort Force enabling continuous escort of convoys across the Atlantic; HX 129 becomes the first transatlantic convoy to receive coverage for its entire journey.
9 May	British capture *U-110* with an Enigma machine and code material.
19–20 May	Convoy HX 126 loses 12 out of 33 merchants; all future transatlantic convoys receive continuous escort.
Late May	Government Code and Cypher School at Bletchley Park is able to read the bulk of German Navy radio traffic with only a few hours delay.
31 May	Axis submarines account for 58 merchant ships of 325,492 GRT during the month.
23–29 June	In a major battle around Convoy HX 133 between 13 escorts and 10 U-boats, 11 merchants are lost in exchange for two U-boats.
30 June	Axis submarines account for 61 merchant ships of 310,143 GRT during the month.
July	American forces occupy Iceland.
25–27 July	Focus of U-boat operations shifts to convoys operating to and from Gibraltar; seven ships are lost from Convoy OG 69.
31 July	Axis submarines account for 22 merchant ships of 94,209 GRT during the month.
18–22 August	Convoy OG 71 comes under heavy attack, losing nine merchants and 2 escorts; no U-boats are lost.
31 August	Axis submarines account for 23 merchant ships of 80,310 GRT during the month.
4 September	American destroyer *Greer* and a U-boat exchange fire south of Iceland; USN ships now authorized to fire on U-boats whenever they are detected.
9–20 September	Convoys SC 42 and SC 44 come under heavy attack off Cape Farewell; 20 merchants and one escort are lost in exchange for 2 U-boats.
25–26 September	As action intensifies off the Mediterranean approaches, Convoy HG 73 loses nine merchants; no U-boats are lost.
30 September	Axis submarines account for 53 merchant ships of 202,820 GRT during the month.
17 October	American destroyer *Kearney* damaged by U-boat attack.

The Wickes-class destroyer USS *Greer*, originally commissioned in 1918, was the first USN ship to engage German naval forces during the Atlantic campaign. In the *Greer* incident on 4 September 1941, *Greer* and *U-652* exchanged fire with neither side incurring damage. In response, President Roosevelt issued a 'shoot on sight' order to the USN, meaning that the Americans were effectively engaged in active hostilities. This is *Greer* later in the war on convoy duty in heavy Atlantic seas. (Naval History and Heritage Command)

31 October	American destroyer *Reuben James* sunk by U-boat attack.
	Axis submarines account for 32 merchant ships of 156,554 GRT during the month.
30 November	Axis submarines account for 13 merchant ships of 62,196 GRT during the month.
7 December	Japan attacks Pearl Harbor, bringing the US formally into the war.
11 December	Germany declares war on the US; Dönitz prepares U-boats for deployment to the US East Coast.
16–23 December	Escorts for Convoy HG 76 defeat heavy attacks, sinking four U-boats; two merchants, one escort carrier and a destroyer are lost in return.
31 December	Axis submarines account for 26 merchant ships of 124,070 GRT in all areas during the month; for all of 1941, merchant losses to submarines total 432 ships of 2,171,754 GRT.
	At the end of the year, the German U-boat force grows to 249 boats of which 91 are operational with the remainder devoted to training or on trials.

OPPOSING COMMANDERS

BRITISH

Winston Churchill was not a naval commander, but this did not stop him from acting as one. On 3 September 1939, the first day of the war, he returned to the post of First Lord of the Admiralty, the same post he had held in World War I. As such, he was the RN's political head. Churchill was constantly proposing new operations, some far-fetched and impractical, but some of value. The First Sea Lord Sir Dudley Pound, the professional head of the RN, would have to deal with these. He became expert in dealing with his political superior, and after a period of adjustment, the two developed a strong working relationship. In May 1940, Churchill left the Admiralty to become Prime Minister. He also retained the position of Minister of Defence, which required a continuing relationship with Pound.

Churchill was intimately involved with the RN's worldwide deployment, including operations in the Atlantic. As Minister of Defence, he was also responsible for the overall allocation of military resources and must bear responsibility for starving the Atlantic campaign of long-range aircraft during the opening phases of the campaign in favour of offensive operations against Germany. He coined the inaccurate term 'Battle of the Atlantic' (the Atlantic Campaign would be more apt) and his post-war writings bolstered the myth that Britain's survival was hanging by a thread at points in the war in the face of the U-boat threat, which was not accurate.

The RN's top-ranking officer at the start of the war was Admiral of the Fleet **Sir Dudley Pound**. After a long career that included commanding a battleship at the Battle of Jutland, he achieved flag rank in 1926 and was given command of the Mediterranean Fleet in March 1936. In June 1939, he was appointed First Sea Lord, becoming the RN's senior officer. Pound was a man of considerable operational experience with a high capacity for work. He was

After a significant delay in instituting convoys to counter the U-boat threat in World War I, the RN almost immediately began convoying after war was declared on 3 September 1939. Both Prime Minister Churchill and First Sea Lord Sir Dudley Pound recognized that neutralizing the U-boat threat was essential for Allied victory. In this photo, Churchill and Pound are being greeted aboard the USN heavy cruiser USS *Augusta* before meeting with President Roosevelt off Newfoundland on 9 August 1941. (Naval History and Heritage Command)

known for his patience and loyalty to his superiors – both tested in his relationship with Churchill. As First Sea Lord, Pound not only saw his duty as issuing orders to the fleet, but also to supervise fleet operations at the expense of the commander on the scene, should conditions warrant.

As First Sea Lord, Pound oversaw all RN operations, but his primary concern was protecting the critical shipping lanes across the Atlantic. He realized that protection of trade was a vital prerequisite for victory over Germany. At the start of the war, he ordered the institution of convoys. This common-sense measure was undermined by the shortage of escorts and the short range of those that were available. It was not until July 1941 that a full convoy system with transatlantic escort coverage was achieved. Even when shipping losses were high, he let his operational commanders handle the day-to-day management of the campaign.

At the beginning of the war, **Admiral Sir Martin Dunbar-Nasmith** was the Commander-in-Chief, Plymouth. His command was responsible for protection of all shipping entering British waters by the South-West or North-West Approaches. By August 1940, use of the South-West Approaches was judged to be untenable with the Germans holding the nearby French coast. As a result, all shipping was diverted to the North-West Approaches. With this, Plymouth, on the south-west coast of England, was no longer suitable as the headquarters of the forces assigned to trade protection. As advocated by the Admiralty, Liverpool was selected as the site for a new headquarters (HQ), which was to be situated in Derby House. In the heart of the HQ was the Operations Room (also called the Plot), which tracked the battle on a massive wall chart of the Atlantic with every convoy, ship and known submarine position depicted. Next to the Plot were two rooms. One was occupied by the Duty Naval Commander and Royal Air Force (RAF) Controller, and the second was set aside for the Naval Commander-in-Chief and the Air Officer Commanding 15 Group, Coastal Command. Work on this complex was not finished until February 1941.

In February 1941, **Admiral Sir Percy Noble** was appointed Commander-in-Chief, Western Approaches. He had joined the Navy in 1894 and brought a wealth of experience to his new assignment. From his new HQ at Derby House, he controlled the RN's battle against the U-boats until being relieved in November 1942 by Admiral Sir Max Horton. Noble was regarded by those who worked with him as a man able to build consensus for his preferred action. His relief was by design and should not hide the fact that his tenure was considered a success. He instituted measures that provided the building blocks for eventual victory in the Atlantic campaign. Among these were reinforcing and expanding the escort groups and improving their training.

In 1941, the RN formed permanent escort groups. These were led by experienced commanders, some of whom went

Admiral Percy Noble held the critical appointment of Commander-in-Chief, Western Approaches for two crucial years, during which he created the conditions for eventual Allied victory in the Atlantic campaign. He was subsequently posted to the US as Head of the RN Admiralty Delegation, as shown in this view. (Britannia Royal Navy College, now in the public domain)

on to build formidable reputations as U-boat killers. The most prominent early escort group commanders were **Donald Macintyre** (commander of the 5th Escort Group), **Addison Joe Baker-Cresswell** (commander of the 3rd Escort Group), and **Frederic John Walker** (commander of the 36th Escort Group).

GERMAN

The commander-in-chief of the *Wehrmacht* (the German Armed Forces), including the *Kriegsmarine* (German Navy), was **Adolf Hitler**. After coming to power in 1933, he began efforts to increase the size of the navy in order to pursue his expansionist aims in Europe and beyond. He formally broke the restrictions of the Versailles Treaty which greatly restricted the size and composition of the navy with the 1935 Anglo-German Naval Agreement. Working with the Commander-in-Chief of the navy, he supported plans for a much larger force capable of conducting large-scale warfare against the RN, although lacking the strength to challenge it directly. Based on Hitler's assumption that Germany would not be in conflict with Britain until 1944 at the earliest, plans for naval expansion were not given top priority in Germany's rearmament, so the Kriegsmarine was not ready for war when it came in 1939.

With regard to U-boat operations, Hitler did not meddle to the same degree as he did with ground operations. It is clear that he understood little of naval operations other than taking an interest in the technical characteristics of large ships. However, he knew enough to understand that the most effective method of striking Britain's vulnerable trade routes was by U-boat attack. In spite of this, he was late in making U-boat production a top priority. There were always other competing requirements that were given higher priority – the campaign in France, preparations for the invasion of Britain, and then the invasion of Russia in June 1941. To be fair, the German war economy simply lacked the resources to support many competing requirements adequately, as much as Hitler declared his desire to increase U-boat production. Essentially, during the period of the U-boat campaign covered in this volume, the size of the U-boat force was too small to achieve decisive results.

Hitler and Erich Raeder worked together to increase the size of the German Navy. Both are shown here on 3 October 1936 at the launch of battleship *Scharnhorst* at Wilhelmshaven. Despite their efforts, the German Navy was almost completely unprepared for war when it broke out in September 1939. Both failed to prioritize U-boat construction before and after the start of the war. (Naval History and Heritage Command)

Although Hitler never dictated the tactical deployment of U-boats, he did influence the Battle for the Atlantic and the U-boat war by directing the navy to support a number of strategic priorities. These changed over time and drew resources away from the war against British shipping. Examples of this are the Norwegian campaign and the war in the Mediterranean in support of Italy, both of which drew U-boats away from the Atlantic shipping war.

Commander of the *Reichsmarine* (as the navy was called during the Weimar Republic) from 1928 was **Erich Raeder**. He joined the *Kaiserliche Marine* (Imperial Navy) in 1894 and through his work ethic and high intelligence was quickly promoted. By the start of World War I, he was the Chief of Staff of the Scouting Force and saw extensive action including at the Battle of Jutland in 1916. Raeder survived the demise of the Imperial Navy and his support for the failed 1920 Kapp Putsch against the Weimar Republic, and on 1 October 1928, was appointed as Chief of the Naval Command of the Reichsmarine. When it became the Kriegsmarine on 1 June 1935, Raeder retained his status as Commander-in-Chief. On 1 April 1939, he was promoted to grand admiral.

Raeder felt betrayed by Hitler when war broke out prematurely in 1939. He was pessimistic about the navy's prospects in a war against Britain and its allies. Faced with developing a strategy to complement Hitler's continental strategy, Raeder failed. He was steeped in the Imperial Navy's focus on the battleship and the battle fleet to win a decisive battle against the RN. In the competing schools of thought in the navy between a fleet centred on the battleship capable of winning a decisive battle against the British and a fleet focused on cruisers and submarines to fight a commerce war, Raeder selected the balanced (battleship) fleet approach. The final result of this preference was the Z Plan of 1939 in which battleships were highlighted.

Raeder's strategy to attack British shipping was ill founded. It failed to consider technology (primarily in the form of radar) and advances in aircraft. The cruiser war of World War I was not possible in World War II. To his credit, when war broke out, Raeder immediately revised the navy's building programme. Only ships that could be finished soon were scheduled for completion. The focus immediately shifted to building more U-boats

and making improvisations to field forces. This was a short-term approach that impeded the development of technology, such as advanced U-boats and radar, which would provide long–term benefits. At the start of the war, Raeder pressed Hitler to lift all restrictions on U-boat and surface operations against British shipping. He aggressively used his small surface fleet and a number of improvised surface raiders converted from merchant ships to attack Britain's lifelines. After the sinking of *Bismarck* in May 1941, Raeder's strategy of using large surface ships as commerce raiders was abandoned and the U-boat was revealed to be the only viable means with which to continue the campaign against British shipping.

Without a doubt, the single most important command figure in the Atlantic U-boat campaign was **Karl Dönitz**. From the first day of the campaign until the last, he either directed or oversaw German U-boat operations. Dönitz had joined the Imperial Navy in 1910 and was commissioned in 1913. He began World War I aboard the light cruiser *Breslau* in the Mediterranean. In late 1916, his request for a transfer to the U-boat arm was approved. By July 1918, he was the captain of *UB-68* assigned to the Mediterranean. Dönitz enjoyed a short career aboard U-boats – on 4 October, his boat was forced to surface while trying to attack a convoy. Dönitz had to scuttle *UB-68* and he and most of his crew were captured by the British. In 1920, he was allowed to return to Germany. During his time as a prisoner of war, Dönitz stated that he came up with a new tactic that he called *Rudeltaktik* (literally 'pack tactic', more commonly known as wolfpack).

Dönitz was selected to remain in the navy after Germany's defeat in World War I. When the Kriegsmarine was legally allowed to possess submarines in 1935, Dönitz was appointed commanding officer of the first U-boat flotilla and was promoted to captain. He oversaw the growth of the embryonic U-boat force, though this expansion was far smaller and slower than he believed necessary.

On 1 October 1939, Dönitz was promoted to rear admiral and assumed the title of *Führer der U-Boote* (Commander, U-boats) directly under the control of the Naval War Staff. As previously mentioned, he had a different vision of what was required to defeat Britain from his superior, Grand Admiral Raeder. In Dönitz's mind, the U-boat war was a 'tonnage war' in which victory would be achieved by the sinking of enemy ships wherever that could be done with the most efficiency and the fewest U-boat losses. Raeder advocated a different approach. His 'commerce war' was concerned with attacking shipping where it had the greatest potential for 'decisive impact'. Examples of this included disrupting supplies heading for the Mediterranean or Russia. Nevertheless, Dönitz was given a very high degree of operational freedom to run the U-boat fleet as he saw fit. His command style required that he be in constant communication with his deployed

The driving force behind the formation and growth of the U-boat force was Karl Dönitz. When Raeder was removed from his post in 1943, Dönitz assumed command of the German Navy and was promoted to *Grossadmiral*, as seen here. Even after this promotion, he refused to delegate control of the U-boat war in the Atlantic. He was worshipped by most of his men, even as he drove them into an increasingly futile struggle. (Naval History and Heritage Command)

U-boats. This need for frequent communication proved to be a critical vulnerability after the British broke German communication codes.

To his men in the U-boat force, Dönitz was an inspirational figure. First, as a former U-boat officer, he was respected as an experienced and hands-on leader. When U-boats returned to base in Lorient in Brittany, Dönitz debriefed their captains personally, serving to establish a firm link with his men. He made every effort to provide returning crews with generous leave and other comforts before their next patrol. In turn, his men appreciated their leader's obvious concern for their welfare. Dönitz was a man of undoubted intelligence and was a clear and independent thinker, and when required, he could be ruthless. Dönitz was a committed German nationalist and was equally loyal to Hitler and the ideas of National Socialism.

For most of the U-boat war, Dönitz commanded the U-boat force from his headquarters at Kernevel Point, located less than a nautical mile south of the submarine berths (and later concrete pens) at Lorient. It was a spartan HQ with a very small staff. Most important among the staff was the operations officer **Eberhard Godt**, who at the start of the war was only a lieutenant commander. He was responsible for running U-boat operations on a daily basis. In July 1940, he was promoted to commander, and to captain in September 1942.

During the first phase of the campaign, several U-boat commanders sunk a huge number of Allied merchant ships, earning them the title of 'ace'. This phenomenon was noteworthy because the achievements of the submarine aces accounted for a large percentage of overall U-boat success. As with many things in Nazi Germany, a cult of personality grew up around the aces and they achieved great fame. Among the most prominent during this period were **Otto Kretschmer** (*U-99*), **Wolfgang Lüth** (mainly as skipper of *U-43*), **Heinrich Liebe** (*U-43*), **Günther Prien** (*U-47*) and **Joachim Schepke** (*U-99*). An indication of the difference that these highly trained and highly motivated men made is highlighted by the fact that top-scoring ace Kretschmer sank 47 ships of over 274,000 GRT and damaged five more.

One of the most successful U-boat commanders in the first phases of the Atlantic campaign was Joachim Schepke. During his 14 patrols, he accounted for 37 ships of almost 156,000 GRT. This is Schepke in the conning tower of *U-100*. (Stratford Archive)

OPPOSITE, BOTTOM
In terms of tonnage, Otto Kretschmer was the most successful U-boat commander with 47 ships sunk accounting for over 274,000 GRT. He was the master of the night surface attack, a tactic used for most of his victories. (Stratford Archive)

OPPOSING FORCES

BRITISH

Naval forces

At the beginning of World War II, the Royal Navy was the largest navy in the world. However, its imposing order of battle was deceiving. The RN was stretched thin, as it had to protect British shipping around the world as well as contending with the Kriegsmarine, and possibly dealing with the Italian and Japanese navies. The RN was built to take on its enemies in fleet actions. Accordingly, of the RN's 100 operational destroyers at the start of the war, 33 were assigned to the Home Fleet and 29 to the Mediterranean Fleet; only one was assigned to the Western Approaches Command (WAC). Although 26 of the 101 operational smaller escorts were assigned to the WAC, the number of anti-submarine warfare (ASW) assets available to escort convoys was grossly inadequate.

The effectiveness of those ASW escorts assigned to the WAC was reduced by the capabilities, training and deployment of those assets. The WAC was composed of a disparate collection of ships – elderly destroyers, sloops, trawlers and corvettes. The lack of numbers and the short range of these

HMS *Bulldog* was a B-class destroyer commissioned in 1931. By 1941, *Bulldog* had assumed duties in the North Atlantic as part of an escort group operating from Iceland. On 9 May, its boarding party recovered an Enigma coding machine and various codebooks from the captured *U-110*. To ensure German ignorance of the capture, *Bulldog*'s commander did not radio the news to his superiors but immediately sailed for Iceland, where he isolated the German prisoners to ensure the still valid codes could be exploited. This is *Bulldog* in 1945. (Stratford Archive)

Force structure and major bases, September 1939

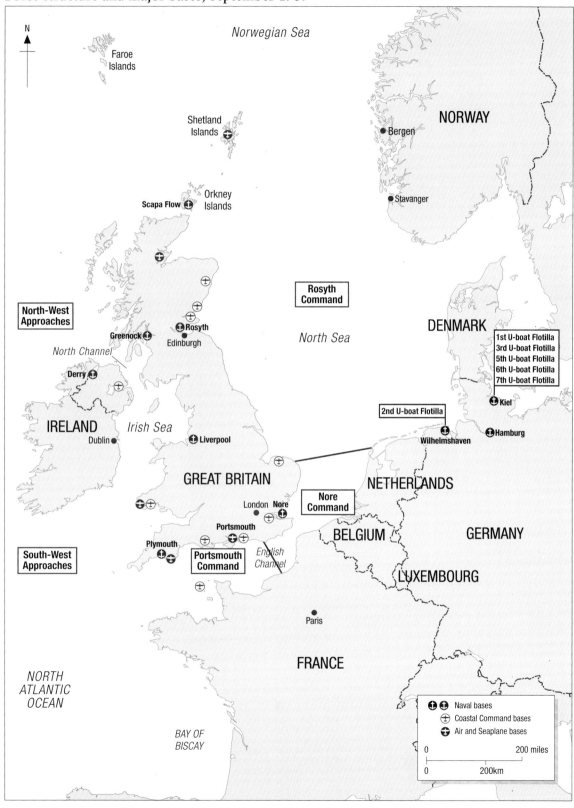

N

Norwegian Sea

Faroe
Islands

NORWAY

Shetland
Islands

Bergen

Stavanger

Scapa Flow
Orkney
Islands

**North-West
Approaches**

**Rosyth
Command**

DENMARK

1st U-boat Flotilla
3rd U-boat Flotilla
5th U-boat Flotilla
6th U-boat Flotilla
7th U-boat Flotilla

North Sea

Rosyth
Edinburgh

Greenock

North Channel

Derry

Kiel

IRELAND *Irish Sea*

Dublin

2nd U-boat Flotilla

Liverpool

Hamburg

Wilhelmshaven

GREAT BRITAIN

NETHERLANDS

London Nore

**Nore
Command**

Portsmouth

BELGIUM

GERMANY

Plymouth

**Portsmouth
Command**

*English
Channel*

LUXEMBOURG

**South-West
Approaches**

Paris

FRANCE

*NORTH
ATLANTIC
OCEAN*

Naval bases

Coastal Command bases

Air and Seaplane bases

*BAY OF
BISCAY*

0   200 miles

0   200km

small ships meant it was impossible to escort a convoy during its entire transatlantic passage. Instead, meeting points were established at the western edge of the Western Approaches covering the parts of the Atlantic thought to be in range of the U-boats. Incoming convoys from North America were escorted from these points to their destination in the British Isles, and outbound convoys only received protection for the first part of their passage.

At the start of the war, the few escorts available were assigned to convoys on an ad hoc basis. There were no established groups – escorts were assigned convoys as they were available and arrived as single ships or in small groups. Because command of the escorts fell to the senior officer present, the officer in charge could change several times during a convoy's transit as escorts came and left the convoy. There was no established doctrine for conducting escort operations; each officer in charge of the escort had his own tactical preferences that had to be shared with all the other escorts in the convoy by flashing lights (radio use was prohibited since this might disclose the convoy's location). Thus, every convoy escort was playing a pick-up game, working with other escorts perhaps for the first time with no standardized tactics or training. This high degree of unfamiliarity produced an uncoordinated defence when tested by the Germans.

In May 1941, the British took measures to improve convoy defences by forming eight escort groups. Each had between four and eight escorts assigned on a permanent basis under the command of a single officer. This stabilization afforded the group the opportunity to develop a standard set of tactics and to train together in their use, thus greatly increasing the level of escort coordination. Also at this time, the Newfoundland Escort Force (NEF) was established with a strength of 30 destroyers, nine sloops, and 24 corvettes. This critical development enabled continuous escort of transatlantic convoys. In late 1941, the NEF was organized into eight escort groups.

By June 1941, the number of escorts in service had increased dramatically. Some 700 escorts of all types were in service, including 248 destroyers and escort destroyers, 48 sloops and cutters, 99 corvettes and 300 trawlers. By 1 October 1941, a total of 19 escort groups had been established. There was no uniform organization with each being assigned between 6 and 11 ships, representing a mix of destroyers, sloops and corvettes, including some which were in overhaul. Of the 19 groups, nine were based at Londonderry, seven at Liverpool and the last three at Greenock.

Several characteristics were desirable for a convoy escort. The most important was the ability to operate over long distances and in the often unforgiving waters of the North Atlantic. High speed, like that possessed by destroyers, was not essential, given the U-boat's mediocre surface speed and very limited underwater speed. Also, sonar could not be used effectively over 20kts, so the destroyer's greater speed offered little practical advantage in submarine hunting. Heavy gun armament was also not required, but it had to be sufficient to engage a surfaced U-boat. A heavy anti-aircraft armament was also not needed since air attack was not expected in the North Atlantic. What was essential was a large depth charge capacity.

Destroyers were in high demand for fleet operations and for convoy escort duties in high threat areas outside the Atlantic. Modern fleet destroyers were not assigned to convoy escort, leaving older destroyers for the WAC. Among these were ships dating from World War I. The RN adapted old V and W classes, dating from 1917 to 1924, for escort work. Many had

Dating from 1918, W-class destroyer HMS *Viceroy* was converted early in the war and served as a convoy escort. Its conversion into an anti-aircraft escort with four 4in guns was not completed until January 1941. This view is *Viceroy* in April 1942 when it was active escorting convoys along Britain's east coast. (Naval History and Heritage Command)

several of their boilers removed in favour of more bunker space to increase range. Eventually, they all received some sort of radar and additional depth charge capacity.

By mid-1940, the RN was facing a destroyer crisis. Twenty-four had already been lost, and after the Dunkirk evacuation another 20 were damaged and forced out of service for repairs. Another 40 were held near Britain's south-east coast on anti-invasion duties. With the requirements for fleet work and considering those in overhaul, this left very few for convoy escort. It was at this moment that the United States made 50 old destroyers available for transfer to the RN. These possessed similar capabilities to the V and W classes. Also, beginning in 1940, the RN brought a large number of escort destroyers into service. Unfortunately, the Hunt class was too short ranged for ocean work and thus most were employed along the east coast of Britain and in the Mediterranean.

During World War I, the RN had introduced a new class of ships designed for escort duty called sloops. They were ideal convoy escort ships and were superior as ASW ships compared to a destroyer. Sloops were easy to build, a critical factor for ASW, for which a large number of escorts was essential. They needed to possess adequate speed, not be fitted with low-angle guns and torpedoes (like destroyers), which were useless for convoy escort, and be good sea boats. Some sloops remained from World War I, and more were built between the wars, but in general the RN's inter-war shipbuilding programme failed to prioritize their construction. The first class to be mass-produced was the Black Swan class, which entered service in January 1940. This 1,750-ton full-load ship could steam at 18.5kts, had a range of 5,500nm

HMS *Wolverine* was typical of the older destroyers that were assigned convoy escort duty when the war began. It began its career as a fleet destroyer in 1920. In 1939, it was reactivated from reserve and assigned convoy duty along Britain's east coast. By 1940, it was escorting Atlantic convoys. This view shows *Wolverine* after conversion to a short-range escort. The forward 4.7in gun has been replaced with a Hedgehog rocket launcher, a Type 271 radar was added on the bridge and the anti-aircraft fit replaced with two 20mm Oerlikon cannons. (Naval History and Heritage Command)

A member of the 12-ship Black Swan class was HMS *Erne*, commissioned in April 1941. Eight of these served in the RN and became the most effective U-boat killers of any escort. (Stratford Archive)

and was heavily armed. Only 42 were completed, but in service they proved to be the best U-boat hunters operated by the RN.

The real workhorses of the Atlantic campaign were the corvettes of the RN, and later the Royal Canadian Navy (RCN). The backbone of the corvette fleet was the Flower class. Designed for mass production and built to mercantile standards, 300 were projected. Beginning in 1940, the first 145 of these 1,195-ton full-load ships left British shipyards, joined eventually by 124 from Canadian yards. In order to meet the Admiralty's required number of escort ships, construction was simplified to the greatest degree possible. The final result was a ship capable of making 16kts with a range of 5,000nm at 10kts. The original armament consisted of one 4in gun, a handful of machine guns and a large number of depth charges deployed by launchers and racks on the stern.

A large number of Flower-class corvettes entered service in 1940. They carried the burden of the U-boat war until 1943. Although the Flowers filled an immediate need, they were not an ideal open ocean escort. Among their shortcomings were a lack of length (which affected seakeeping), speed and endurance. The improved River-class corvette was in production, but these were not operational until well into 1942.

All RN anti-submarine escorts carried ASDIC (named after the Allied Submarine Detection Investigating Committee), now better known as sonar. Using soundwaves, sonar could detect U-boats under water. Developed late in World War I, the British believed it was a potentially decisive weapon in any future U-boat war, since it took away their cloak of invisibility. This was an extremely unrealistic assessment, since in practice the range of sonar

This painting of a Flower-class corvette depicts HMS *Hydrangea*. Commissioned in January 1941, it was quickly thrown into action in March after using February for anti-submarine training. The Flower class was based on a whaler design, making it suitable for mass production. Originally intended as a coastal escort, it was forced into open-ocean duties. In heavy seas, living conditions were horrific, as hinted at in this scene. (Naval History and Heritage Command)

Another Flower-class unit was HMS *Chrysanthemum*, renamed *Commandant Drogou*. This beam view of the ship shows its primary features. The main gun was a 4in single mount forward. Early ships had the mainmast placed forward of the superstructure. This ship has already received some modification with the Type 271 radar abaft the bridge and a 2-pdr anti-aircraft mount abaft the stack. On the stern are depth charge racks; the original depth charge capacity of 25 was increased to 50 in August 1940. (Naval History and Heritage Command)

is subject to a number of operational and environmental conditions. Under actual conditions, the range of the sonars on RN escorts was limited to about 1,000–1,500yds.

Another reason that sonar was not the decisive instrument the RN had expected it to be was that the U-boats' preferred tactic of attacking at night on the surface made sonar useless. Given this preferred tactic, it was vitally important that the RN develop radar small enough to fit on escort ships. In 1940, the primitive Type 286 radar began to be deployed aboard escorts. However, it was unreliable, possessed a short range and could not be trained. In May 1941, the improved Type 271 went to sea on trials. This was the first centimetric naval radar, which gave it much better definition. For the first time, escorts could reliably detect surfaced U-boats and under certain sea conditions, could even detect the periscopes of submerged U-boats.

RAF Coastal Command

One of the enduring lessons of World War I was the effectiveness of aircraft in combating the U-boat threat. Just the presence of aircraft forced U-boats to submerge to avoid attack, thus greatly reducing their effectiveness. Despite this legacy, the RAF gave a very low priority to ASW aircraft in the inter-war years. In 1939, most of the aircraft of Coastal Command (responsible for trade protection) were obsolete. Just over 240 aircraft were available in 19 squadrons. The most numerous aircraft was the Avro Anson, making up half of Coastal Command's strength. It possessed a totally inadequate range of 510nm, a top speed of 144kts and a pathetic payload of just 360lb. On an emergency basis, Lockheed Hudsons were ordered from the US, but only

Ordered in 1940 and built in Montreal, HMCS *Chambly* was one of the first Canadian corvettes ready for Atlantic service. It was a remarkable achievement for the Canadians to build 79 original design Flower-class units from a very small industrial base. This is a view of the ship as completed with minesweeping gear and no weapon yet fitted to the aft bandstand. (Canadian Naval Heritage)

23

Depth charges were the only means available early in the war to attack submerged U-boats. The standard RN depth charge of the period was the Mark VII with 290lb of explosives. The lethal radius of a depth charge depends on the depth of the detonation and the type of submarine that is being targeted. Against a German Type VII boat, the lethal radius was approximately 10–13ft, making accuracy essential. This was difficult to do against a target moving in three dimensions. (Stratford Archive)

one squadron had been re-equipped when the war broke out. The Hudson was a dramatic improvement on the Anson, since it possessed twice the range and five times the bomb load. The only modern long-range aircraft was the Short Sunderland flying boat, but only two squadrons were available when war began. To make up for the shortage of long-range patrol craft, the British ordered the Consolidated PBY Catalina from the US.

In addition to the lack of aircraft, those available were equipped with weapons of very limited effectiveness. The standard ASW weapons were 100lb and 250lb anti-submarine bombs and an air droppable 450lb depth charge. Unfortunately, the bombs were more deadly to the aircraft dropping them than to U-boats. In 1939, half a dozen aircraft were brought down by their bombs bouncing off the water and exploding. The Anson could not even carry the larger bomb. Only the Sunderland could carry the depth charge at the start of the war. On top of this, the bombsight on both types failed to perform effectively.

It was not until November 1941 that Coastal Command transformed itself into a force capable of attacking U-boats from the air. This had been accomplished by the development of a new 250lb depth charge, deploying radar on aircraft, and implementing new tactics to attack U-boats when they were detected.

Introduced into RAF service in 1936, the Avro Anson was Coastal Command's mainstay aircraft at the start of the war. In this role, it was totally inadequate. The British had already made this assessment and had placed orders for 200 Lockheed Hudson aircraft before the war. This image, taken in 2015, is of the only flyable Anson. (L-Bit, CC BY-SA 3.0 https://creativecommons.org/licenses/by-sa/3.0, via Wikimedia Commons)

Intelligence

A huge factor in the Atlantic campaign was the intelligence war fought between the British and the Germans for information on each other's deployments and intentions. Intelligence was collected in many ways, but in a theatre as vast as the Atlantic, the most significant method was through 'radio intelligence', known today as 'signals intelligence'. Three methods were used to gain radio intelligence. The easiest was traffic analysis that examined the volume, precedence and recipients of radio messages. By using this method, it is possible to discern levels and timing of enemy activity. The second method was finding the direction of the ship or

unit sending a radio message. If two or more bearings were gained, the general location of the transmitter could be ascertained. To do this, the RN established direction-finding stations (called 'Y' stations) at three locations in Britain, two in the Mediterranean, and others in Gibraltar, Bermuda, Sierra Leone, Kenya and later in northern Russia. This network covered the Atlantic with varying degrees of accuracy (the closer the transmitter is to the collecting station, the more accurate the line of bearing). By using direction finding, the location of every deployed U-boat could potentially be plotted, since during this phase of the war U-boats were required to report their positions and status at least daily and more if they were in contact with the enemy. Fixes from direction-finding stations were not sufficient for tactical purposes, but this problem was addressed when escorts were equipped with direction-finding capabilities.

Decoding the content of radio messages was potentially the most lucrative method of gathering radio intelligence. The breaking of German naval codes transmitted with the Enigma coding machine has become legendary, but in the early phases of the war this was not a major factor for the British. To decode German naval messages, the British had to acquire an Enigma machine and code material. Leading what became an enormous effort to decipher the Enigma codes was the Government Code and Cypher School at Bletchley Park. By various means, Bletchley Park acquired the material it needed; a big break came on 9 May 1941 when the Enigma machine on *U-110* was seized along with the codes. Combined with the seizure of code material on a small weather ship two days earlier, the British were able to develop a capacity to read Enigma messages on a consistent and timely basis.

The speed by which Enigma codes were broken and rendered into 'Ultra' intelligence was critical and varied throughout the war. Only beginning in February 1941 was Ultra information gained, and this was intermittent. Decoding took at least 48 hours, meaning its usefulness was limited. In June, this was reduced to as little as 24 hours. From the last part of May 1941, the British were able to read the bulk of traffic transmitted in the primary German naval code. From this point until the end of the war, the British knew about nearly all the U-boat locations and operations. For the remainder of 1941, this translated into the seemingly uncanny ability of the RN to route convoys

Ordered as a replacement for the obsolescent Anson, the Lockheed Hudson began to be delivered to Coastal Command units in May 1939. The Mark I featured a range of 1,960nm and a bomb load of 1,400lb, far in advance of the Anson. The USN also used the Hudson, as seen in this view. (Naval History and Heritage Command) out of danger from U-boat packs deployed to detect and attack them. There is no doubt that radio intelligence, and Ultra in particular, played a critical role in deciding the Atlantic campaign.

GERMAN

Naval forces

By 1934, Raeder and Hitler had agreed to expand the German Navy, even in the face of British opposition. In June 1935, the Anglo-German Naval Agreement allowed the Germans to build up to 35 per cent of the RN and to allow for the construction of U-boats. Hitler was not content with a clearly inferior navy, so supported Raeder's plans for a much larger fleet capable of waging war against the RN. The resulting Z Plan of 1939 recognized that it was not possible to build a battle fleet capable of directly challenging the RN. What Raeder did envision was a fleet built for cruiser warfare against British worldwide sea lanes, supported by a traditional battle fleet smaller than the RN's but comprising superior ships on an individual basis. Despite their success in World War I, U-boats were not a focus of the programme. Even so, it was planned to build 249 U-boats by 1948, of which 133 would be completed by 1942–43. In 1939, the plan was modified and before the start of the war in September, 131 U-boats were ordered.

However, the grandiose Z Plan did not give the Germans a fleet ready for war on 1 September 1939. Few ships ordered were ready at this time because of a shortage of shipyard capacity, skilled workers and necessary materials, especially steel. On the first day of war, the Kriegsmarine was made up of two modern battleships, three *Panzerschiffe* ('armoured ships', called 'pocket battleships' by the British that were essentially heavy cruisers), one heavy and six light cruisers, 21 destroyers, 12 torpedo boats and 57 submarines. Against this small fleet was arrayed the might of the RN and the French Navy.

After all the planning for a future war with Britain, the German Navy was caught unprepared for war when it did come at the beginning of September 1939. The total U-boat force included 57 units. Ironically, even after the success of their submarines in World War I, the German Navy possessed the fewest number of submarines of any of the five major naval powers in September 1939. Even the total of 57 was deceptive; of these, 32 were too small for operations in the Atlantic. In addition, 79 U-boats were under construction or had been ordered. Within 18 months, German shipyards were to deliver nine boats per month – three small Type II boats, four medium-size Type VIIC units and two large Type IX boats.

Both existing force levels and the planned construction programme were clearly inadequate for achieving significant results. In the first week of the war, Dönitz issued a memorandum stating that 300 U-boats were needed for operations in the North Atlantic to force the British to their knees. Of these, one-quarter needed to be Type IX boats with the rest being the standard Type VII. In addition, Dönitz stated a need for 48 large boats capable of operations in distant waters. Raeder accepted this requirement and in a meeting with Hitler on 23 September explained that the existing construction programme was inadequate and that a monthly production rate of 20–30 boats was necessary. Although Hitler seemed convinced of the necessity of ramping up U-boat production, his first priority was re-equipping the army after the Polish campaign. In the competition for tight resources, the navy was a loser. A final decision on allocation of raw materials was put off until May or June 1940. As a result, Dönitz did not have a firm understanding of the size of his force available for future operations.

The U-boats

The U-boats available to Dönitz at the start of the war were little changed from those used by the Imperial Navy in World War I. It is important to remember that to call German U-boats of World War II submarines is misleading. In fact, they were designed to spend the great majority of their time on the surface, only submerging to escape attacks or to launch them.

The first oceangoing submarine built by the Germans after World War I was the Type IA U-boat. Based on the German-designed, Spanish-built submarine for Turkey, the design was satisfactory, but only two were built (*U-25* and *U-26*), as Dönitz chose to focus on the smaller Type VII and larger Type IV boats. The Type I design served as the basis for more successful boats to follow, most notably the Type IX.

Nazi Germany's first mass-produced U-boat was the Type II. Fifty of these boats were produced in four variants with the first being completed in 1934. Because of their small size (only 250 tons on the surface for the Type IIA), limited range (1,600nm for the Type IIA, but increasing to 5,650nm for the Type IID) and small weapons load (only five torpedoes), they possessed little combat capability. In practice, they were restricted to operations in the North Sea, but when the Germans acquired bases in Norway, the Type II boats extended their reach to the North-West Approaches. The real value of these small boats was as training units for Dönitz's growing U-boat fleet.

This pre-war photograph shows Type IIB U-boat *U-7*. Though slightly wider and longer than the original Type IIA design, these boats possessed minimal open ocean combat capabilities because of their lack of range and load of only five torpedoes. *U-7* served almost exclusively as a training boat in the Baltic except for two patrols during which it sank two small freighters. (Naval History and Heritage Command)

A Type IIB-class submarine, probably during the winter of 1940/41 in the Baltic Sea. Called 'dugout canoes' by German submariners due to their small size and surface instability, Type II boats were useful mainly for training. The Type II C and D boats possessed the range for operations around Britain and were used in combat roles throughout 1941 before being retired to training duties. (Naval History and Heritage Command)

The bedrock of the U-boat fleet was the Type VII boat. This was based on a World War I Type UB III design and then modified after the war in spite of the Treaty of Versailles, which forbade Germany from submarine design work. Ten Type VIIA boats were built between 1935 and 1937. The modified Type VIIB improved the boat's range, speed and weapons load. In total, 24 were built between 1936 and 1940.

By far the most important German submarine of the war was the Type VIIC. With 568 units built between 1940 and the end of the war, it was easily the most produced submarine in history. Although well liked by its crews, and epitomizing the features that Dönitz thought were important, it was actually a mediocre design. In fact, the design was nearly obsolescent at the start of the war and it fell further behind as the war progressed. Dönitz wanted a small boat that was easy to produce and that carried a large torpedo load. It had to be quick to dive to avoid attack and manoeuvrable. At 769 tons surfaced and 871 tons submerged, the Type VIIC was big enough

The most produced submarine in history was the Type VIIC with 568 built between 1940 and 1945. This is a Type VIIC entering Trondheim, Norway. Although an effective fighting machine in capable hands when first introduced, the growing obsolescence of this design became more apparent as the war progressed. (Naval History and Heritage Command)

to carry fuel for a range of 8,500nm at 10kts. The two diesel engines could drive the boat at a top speed of 17.7kts on the surface. On battery power, the boat could only make 80nm at 4kts. Its top submerged speed was 7.6kts, but this severely reduced its underwater range. The boat could safely dive to a depth of 400ft, although emergency dives to over 750ft were recorded.

With the use of four bow tubes and an exterior stern tube, 14 21in torpedoes could be embarked. A single 88mm deck gun was fitted in front of the island and 220 rounds carried. Six Type VII U-boats (Type VIID) were modified into minelayers with a capability to carry up to 15 mines in vertical tubes and up to another 39 in the torpedo tubes.

Complementing the medium-range Type VIIC was the longer-range Type IX. Built from 1937, 194 were completed by the end of the war. Four variants were designed, with the first Type IXA being commissioned in 1938. Displacing 1,032 tons on the surface, it possessed enough fuel for a range of 10,500nm at 10kts. Top speed was 18.2kts on the surface. Once submerged, speed was limited to 7.7kts for a distance of 65–78nm.

The larger Type IXA carried six torpedo tubes (four on the bow and two on the stern) and could carry 22 torpedoes. The size of the deck gun was increased to 105mm. Only eight boats of this class were completed.

In 1938, the first of the improved Type IXB boats entered service. The main difference from the earlier Type IX variant was an increased range to 12,000nm. Fourteen of these boats were built with construction ending in March 1940. The Type IXB class was the most successful U-boat class of the war with each boat averaging over 100,000 GRT of Allied shipping sunk. During 1941, the first of the 54 Type IXC boats were commissioned into service. With the capability to carry an additional 43 tons of fuel, range was further increased to 13,450nm. The Type IXD boats were simply enlarged Type IXC boats modified for cargo transport; they had no torpedo tubes, and a reduced battery capacity.

Beginning in 1938, the Germans began to commission Type IX boats. Eventually, 194 of five variants were completed. Much larger than the preceding Type VII, they possessed greater range that enabled them to operate in the South Atlantic and off the east coast of the United States. Operating in these poorly defended areas allowed them to stack up amazing scores. (Naval History and Heritage Command)

A Type IX boat departing base with the crew in formation on deck. Although less manoeuvrable and slower diving than the Type VII, the 14 Type IXB boats were the most successful of any type of U-boat and averaged over 100,000 GRT sunk. Three of the top six U-boat commanders in terms of shipping sunk made their mark on Type IX boats. (Naval History and Heritage Command)

Of note, U-boats during this period of the war did not carry radar. They only received radar in late 1942. Nor did they carry radar detection devices to provide warning of approaching British radar-equipped ships and aircraft. Other than the bridge crew equipped with binoculars, the only sensor was an active and passive sonar.

The main German U-boats were not outstanding weapons. Salient weaknesses of the Type VII were its limited range and relatively small weapons loadout. These restricted where it could effectively operate. The larger Type IX boat was able to operate much farther from bases in France and carried enough weapons for a prolonged patrol. This gave Dönitz the capability of operating U-boats in areas where British defences were much weaker.

U-boat tactics

The mainstay Type VII boat was little more than a torpedo boat with the capability of temporarily submerging to escape danger. It possessed a fairly high surface speed, which it used to reach its assigned patrol area and then to react to reports from other boats of new targets. However, its submerged speed of only 8kts (and this for only a short period) meant that it was all but impossible to manoeuvre to a favourable torpedo firing position in daylight while under water. Dönitz trained his crews to act as torpedo boats by gaining contact on a target during the day and then maintaining contact at extreme range. Once it was dark, the U-boat closed the target on the surface relying on the stealth provided by its low silhouette. If light conditions were unfavourable, the boat would use its higher surface speed to move into a position ahead of the target and then conduct a submerged attack. If sufficient darkness was available, the boat would conduct its attack on the surface.

Dönitz gave much thought to new tactics for attacking convoys. As evinced in World War I, a single boat attacking a concentration of merchant ships and escorts could not deliver decisive results. The answer was to mass a number of U-boats to attack a convoy to overwhelm its defences and inflict serious losses on the merchants. These group tactics had been experimented with in 1918 but had proved unsuccessful. Dönitz refined them with the assistance of better radio communications. In its initial form and as first executed in October 1939 by a group of six U-boats, the concept of several U-boats operating under a single officer to conduct a coordinated attack on a convoy proved impractical. The failure of the first wolfpack and of two others the following month made Dönitz modify his approach. U-boats patrolled separately in the expected area of convoy activity. Once a U-boat spotted a convoy, it would shadow it and radio reports of its location to Dönitz's headquarters. Using this contact information, other nearby boats would be ordered to converge on the convoy, forming a wolfpack. Each U-boat captain was free to attack whenever favourable tactical conditions existed. Once the maximum number of boats had gathered around the convoy, a general attack was ordered from U-boat command. Other than to mass as many U-boats as possible on a single convoy, no effort was made to mount a truly coordinated attack.

Using this tactic, the Germans gained several important successes in late 1940 and 1941. However, these tactics possessed several vulnerabilities. Foremost was the need for a high volume of radio communications from the deployed boats to headquarters and from Dönitz's command staff to the boats. The Germans thought that this was not an issue, since they assessed their communications were secure. At the tactical level, the frequent use of radios was a potential weakness, since the position of the boats could be determined by high-frequency direction finders (HF-DF). Eventually, the Allies deployed HF-DF on escorts, which provided them with an immediate line of bearing on a nearby U-boat, which could be used for an attack. Pack tactics were usually successful in overwhelming inadequate or poorly trained

The long-range Fw 200C Condor was used by the Luftwaffe to threaten ships in the Western Approaches. It carried 2,200lb of bombs, but with its crude bombsight was forced to attack at very low altitude, thus exposing the vulnerable aircraft to defensive fire. Using this method, Condors accounted for 20 ships in 1940 and another 58 ships sunk in 1941. (© Imperial War Museum, HU 39426)

escorts. Once the Allies increased the number of escorts and improved their proficiency, U-boats faced increasing losses. Further, U-boats transited on the surface to mass against a detected convoy. Once Allied aircraft were introduced in sufficient numbers to make surface transits untenable, the U-boats lost their ability to manoeuvre and mass freely.

German air forces

Throughout the war, the U-boats found it difficult to locate convoys. This weakness could have been alleviated by the employment of German Air Force (*Luftwaffe*) long-range aircraft to provide reconnaissance support. However, coordinated operations between the U-boats and the Luftwaffe proved to be an illusion. The head of the Luftwaffe, *Reichsmarshall* Hermann Göring, consistently refused to allow his aircraft to come under the operational control of the navy. At issue was control of the only group, I/Kampfgeschwader 40 (I/KG 40), to fly the Fw 200 Condor long-range bomber/reconnaissance aircraft. Only these aircraft, which had been flying from an airfield just west of Bordeaux since August 1940, possessed the range to fulfil Dönitz's scouting requirements.

After presenting his case to the Wehrmacht operations staff, Dönitz obtained a Führer Order on 7 January 1941 to place I/KG 40 under his operational control. However, the low availability of these aircraft (an average of two per day) and the weak navigational skills of their crews paid fewer dividends than expected. By March, Göring had largely undermined the January order. He was determined to prevent the development of an independent naval air arm. The Luftwaffe preferred to concentrate on attacking shipping rather than the unglamorous job of flying reconnaissance missions for the U-boats. This approach was not entirely fruitless – between June 1940 and March 1941, the Fw 200s sank 52 ships of 207,889 GRT. However, to make more effective use of the limited numbers of Fw 200s, in mid-1941, the crews were instructed to avoid all combat, and the Condors were used solely to report Allied shipping movements.

The Condors were of great concern to the British, who took several measures to counter them. Sporadic bombing of their bases was ineffective. Air cover was needed, and the most effective method was to get fighters on ships. This led to the development of catapult aircraft merchantman (CAM) and later escort carriers.

Intelligence

British intelligence efforts have been rightfully renowned for their efforts during the Atlantic campaign. However, often forgotten are the efforts of German naval intelligence, which in the first phase of the campaign outshined their British counterparts. The most successful arm of German naval intelligence was its cryptanalysis unit known as the *B-Dienst* (short for *Beobachtungsdienst*: 'Observation Service'). During the first part of the war, it was based in Berlin and by late 1942 employed 1,100 personnel. This number was insufficient to attack the many British naval codes then in use, so lack of resources restricted German success in this key area. In mid-October 1939, B-Dienst achieved its first success against the RN's Naval Cypher which was used for operational messages. The Germans maintained some degree of access into this system until 1941. The RN's Naval Code was used for administrative messages including communications to merchant shipping.

With some gaps, this system was being read by B-Dienst from the start of the war until December 1943. Such access provided the Germans with an awareness of convoy movements. Introduced in October 1941, Combined Naval Cipher No. 3 was used by both the RN and USN for communications with transatlantic convoys. By February 1942, it too was penetrated by B-Dienst. German codebreakers provided Dönitz with a huge advantage in the vital task of detecting convoys, especially during the periods when only a small number of boats were operating in the Atlantic.

ORDERS OF BATTLE

ALLIED

Royal Navy, 1 September 1939

(only those commands directed at trade protection are shown)
Portsmouth Command (Admiral Sir William James)
12th and 16th Destroyer Flotillas (16 destroyers)
5 anti-submarine trawlers
4 minesweepers
4 minesweeping trawlers
Nore Command (Admiral Sir H. Brownrigg)
19th Destroyer Flotilla (9 destroyers)
5 escorts
3 minesweepers (Dover)
3 minesweepers, 9 minesweeping trawlers (Thames Estuary)
Rosyth Command (Vice Admiral C.G. Ramsey)
15th Destroyer Flotilla (8 destroyers)
8 escorts
Western Approaches Command (Admiral Sir M. Dunbar-Nasmith, VC)
3rd, 11th, 12th and 17th Destroyer Flotillas (32 destroyers)
6 escorts
3 anti-submarine trawlers
3 minesweeping trawlers

Royal Canadian Navy

7 destroyers
5 minesweepers

GERMAN

German U-boat force, 3 September 1939

1st U-boat Flotilla (Kiel)
8 Type IIB, 2 Type IIC
2nd U-boat Flotilla (Wilhelmshaven)
5 Type VIIA
3rd U-boat Flotilla (Kiel)
7 Type IIB
5th U-boat Flotilla (Kiel)
2 Type 1A, 5 Type VIIA
6th U-boat Flotilla (Kiel)
5 Type IX
7th U-boat Flotilla (Kiel)
7 Type VIIB
Training Duties
6 Type IIA, 3 Type IIB, 4 Type IIC, 3 Type IX

OPPOSING PLANS

BRITISH

In January 1939, the Admiralty issued war plans in the event of a European war. It was assumed that hostilities would commence against Germany and Italy, and that Japan would enter the war at a later phase. The first priority was defence of the home islands, including defence of the shipping lanes, which would be crucial for sustaining the British war effort. The RN was spread thin as it had to guard home waters, control the Mediterranean and protect thousands of nautical miles of trade routes around the globe. Defence of trade was an enormous responsibility. In 1939, British shipping totalled 21 million GRT with 2,500 ships at sea at any time. Britain's total merchant fleet was composed of 3,000 oceangoing cargo ships and tankers and another 1,000 smaller ships devoted to coastal trade.

Defence of Britain's home waters was the responsibility of several commands. The most important was the Home Fleet, which was tasked to engage the German fleet whenever possible and to institute a blockade against

Convoying merchant ships under naval escort was an age-old tactic. It took heavy shipping losses in 1917 to finally force the RN to adopt this measure. This view of an American merchant convoy nearing its destination in England during World War I gives the appearance of a typical convoy. Although a large formation, it is a small target in the expanses of the Atlantic. By putting ships into convoys, the rest of the ocean was swept clean of potential targets. Falsely seen as a defensive measure, convoys also force submarines to make attacks on the best-defended areas of the ocean. (Naval History and Heritage Command)

Because of their high speed and ability to carry large guns up to 6in, the RN converted 53 passenger liners into armed merchant cruisers beginning in 1939. Three more were converted by the RCN. For the initial period of the war, these ships provided the only escort for convoys until they reached the Western Approaches. Although somewhat useful against surface raiders, they possessed no real anti-submarine capabilities, so losses were heavy with 14 armed merchant cruisers being lost. This is HMS *Cilicia* in November 1942. It was heavily armed with eight 6in guns. (Naval History and Heritage Command)

German shipping by controlling the North Sea. Four shore commands, Portsmouth, the Nore (Chatham), Rosyth and the Western Approaches, were charged with defending shipping. The introduction of convoys was seen as an integral part of this defence. This did not include shipping in low-threat areas or in areas where British forces were inadequate to defend convoys. In areas beyond home waters, the Admiralty planned to only patrol chokepoints and rely on 'evasive routing' elsewhere.

Measures to thwart German U-boats included laying mines along the east coast of Britain and instituting convoys for all coastal shipping immediately, mining the Strait of Dover to close down the English Channel as a transit route to the Atlantic, and guarding the northern exits to the Atlantic with ships of the Northern Patrol.

The first convoys were established along the east coast of Britain between the Thames Estuary and the Firth of Forth. These began on 6 September; both south- and northbound trips were organized every second day. The first open-ocean convoy was established on 7 September. These departed from the Thames (named OA) and Liverpool (OB) and steamed through the Irish Sea and on to North America. In the first phase of the war, these convoys were only escorted to a point at 12.5 degrees west longitude, after which the convoy dispersed and the ships proceeded to their destinations independently. The escort lingered at the dispersal point and picked up the next convoy bound for Britain. Convoys headed to Britain from Canada were given only a weak escort to defend against raiders (usually in the form of a merchant cruiser) before picking up their ASW escort. Commencing in July, ships departing from Britain headed south were formed into OG convoys headed to Gibraltar.

Merchant ships carrying commodities to Britain from South America, the Indian Ocean and Africa were staged at the protected anchorage of Freetown, Sierra Leone, to be convoyed north to Britain. On 14 September, the first convoy (dubbed 'SL') departed Freetown and headed north to Britain. Ships as slow as 7.5kts could proceed in this convoy.

The most important convoys in the entire British scheme were those from Nova Scotia to Britain. The first of these, Convoy HX 1, departed Halifax on 16 September under the local escort of Canadian ships. Ships capable of 9–10kts were usually included in the HX convoys. On 19 September, the first fast convoy from Halifax (HXF 1) left for Britain. The last major inbound convoy route was from Gibraltar, dubbed 'HG'. HG 1 left Gibraltar on 26 September.

It was impossible to get every ship already under way into a convoy by 3 September when war began. Those that were not in convoy and that were unescorted were the most vulnerable and took the great majority of losses at the hands of the U-boats. The importance of convoy operations was immediately apparent – by the end of 1939, 5,756 ships were organized into convoys and only four were lost to U-boat attack. The requirement to sail in convoy extended only to British merchants. The British tried to persuade neutral shipping to also use convoy protection, but this was only partially successful until these countries were occupied by the Germans. Once this occurred, the British took control of these formerly neutral ships.

It is important to note that initially only ships capable of making more than 9kts and less than 15kts were placed into convoys. Slower ships were not convoyed, since they would have restricted the speed of the entire convoy. Faster ships were thought to be relatively immune to U-boat attack. Both slow and fast ships were routed independently in areas thought to be clear of German submarines. This approach worked well with fast ships, but slow ships continued to suffer heavily. From November 1940 to May 1941, ships sailing on the Halifax and Freetown routes averaged a loss rate of approximately 6 per cent on a round-trip voyage while in convoy, but if sailing independently averaged 14–15 per cent loss rates. Contributing to this was the decision in November 1940 to reduce the maximum speed for ships to be included in a convoy from 15 to 13kts. Seeing losses to independents so high, in May 1941, the speed requirement reverted to 15kts.

The scope of the convoy system gradually expanded. By May 1940, anti-submarine escort was only provided out to about 200nm west of Ireland. In July 1940, the limit of close escorts for convoys headed outbound was extended from 15 to 17 degrees west longitude; in October, it was extended again to 19 degrees. To relieve congestion in Halifax, a new convoy from Sydney, Nova Scotia, was instituted on 15 August 1940. The new convoy was named 'SC' and was intended for ships in the 7.5–8kt range. SC convoys were originally intended to run for the summer of 1940, but went well beyond that. Presenting a large and slow target, SC convoys figured prominently in the Atlantic campaign. For all eastbound convoys from Canada, the limit of close escort was extended to 53.5 degrees west longitude.

By 1941, the convoy system had evolved to the structure shown below.

Principal Convoy Routes to and from Britain in 1941

Convoy code	Route	When begun
Inbound		
SL	Sierra Leone to Britain	14 September 1939
HX	Halifax to Britain	16 September 1939
SC	Sydney to Britain	15 August 1940
HG	Gibraltar to Britain	26 September 1940
Outbound		
ONF	Britain to Halifax (fast ships)	27 July 1941 (replaced OB convoys from Liverpool)
ONS	Britain to Halifax (slow ships)	26 July 1941
OG	Britain to Gibraltar	1 October 1939
OS	Britain to Sierra Leone	24 July 1941

Early war convoy routes

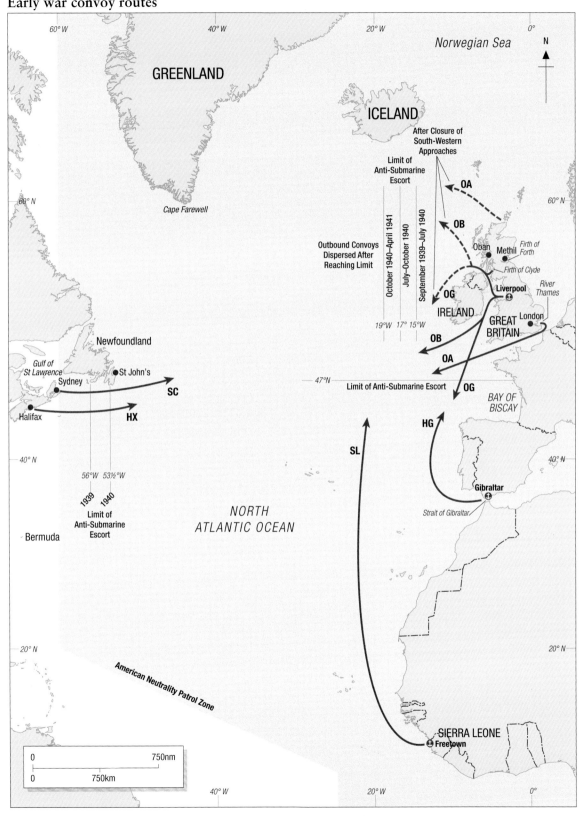

GREENLAND

Cape Farewell

ICELAND

Norwegian Sea

N

After Closure of
South-Western
Approaches

Limit of
Anti-Submarine
Escort

OA

OB

Outbound Convoys
Dispersed After
Reaching Limit

October 1940–April 1941

July–October 1940

September 1939–July 1940

19°W 17° 15°W

Oban

Methil

Firth of
Forth

Firth of Clyde

River
Thames

Liverpool

OG

IRELAND

GREAT
BRITAIN

London

60° N

60° N

Newfoundland

Gulf of
St Lawrence

St John's

Sydney

SC

Halifax

HX

OB

OA

47°N

Limit of Anti-Submarine Escort

OG

BAY OF
BISCAY

HG

SL

56°W 53½°W

1939 1940

Limit of
Anti-Submarine
Escort

NORTH
ATLANTIC OCEAN

40° N

40° N

Bermuda

Gibraltar

Strait of Gibraltar

20° N

American Neutrality Patrol Zone

20° N

0   750nm

0   750km

SIERRA LEONE

Freetown

40° W

20° W

0°

60° W

40° W

20° W

0°

Convoy routes, June 1940–December 1941

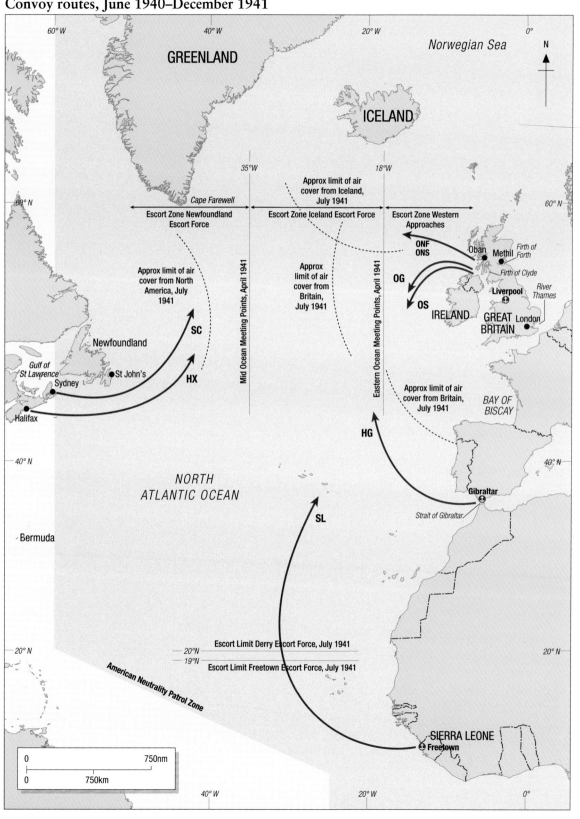

60° W

GREENLAND

40° W

20° W

Norwegian Sea

N

ICELAND

35°W

18°W

Approx limit of air
cover from Iceland,
July 1941

60° N

Cape Farewell

60° N

Escort Zone Newfoundland
Escort Force

Escort Zone Iceland Escort Force

Escort Zone Western
Approaches

ONF
ONS

Oban

Methil

Firth of
Forth

Firth of Clyde

River
Thames

OG

Approx limit of air
cover from North
America, July
1941

Approx
limit of air
cover from
Britain,
July
1941

Liverpool

SC

Mid Ocean Meeting Points, April 1941

Eastern Ocean Meeting Points, April 1941

OS

IRELAND

GREAT
BRITAIN

London

Newfoundland

Gulf of
St Lawrence

St John's

HX

Sydney

Halifax

Approx limit of air
cover from Britain,
July 1941

BAY OF
BISCAY

HG

40° N

40° N

NORTH
ATLANTIC OCEAN

Gibraltar

Bermuda

SL

Strait of Gibraltar

American Neutrality Patrol Zone

20° N

20° N

20°N

Escort Limit Derry Escort Force, July 1941

19°N

Escort Limit Freetown Escort Force, July 1941

0   750nm

0   750km

SIERRA LEONE
Freetown

40° W

20° W

0°

A North Atlantic convoy proceeds in heavy seas peacefully under the watchful protection of an escort. Most transatlantic convoys never came under attack from U-boats. By late 1941, the U-boat threat in the North Atlantic was much reduced by the relatively small numbers of U-boats available and British skill in routing convoys around known U-boat concentrations. (Stratford Archive)

OPPOSITE
As more escorts became available, continuous escort was provided to convoys inbound from North America beginning in May 1941 and from Freetown in July 1941. For convoys transiting the North Atlantic, three groups of escorts were required to provide continuous coverage. Although Coastal Command expanded its coverage, air protection of North Atlantic convoys was still limited. A large air gap remained; the Germans were poised to exploit this weakness in 1942.

As more escorts became available, the level of protection increased. A lack of escorts meant that convoys proceeded for most of their voyage with no or very minimal protection provided by auxiliary cruisers (passenger liners fitted with weapons). It was not until May 1941 that the first HX convoy was provided with an anti-submarine escort for its entire transatlantic trip. This important development followed the expansion in the overall escort force, and by the RCN in particular. Covering a single convoy across the Atlantic was a considerable effort. When a convoy departed Halifax, it was protected by an RCN escort group to a Western Ocean Meeting Point off Newfoundland. Here, another escort group relieved the first one and provided protection until reaching the Mid-Ocean Meeting Point (MOMP) off Iceland somewhere near 35 degrees west longitude. In April 1941, escorts began using bases in Iceland, which extended escort coverage to the west. The precise location of the MOMP was always different so that the

Between 8 and 12 July 1941, US Marines occupied Iceland, relieving the Canadian garrison on the island. US naval and air forces began to use bases on the island, further deepening the United States' involvement in the Atlantic campaign months before Pearl Harbor. In this view, USN destroyers are visible in Reykjavik Harbour during the initial occupation of Iceland in July 1941. An RN anti-submarine trawler is on the left. (Naval History and Heritage Command)

USS *Kearny*, an American Gleaves-class destroyer, was the first USN ship to be damaged by German naval forces in the Atlantic campaign. On 17 October, *U-568* hit the destroyer with a torpedo, killing 11 and wounding 22. The crew was successful at containing the flooding and the ship survived. This view shows *Kearny* en route to Reykjavik, Iceland, at 10kts after being damaged. (Naval History and Heritage Command)

Germans could not wait at a known point. At the Eastern Ocean Meeting Point (EOMP) at approximately 18 degrees west longitude, a third escort group took responsibility for the convoy.

Throughout 1941, the United States took increasingly belligerent measures against German naval forces in the Atlantic. This occurred well before the Pearl Harbor attack in December, which formally brought the Americans into the war. The destroyers-for-bases deal and the American occupation of Iceland in July 1941 were both designed to support British efforts in the Atlantic. On 4 September, the USN was allowed to escort convoys comprising not only American-flag ships. Starting with HX 150, the USN provided escort for certain convoys up until the MOMP. After escorting convoys eastward, the American escorts refuelled in Iceland and then took Convoy ON to Canada. Later, the USN also agreed to escort convoys to about 22 degrees west longitude. Moving the rendezvous to the east meant that the WAC escort groups did not have to refuel in Iceland and could spend more time at sea. In turn, this freed three escort groups from the North Atlantic to strengthen the SL and HG convoys. Inevitably, this led to clashes between German and American naval units. On 4 September, American destroyer *Greer* was attacked by a U-boat while proceeding to Iceland. The destroyer responded with depth charges, but neither side incurred damage. However, on 17 October, destroyer *Kearny* was damaged by a torpedo, and on 31 October, destroyer *Reuben James* was sunk by a U-boat while escorting HX 156. The United States was an active belligerent in the Atlantic in all but name months before the Pearl Harbor attack.

GERMAN

Dönitz had plenty of time between the wars to devise a new operational concept for the next time German submarines went to war against British shipping. His new scheme was based on several assumptions. First, he assumed that the prize regulations that restricted wartime submarine operations would be discarded by Germany and all other signatories. This assumption was correct. Second, Dönitz also believed that the British faith

LORIENT - KÉROMAN

in ASDIC was misplaced. He assessed that ASDIC did not negate the U-boat threat as the British believed, but that it was only effective in locating submarines in tactical situations. In order to attack convoys, the primary tool used by the Allies to defeat the U-boat in World War I, Dönitz planned to mass submarines (the genesis of the wolfpack tactic) and attack convoys at night. Attacking on the surface, the submarines would be protected at night, since their small surface profile made them difficult to spot. This assumption was initially well founded, but the development of radar made its continuing viability dubious. As early as 1938, the Germans were developing devices capable of locating ships and submarines by radio waves. The British were also developing radar. Though not widely deployed at the start of the war, it would eventually remove a surfaced U-boat's nocturnal protection and invalidate one of Dönitz's key assumptions.

Third, based on a wargame conducted in early 1939, Dönitz believed he could achieve decisive results against British shipping with a force of 300 operational U-boats. In such a campaign, U-boats would play the primary role, since surface ships would have difficulty getting into the Atlantic and being supplied there. As in World War I, the English Channel would be closed to U-boats, so all transits would have to move through the North Sea, the chokepoints out of which could be mined by the British. The best way to circumvent the British blockade of the initial U-boat bases was to secure bases in France. Dönitz was aware of the danger posed to U-boats by aircraft and foresaw a need for building protective shelters at submarine bases.

The basic viability of Dönitz's pre-war planning for a U-boat campaign against the British can be questioned for a number of important reasons. The initial number of submarines available was utterly inadequate for such a campaign. Production was not planned to reach Dönitz's desired

As part of his plan to move U-boats to operational bases in France as quickly as possible, Dönitz foresaw the need to build protective shelters for the boats where they could undergo maintenance undisturbed by possible bombing. In November 1940, work began on docks protected by concrete roofs (the two curved roof structures in the centre of the drawing). In February 1941, work began on the first of three enclosed pens at Lorient with bomb-proof, steel-reinforced, layered concrete roofs (the three structures in the foreground). Eventually, 30 boats could be enclosed under cover. Despite heavy bombing of Lorient, no U-boats were lost at their base. (Naval History and Heritage Command)

300 submarines until 1942. Any war would stretch German resources to the limit with the navy being allocated the fewest resources of any of the three services. In comparison, the British could call upon many more maritime resources, and after the entry of the United States, the resource advantage between the Allies and the Germans expanded exponentially. Another resource disadvantage for the Germans was fuel. German production of diesel and fuel oil was insufficient to meet the needs of the Wehrmacht, particularly the navy. This shortage affected fleet operations as early as 1941, although the U-boat arm was the least impacted. However, it did mean that support to the U-boats from the other parts of the navy was limited.

Dönitz dismissed, or at least downplayed, the impact of technology on the U-boat war. Sonar did prove effective once sufficient platforms were deployed to use it. Use of radar became widespread and forced Dönitz to alter the basic operating parameters of his U-boats. Surface attacks were rendered impossible. When forced to submerge, the submarines of the period were much less effective.

Against the growing tide of technology the Allies brought to bear against the U-boats, Dönitz was forced to conduct his campaign with submarines barely improved since World War I. Not until much later in the war did the Germans bring into service true submarines, and when this occurred, the war was almost over.

THE CAMPAIGN

THE FIRST SIX MONTHS

Up until the last minute, Raeder was content to accept Hitler's assurance that the Polish crisis would not result in war with the British or French. Accordingly, forces in the Baltic Sea were brought up to full readiness in preparation for a war with Poland. As a precautionary measure, Raeder agreed to move some forces into the Atlantic. On 19 August 1939, these forces, in the form of 14 U-boats and pocket battleships *Graf Spee* and *Deutschland*, were ordered to leave port. Two more U-boats departed on 22 and 23 August.

Raeder's first concern was to keep the RN out of the Heligoland Bight to defend key German ports and bases in the North Sea. German surface forces completed the deployment of the 'Westwall' mine barrage by 24 September. German submarines also began to lay mines off the east coast of Britain. The forces deployed into the Atlantic were restricted in their operations.

In this somewhat fanciful German painting from World War II, a German U-boat sinks an English freighter. Apparently, the attack was conducted with prize regulations in mind since the crew has been allowed to take to lifeboats. Having to remain on the surface for this process to play out, the vulnerability of the U-boat is obvious as in this scene. (Naval History and Heritage Command)

This is a pre-war view of passenger liner SS *Athenia*. On 3 September, it became the first ship lost to U-boats in the Atlantic campaign. Although under orders not to attack passenger liners, the captain of *U-30* attacked without warning. (Clifford M. Johnston/Library and Archives Canada/PA-056818)

The pocket battleships were withheld from attacking British shipping and the U-boats were ordered to conduct their attacks in accordance with prize regulations and not to attack any passenger ships or any French shipping. On 23 September, Raeder was able to convince Hitler to give the navy permission to attack French ships and for U-boats to attack merchant ships without warning. The prohibition on attacking passenger ships remained.

As Hitler and Raeder negotiated the rules of engagement for U-boats, the first significant event of the Battle of the Atlantic occurred on 3 September when *U-30* came across the British passenger liner *Athenia* in the Western Approaches. The skipper, Fritz-Julius Lemp, believing he had sighted weapons aboard the ship, assessed it to be an armed merchant cruiser and therefore fair game. Without warning, Lemp launched two torpedoes. One hit, causing fatal damage. When Lemp surfaced, it was obvious that he had attacked a passenger ship. In total, 118 passengers died, including 22 Americans. Lemp's attack was in direct violation of Hitler's orders to abide by prize regulations. Killing innocent women and children, and Americans, reminded the Germans of World War I U-boat attacks that prompted the United States to enter the war. Dönitz was forced to deny Lemp's involvement in the attack and went so far as to falsify *U-30*'s deck logs. With this first uncertain step, the Atlantic campaign was under way.

The sinking of *Athenia* led the RN to accelerate the introduction of the convoy system on 6 September. The British also began arming merchant ships. Gradually, the restrictions on U-boats were lifted. As of 17 September, U-boats were permitted to attack merchant ships (except passenger liners) in the waters around Britain and later in the month this was extended to ships in the same waters steaming without lights. It was not until May 1940 that all restrictions were lifted on attacks against shipping in the waters around the British Isles and in the Bay of Biscay.

Dönitz deployed his full strength in the opening weeks of the war. By the first week of September, 21 U-boats were stationed in three groups west of the British Isles, west of the Bay of Biscay and west of the Iberian Peninsula. These boats sank 35 merchants and captured three more. Although the overall number of boats on patrol was not large, they enjoyed initial success, since the British did not have time to bring all shipping under naval control or to organize convoys. By 18 September, only 11 boats were still on patrol in the Atlantic.

Although the focus of German efforts was against shipping, U-boats struck important blows against the RN in the first couple of months. At the start of the war, the RN organized submarine hunter groups centred on fleet carriers. On 14 September, *U-39* spotted aircraft carrier *Ark Royal* west of Ireland on anti-submarine patrol. The U-boat fired a salvo of three torpedoes at the RN's most valuable warship, but they exploded prematurely, disclosing the submarine's presence. In return, *U-39* was quickly sunk by the carrier's escorts. Just three days later, *U-29* sighted carrier *Courageous*, also operating as part of a submarine hunter group west of Ireland. The submarine fired a spread of three torpedoes at the carrier, and this time two hit. Within 20 minutes, the carrier sank with the loss of 519 crewmen. This was the end of using fleet carriers as part of submarine hunter groups in 1939. Once more expendable escort carriers were available, the concept was reintroduced with more success.

On 14 October, another disaster befell the RN. In a carefully planned operation, Dönitz dispatched *U-47*, under the command of Günther Prien, to attack the Home Fleet inside its main base at Scapa Flow. After a remarkable feat of navigation, Prien came across the unsuspecting battleship *Royal Oak*. Forced to make three separate attacks because of his malfunctioning torpedoes, Prien was rewarded for his daring when the last three hit the battleship, which went under with almost 900 of the crew. As a result, the Home Fleet was forced to abandon its principal base until its defences could be strengthened.

In the first few months of the shipping war, Dönitz decided to deploy his few available boats singly in the Eastern Atlantic. When the British instituted convoys, Dönitz was not surprised and decided to test his wolfpack tactic. In early October, the first wolfpack operation got under way with six boats deployed south of Ireland under the senior officer Werner Hartmann in *U-37*.

U-47 arrives at Kiel on 23 October 1939 after sinking battleship HMS *Royal Oak* nine days earlier. In the background is battleship *Scharnhorst*. Under the command of Günther Prien, *U-47* was the tenth most successful U-boat in terms of tonnage sunk with 162,769 GRT in 30 merchants and *Royal Oak* at just under 30,000 GRT. (Naval History and Heritage Command)

SCHARNHORST
Germany – BB
(GNEISENAU Class)
(1939)

THE LOSS OF *COURAGEOUS*, 17 SEPTEMBER 1939 (PP.46–47)

An early indication that ASDIC might not be the game-changing technology that the Admiralty claimed it would be came on 17 September 1939. *U-29* under Otto Schuhart was on patrol in the Western Approaches some 190nm west of Ireland. He soon encountered RN carrier *Courageous* and two escorting destroyers. *Courageous* was one of two fleet carriers deployed to the Western Approaches as the centre of a 'hunter killer' group to seek out and destroy U-boats. The tactic was a disaster. At 1800hrs on 17 September, *Courageous* was sighted by *U-29* as the carrier was heading back to Devonport. Two of its destroyers had been dispatched just over two hours earlier to investigate a reported U-boat attack on a freighter, leaving just two to escort the carrier. Schuhart began to stalk his target, which he had identified as a carrier. *Courageous*, unaware of the presence of the submarine, was proceeding at high speed (20kts) **(1)** and was zigzagging and seemed to be on the verge of escape. Suddenly, at 1922hrs,

the carrier changed course into the wind to recover aircraft and headed right for *U-29*. With this good fortune, Schuhart calculated his attack and launched three torpedoes at 1950hrs. After a running time of two minutes, two of the torpedoes struck *Courageous* **(2)**. This was the first indication the British had of *U-29's* presence. The escorting destroyers made three depth charge attacks, none particularly close, and *U-29* escaped unharmed to report this success. *Courageous'* demise was quick; 19 minutes after being struck, it sank. The two torpedoes struck the carrier on the port side abaft the bridge. Power was lost and a severe list quickly developed. From the crew of 1,216 men, 518 were lost, including the captain, who remained on the bridge as the ship went down. For his part, Schuhart survived the war, having been assigned training duties in 1941, and later joined the post-war West German *Bundesmarine*. This scene shows the impact of the first torpedo. *Ivanhoe* or *Impulsive* is in the background **(3)**.

Things went bad quickly when *U-40* was sunk by a mine when trying to use the English Channel and *U-42* and *U-45* were sunk by escorts on their way to the rendezvous point. With his three remaining boats, Hartmann attacked inbound Convoy HG 3 on 17 October when it was well west of Ireland and was unescorted. Each of the three U-boats was able to sink a single ship before being driven off by aircraft. Though not a smashing success, the basic concept of wolfpack attacks had been demonstrated.

The following month, Dönitz ordered another wolfpack operation, this time with five boats. Again, only three boats were able to attack French Convoy KS 27 west of Gibraltar. The submarines did not score any success against the well-defended convoy, but hit stragglers and independent ships in the area, with two of the U-boats sinking seven merchants. These early attempts to use packs in October and November ended in failure, because the number of boats available to execute a true wolfpack attack was too small. It also became clear that the concept of a tactical officer in charge of the group attack was largely impractical. After flirting with the wolfpack tactic, Dönitz reverted to sending out individual boats as soon as they were ready. He hoped to employ wolfpack tactics in 1940 when more boats were available.

At this point in the campaign, it did not matter if wolfpacks were successful or not. The Atlantic still teemed with ships sailing independently, giving the few U-boats at sea plentiful targets. This state of affairs was true well beyond 1939 – it was not until 1943 that the majority of Allied shipping was placed in escorted convoys.

During the last four months of 1939, total Allied merchant losses to U-boat attacks were 114 ships totalling 421,156 GRT. However, of these, only 12 were lost in convoy and another four were lost after straggling from convoy. In exchange, nine U-boats were lost. It is important to note that for the last two months of 1939, German mines accounted for more losses than U-boat attacks. From the British perspective, the results of the opening round were not discouraging. Most importantly, losses of merchants in convoy were negligible, as indicated in the table below.

Losses to Allied Merchant Ships in Convoy, September–December 1939

Convoy route	Ships in convoy	Lost in convoy	Lost as stragglers	Lost out of convoy
HX (Halifax to Britain)	431	0	0	3
HG (Gibraltar to Britain)	473	0	0	3
OA/OB (outbound from Britain) OG (Britain to Gibraltar)	2,516	2	3	3
SL (Sierra Leone to Britain)	302	1	1	0

In the first two months of 1940, the total number of U-boats available and those on patrol were reduced. For those few boats on patrol, there were still plenty of targets in the form of ships steaming independent routes. Occasionally, U-boats spotted and tried to attack convoys. On 30 January, *U-55* attacked Convoy OA 80G and sank two ships. The alerted escort mounted a counter-attack and with the help of a Sunderland flying boat sank *U-55*. *U-41* went after Convoy OA 84 on 5 February and suffered a similar fate after sinking a single merchant. On 17–18 February, Dönitz mounted his

Throughout 1941, when targets were plentiful in most areas, the length of a patrol for a U-boat was largely dependent on the number of torpedoes remaining. A Type VII boat, like that shown here, only carried 14 torpedoes. If possible, the deck gun was used to finish off crippled ships to avoid the use of a precious torpedo. Once a boat had exhausted its load of torpedoes, it might be ordered to remain at sea to report weather conditions in the Atlantic, which was useful information for German meteorologists. (Naval History and Heritage Command)

third attempt to employ a wolfpack against a convoy under the control of a tactical commander. This time, five boats were earmarked for the operation under the command of Hartmann. Although the B-Dienst provided the location of two convoys west of Portugal, the wolfpack failed to assemble as planned. Only two U-boats were able to mount a joint operation, and they were unable to attack either convoy. Four stragglers or independents were dispatched.

During the first two months of 1940, 85 ships were lost to U-boats, the highest losses of the war to date over a two-month period. Of these, only seven were in convoy, a clear indicator of the value of convoys and of the continued wealth of targets proceeding independently.

In March, the Germans turned their attention to preparations for the invasion of Norway scheduled for the following month. In the first six months of the Atlantic campaign, U-boats sank 199 Allied merchant ships. If not for the torpedo problem, probably another 50 to 60 ships would have been sent to the bottom. Sinking 199 ships seems like an impressive total, but it was only an average of some 116,000 GRT per month. This was far below what Dönitz estimated was required to bring Britain to its knees and far below the peak German successes in World War I. At this point, British construction of merchant shipping was greater than its losses. Both sides had reason to be satisfied with the results of the first six months of the Atlantic campaign. The Germans had inflicted real losses on Allied shipping with only a handful of submarines. To the British, these losses in no way imperilled the viability of their trade routes. However, the British, beginning with Churchill, realized that the opening months of the campaign did not constitute the main German attack. The British were banking on their assessment that by the time the Germans increased U-boat construction, the RN would have enough time to deploy a significantly larger and more effective escort force.

U-boat losses had been fairly heavy during the first few months of the war, given the immature state of British defences. Fifteen were sunk in the Atlantic by February. Of these, nine were accounted for by convoy escorts. Early war British submarine hunter groups accounted for three, and aircraft for a single U-boat. It was obvious that the seemingly defensive concept of convoys was actually the most effective way to kill U-boats, since it forced the submarines to come to the most heavily defended sections of the ocean.

THE NORWEGIAN DIVERSION

One of the hallmarks of the campaign from the German perspective was the periodic diversion of U-boats for missions other than direct attacks on shipping in the Atlantic. The first major example of this was the Norway campaign from April to June in 1940. On 1 March, Hitler issued his directive for *Weserübung* – the occupation of Denmark and Norway. For the Kriegsmarine, this was a very risky operation, and one that required all its strength. As a result, the war in the Atlantic against British shipping was essentially placed on temporary hold.

For the Kriegsmarine to land troops successfully at several points in Norway, including as far north as Narvik, in the face of the much larger RN was an incredibly bold and even reckless operation. Commencing on 9 April, the Germans gained lodgements as planned and then established air superiority, which led to eventual victory. This risky operation resulted in heavy German losses – one heavy cruiser, two light cruisers, ten destroyers and four U-boats.

The impact of the campaign was significant. Virtually the entire ocean-going submarine force – 31 boats – was employed in the invasion of Norway. This gave the shipping in the Atlantic a three-month respite. During this period, Allied shipping losses at the hands of submarines were light – only 23 in March, 7 in April and 13 in May. Of these, only 2, 4 and 9, respectively, were sunk in the North Atlantic. There was no compensation for the U-boat force by sinking RN warships or transports off Norway. U-boat attacks during the Norwegian campaign accounted for only one RN submarine and six other ships. Faulty torpedoes were the primary culprit for this lack of success. Reports from the frustrated U-boat skippers indicated that at least 20 certain torpedo failures were recorded against British warships and transports. In exchange for these scant successes, four U-boats were lost during the Norwegian campaign.

A significant side benefit of the Norwegian campaign for the Kriegsmarine was the occupation of the country and the opening of its ports and airfields for German use. For the U-boats, this meant they could circumvent the British blockade of the North Sea. Using Norwegian bases did not give the U-boats direct access to the Atlantic, but it dramatically reduced the difficulty of reaching their desired operating areas.

DÖNITZ PREPARES FOR THE NEXT PHASE

Conditions in the Atlantic campaign changed dramatically by the middle of 1940. German conquests of Norway and France eliminated the geographic constraints of trying to sortie U-boats from the North Sea from which all exits were patrolled by the RN. Transiting from bases on the North Sea to the Western Approaches took at least nine days and consumed roughly a third of a Type VII's fuel; operating from France, transit time and fuel expenditure were greatly reduced. After the armistice with France in June 1940, Dönitz moved quickly to open French bases for his U-boats. Operating from bases in France, U-boats had direct access to the Atlantic. By July, U-boats were using Lorient for resupply. The following month, the shipyard in Lorient was placed back in operation under German supervision for the overhaul

Merchant and U-boat losses, September 1939–May 1940

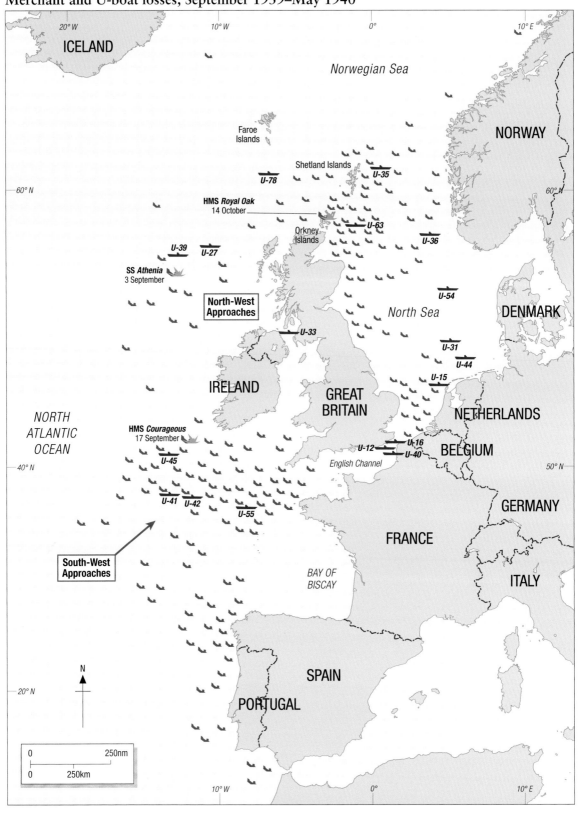

ICELAND

20° W

10° W

0°

10° E

Norwegian Sea

Faroe
Islands

NORWAY

Shetland Islands

U-78

U-35

60° N

60° N

HMS *Royal Oak*
14 October

U-63

Orkney
Islands

U-36

U-39

U-27

SS *Athenia*
3 September

U-54

North-West
Approaches

North Sea

DENMARK

U-33

U-31

IRELAND

U-44

GREAT
BRITAIN

U-15

NORTH
ATLANTIC
OCEAN

NETHERLANDS

HMS *Courageous*
17 September

U-12

U-16

U-40

BELGIUM

40° N

U-45

English Channel

50° N

U-41 *U-42*

GERMANY

U-55

FRANCE

ITALY

South-West
Approaches

BAY OF
BISCAY

N

20° N

SPAIN

PORTUGAL

0   250nm

0   250km

10° W

0°

10° E

All 24 Type VIIB boats were completed by early 1940, making them a mainstay in the opening phases of the Atlantic campaign. With an additional 33 tons of fuel, these boats possessed an increased range of 8,700nm, which enabled them to operate well into the Western Approaches. Note the 88mm deck gun forward of the conning tower. Many of the top aces achieved their scores in Type VIIB boats. (Naval History and Heritage Command)

of submarines. In time, it proved more efficient than German shipyards. Final proof that the centre of gravity for U-boat operations had shifted to France was provided when Dönitz moved his headquarters to Kernevel Point, adjacent to Lorient.

Even with the reduced state of British anti-submarine defences during the second half of 1940, the Kriegsmarine lacked the means to take full advantage. Raeder and Dönitz fought a continual battle with Hitler and the German army and air force to allocate additional resources to the expansion of the U-boat fleet. The basic constraint was that the German war economy was inadequate to support a multi-front war. Until July 1940, expansion of the U-boat force was not seen as a top priority.

During the last four months of 1939, Dönitz lost nine boats; during the first half of 1940, another 18 were lost. Production of new boats was not keeping up with losses. In part because of the unusually cold winter of 1939/40, production was not as robust as expected. Only seven boats were delivered in the last months of 1939 and 13 during the entire first half of 1940. This translated into a net reduction of the U-boat force by seven boats.

From 1 June 1940 until 31 March 1941, 72 boats were commissioned. Since losses during this period was only 13 boats, the total force increased to 109. However, there were growing pains during this expansion, as some boats had to be retired from front-line service for training purposes and many of the new boats were still in the process of sea trials and crew training. The Norwegian campaign had another result – after it was concluded, the participating U-boats required an overhaul. The effect of all these factors resulted in the decline of boats in the North Atlantic. In January 1941, there were a mere eight boats on station in the entire Atlantic, the lowest point in the entire campaign. The total number of boats on front-line duty fell to 22 in February 1941 – also the lowest level of the war. The total U-boat force was up to 89, but most of these were either conducting trials or devoted to training in the Baltic Sea. Monthly production for the preceding quarter was less than eight boats per month.

PREVIOUS PAGE, BOTTOM
The crew of a Type VIIC loads a G-7 torpedo. On the Type VII boat, a torpedo was loaded into the four bow tubes and the single stern tube. Up to nine spare torpedoes could be carried internally. Both variants of the G-7 were straight running. The G-7a was driven by super-heated steam and had a top speed of 44kts. It left a visible wake. The G-7e was an all-electric torpedo that was simpler, cheaper to build and was wakeless. It required more maintenance and possessed a shorter range. Both variants were carried on German submarines at the start of the war. (Naval History and Heritage Command)

Another issue reducing the effectiveness of the U-boats was the unreliability of their torpedoes. The difficulty of American submarine torpedoes during the first years of the war is well known, but the Germans faced a similar issue that took almost as long to address. The standard German torpedo, the G7, possessed both contact and magnetic detonators – both had severe problems. The magnetic detonator offered great promise as it was designed to explode under a ship, which increased its explosive effect. But as early as September 1939, it was apparent that the magnetic detonator was faulty. All too often it exploded well short of the target. Aside from resulting in the failure of the attack, it also served to alert the defenders to the presence of a U-boat, and on several occasions the boat was lost as a result. As early as 2 October 1939, Dönitz ordered that only torpedoes with contact detonators be used, but soon it was clear that these also had issues. Because of a leak in the depth-control mechanism, the torpedo ran too deep. The contact fuse for the torpedo failed to operate if the torpedo struck the target at an angle of less than 50 degrees, well below its supposed capability of exploding, even if it struck at 21 degrees.

THE BRITISH PREPARE

During the months following the fall of France, the RN was stretched to its limit. Losses to destroyers and other escort ships had been heavy during the Norwegian campaign and the evacuation of the British Expeditionary Force from France. After the fall of France, Britain was exposed to the real threat of invasion. This required the Admiralty to retain large numbers of destroyers in home waters to repel any invasion. All this reduced the number of destroyers and other escorts available for convoy protection. Until October 1941, lack of escorts forced the RN to reduce the coverage of escorts for convoys departing from and arriving to Britain. The increased threat of air attack from bases in France also forced shipping to stop using the approaches south of Ireland after 15 July. As a result, all shipping was forced to use the North Channel into the Irish Sea, making it easier for U-boats to find targets.

HMS *Roxburgh* was one of the 50 ex-USN destroyers provided to Britain in 1940. Many of these were modified by the British before entering service in the RN. This 1942 view of *Roxburgh* shows the ship after most of its original USN armament had been removed in favour of additional anti-submarine and anti-aircraft weapons. Note the Type 271 radar fitted on the bridge. (Naval History and Heritage Command)

HMS *Hamilton* was an American destroyer handed over to the RN on 23 September 1940. Following repairs from a collision, it was given to the RCN in July 1941. *Hamilton* was one of the 50 ex-USN destroyers given to the RN at a critical point in the Atlantic campaign. (Naval History and Heritage Command)

Despite shipping losses up to this point, British commerce was not significantly impacted. Only in June and October 1940 did losses surpass 300,000 GRT. This was far below the worst losses recorded during World War I.

In contrast, British defences were thickening. On 5 September, an agreement was reached with the United States for the transfer of 50 destroyers in exchange for the use of eight bases in the Western Hemisphere, namely in the Caribbean and Bermuda. Within the month, eight were turned over to the RN, and by the end of the year, most arrived in Britain. In November, the first radar was installed on British destroyers. Coastal Command was also gathering strength and in April 1941 began to fly missions from bases at Reykjavik and Kaldadarnes in Iceland.

THE BATTLE RESUMED

Following the pause in U-boat operations in the Atlantic during the Norwegian campaign, on 15 May 1940 the first U-boats departed their bases to resume the attack on British sea lanes. Since the South-West Approaches were closed, forcing all inbound shipping to be funnelled through the North Channel into the Irish Sea, Dönitz concentrated his available boats on the approaches to the North Channel.

By mid-August, nine boats were operating in this area. Using newly acquired bases in Norway, even the short-range Type II boats were able to take part in the campaign. Usually, it was difficult for the Germans to find convoys with only a few boats on station. In this instance, the convergence of convoys and independently routed ships into the North-West Approaches made the problem much simpler. In August and September, some 100 ships were sunk in this area.

Following the Norwegian campaign, *U-37* was the first to return to the Atlantic. Between 19 May and 2 June, while operating west of the Bay of Biscay, it sank nine merchants. In late May, five boats were deployed to form the first named wolfpack – the *Rösing* pack. In the middle of June, the boats operated together north-west of Cape Finisterre against troop Convoy US 3. No success was recorded against the heavily defended convoy, but during this deployment, the five boats sank a total of 27 ships. Two of them covertly refuelled and took on water and foodstuffs from a German supply ship in Vigo, Spain, during their deployments. These replenishment operations, a

Life for both Allied and German submarine crews participating in the Atlantic campaign was both brutal and monotonous. For the Germans, the approximately 44 men on a Type VII submarine lived together in a cramped hull until fuel or torpedoes ran out and the patrol concluded. In this view, a member of the U-boat bridge crew surveys the ocean for targets. With no radar, finding the enemy was largely dependent upon the visual acuity of the watch. (Naval History and Heritage Command)

blatant breach of Spanish neutrality obligations, were to continue periodically throughout 1944.

A second wave of seven boats departed in the first week of June to operate west of the English Channel and in the Bay of Biscay. While en route to their assigned patrol areas, the group encountered other convoys west of the British Isles. Attacks against the convoys were not lucrative, but there were still many other targets. The seven boats accounted for 32 ships of over 170,000 GRT. From this group, *U-30* was the first U-boat to enter Lorient on 5 July.

Dönitz's tonnage war played out wherever he thought British defences were weak. One of these areas was the South Atlantic, which was beyond the range of most U-boats. The first boat ordered to patrol in this area was *U-A*, a Type IX boat modified to Turkish requirements but commissioned into the Kriegsmarine in 1939. Departing on 11 June, it ranged as far south as Freetown where it was replenished from an auxiliary cruiser on 19 July. All told, seven ships (over 40,000 GRT) were sunk during this deployment.

In mid-June, Dönitz prepared a third wave of eight U-boats for operations in the North Channel and off Cape Finisterre. This group feasted on independent ships, while occasionally attacking convoys. The tally for these boats was 23 ships sunk, including one destroyer. However, the RN exacted a high price. On 23 June, Flower-class corvette *Arabis* probably sank *U-122*, marking the first success for a ship of this class. On 1 July, V-class destroyer *Vansittart*, part of the escort for Convoy SL 36, sank *U-102*. The same day, *U-26* attacked Convoy OA 175, sinking one ship and damaging another. However, another Flower-class corvette, supported by a Sunderland, sank the U-boat before it could exact any more damage. When either low on fuel or out of torpedoes, the U-boats were forced to break off their deployments. Four of the surviving boats of this group arrived at Lorient.

Between 10 and 23 July, five Type IIC boats were deployed off the North Channel. Only six ships were sunk before the boats were forced to return to base. In late July, four of the boats based at Lorient deployed to the waters off the North Channel. *U-34* sank four ships in Convoy OB 188 between 26 and 27 July. From 28 to 31 July, *U-99*, under the rising star Otto Kretschmer, sank four ships and then, on 2 August, dispatched three tankers from OB 191. The other two boats also attacked convoys successfully.

In response to the Germans using French ports, the RN began to deploy submarines off German-occupied ports in the Bay of Biscay in late July. On 20 August, *Cachalot* sank *U-51*.

In August, four submarines were deployed from Germany and five from Lorient in the North Channel. Each of the boats enjoyed some success against ships steaming independently and in convoys. No U-boats were lost to British counter-attacks, but on its return to Germany, *U-57* collided with a Norwegian freighter north-west of Hamburg on 3 September and was lost (though it was raised and returned to service in January 1941).

THE FIRST HAPPY TIME

The summer of 1940 was a period of German success in the Atlantic campaign. So extraordinary was this period that U-boat crews called it the 'Happy Time'. It was also during this period that Dönitz's wolfpack tactic began to work. The first really successful wolfpack operation took place over three days from 6 to 8 September against Convoy SC 2. The convoy had 53 ships and an escort of two destroyers, two sloops, one corvette and two ASW trawlers. Dönitz received cueing information from B-Dienst on 30 August and had time to deploy four boats against the convoy. The battle opened on 6 September when the escorts drove the first encroaching U-boat away. Just before midnight, two boats tried again, and this time Prien's *U-47* penetrated the screen to sink three freighters. The following day, long-range flying boats gave the convoy a day of respite. On 8 September, the first two U-boats again pressed their attacks and Prien torpedoed another ship. Later that night, two more boats arrived, and *U-28* sank another ship. This was a case study of U-boat tactics and why the British were unable to counter them. All attacks against the convoy were made at night on the surface. As such, sonar aboard the escorts was useless. On a dark night, and with the small silhouette of the U-boats, spotting them was very difficult. As a result, Convoy SC 2 lost five ships of almost 21,000 GRT without loss to the Germans.

In this image, Fritz-Julius Lemp, captain of *U-30*, is awarded the Knight's Cross of the Iron Cross on 14 August 1940 by Dönitz. Lemp was a controversial figure known for his role in the *Athenia* incident and for the loss of his second boat, *U-110*, which gave the British a major intelligence victory. He was also a successful U-boat commander with 20 ships sunk (96,639 GRT). (Naval History and Heritage Command)

AN ACE STRIKES, 21/22 SEPTEMBER 1940 (PP.58–59)

Convoy HX 72 departed Halifax on 9 September 1940 with 43 ships. As was the norm for this period of the war, the initial escort for a convoy headed to Britain was an armed merchant cruiser (in this case *Jervis Bay*) for protection against surface raiders until it reached the Western Approaches and picked up an anti-submarine escort. On 20 September, *Jervis Bay* departed to escort a westbound convoy. Since the anti-submarine escort was not scheduled to meet the convoy until the afternoon of 21 September, HX 72 was entirely unescorted when it was spotted by *U-47* at dusk on 20 September. In response, Dönitz ordered another five boats to converge on HX 72. The first to make contact at about midnight was *U-99*. Otto Kretschmer's boat launched an attack and hit three ships. The following day, more boats joined the attack, including *U-100* under Joachim Schepke and *U-48*. *U-48* attacked from outside the convoy,

but only succeeded in damaging a single ship. As scheduled, the British escort, comprising a destroyer, a sloop and three corvettes, joined the convoy in the afternoon, giving the convoy a brief respite. After dark, Schepke began his attack. He boldly slipped inside the columns of the convoy to make his attacks from close range in order not to waste a single torpedo. Within minutes, three ships were torpedoed. The escorts searched for the attacker without success since *U-100* was already inside the convoy. Schepke struck again just after midnight. This time, three more ships were torpedoed, but *U-100* was spotted and forced to break off its attack. Later, Schepke sank a seventh ship. This scene depicts *U-100* on the surface making its midnight attack **(1)**. One ship has already been torpedoed and is on fire **(2)**. The second had just been hit by one of Schepke's torpedoes **(3)**. In total, HX 72 lost 11 ships, seven to Schepke.

The four boats that had attacked SC 2 were joined by another six and continued operations off the North Channel. In mid-September, three boats attacked three different convoys. On 20 September, Prien spotted Convoy HX 72 and maintained contact, allowing Dönitz to order another five boats to join the attack. Kretschmer in *U-99* opened the assault on the convoy later that day before the escort group reached the inbound convoy. He torpedoed three of the convoy's 43 ships, all of which eventually sank. *U-48* sank another ship early on 21 September before the escort group of one destroyer, one sloop and three corvettes finally arrived. With the destroyer assigned to assist the previously torpedoed ships, only four escorts remained to protect the convoy. After darkness on 21 September, Joachim Schepke in *U-100* began a virtuoso performance. Over four hours, Schepke torpedoed seven ships amounting to over 50,000 GRT. When the carnage was over, HX 72 had lost 11 ships of almost 73,000 GRT. September was the most successful month to date for the U-boats with a total of 59 ships sunk for a total of 295,335 GRT.

From late September to mid-October, ten U-boats took up patrol off the North Channel. All but two of these boats gained some level of success. As during the previous month, Dönitz was able to mass his boats on convoys and achieved several successes. The first began when *U-48* spotted Convoy SC 7 with over 30 merchants on 17 October. The convoy was initially only lightly protected with two sloops and a corvette, but the escort was later reinforced with another sloop and a corvette. What was to become a massacre began later on 17 October when *U-48* sank two ships. Upon receipt of *U-48*'s contact report, Dönitz set up a patrol line with five more boats. On the evening of 18/19 October, the convoy ran into the patrol line. All six boats were able to launch attacks during the night, some more than once. In total, 20 ships from Convoy SC 7 were sunk and three damaged. Kretschmer's *U-99* was the most successful boat with six ships sunk and another torpedoed. Again, the small escort was unable to contend with the bold attacks of the German submarines mounted on the surface.

Just a day later, it was the turn of Convoy HX 79 to be subjected to concerted attack. The large convoy of 49 ships looked to be well defended with two destroyers, four corvettes, three ASW trawlers, one oceangoing minesweeper and a submarine. *U-47* was the first to spot the convoy and by the night of 19/20 October, four more boats had arrived to join Prien's attack.

All five boats scored heavily with *U-47* penetrating the convoy to sink three ships and torpedo three more. During the night, 12 ships of just over 75,000 GRT were lost. Most submarines were out of torpedoes after the two big convoy battles, leaving only a handful in the

The fate of the *Empress of Britain*, a 42,348 GRT passenger liner, provided testimony to the potential of coordination between the U-boat force and the Luftwaffe. On 26 October 1940, the ship was struck by bombs from a single Fw 200. Alerted to the presence of the burning ship, *U-32* was vectored to finish it off. (Author's collection)

SS *Scoresby* was a typical merchant ship plying the North Atlantic in the first phases of the Atlantic campaign. Capable of only 8.5 kts, *Scoresby* was placed in an SC convoy. While part of SC 7, it was torpedoed by *U-48* and sunk. The entire crew was rescued by an escort. (Author's collection)

EVENTS

16 October

1. Of the 36 merchant ships originally in convoy, 35 remain. The only escort is sloop *Scarborough*.

2. *U-124* sinks Canadian ship *Trevisa* when the ship lags behind. Just 14 survivors are later rescued by *Bluebell*.

17 October

3. *Fowey* and *Bluebell* arrive to reinforce the escort.

4. *U-38* sinks the Greek ship *Aenos*.

5. *U-48* spots SC 7 and fires a salvo of three torpedoes; one each hits *Languedoc* and *Scoresby*, third torpedo misses. *Languedoc* is assessed to be beyond repair and is sunk by gunfire from *Bluebell*. The crews of both ships are rescued by *Bluebell*. *Scarborough* attacks *U-48* with depth charges but afterward loses contact with the convoy.

18 October

6. *Leith* and *Heartsease* arrive to reinforce the escort.

7. *U-38* torpedoes British ship *Carsbreck*; *Leith* and *Heartsease* conduct depth charge attacks with no success. *Heartsease* is assigned to escort the damaged ship back to port and it survives.

8. Six U-boats attack SC 7 over the span of six hours during the night of 18/19 October. Most of the attacks are made on the surface from within the convoy.

9. *U-46* sinks *Beatus*, *Convallaria* and *Gunborg*.

10. *U-99* sinks *Empire Miniver*, *Fiscus* and Greek ship *Niritos*.

11. *U-100* damages Dutch *Boekelo* and *Shekatika*.

12. *U-101* damages *Blairspey* and sinks *Creekirk* at 2112hrs with the loss of all hands.

19 October

13. 0122hrs: *U-101* fires three torpedoes, followed by a fourth. One hits *Assyrian*, and another *Soesterberg*, both of which later sink. Another merchant ship spots the boat and opens fire; it avoids torpedoes by turning away.

14. *U-99* sinks *Empire Brigade*, Norwegian *Snefjeld* and Greek *Thalia*. *Clintonia* is damaged.

15. *U-123*, on its first patrol, sinks four ships. *Clintonia* straggles behind after being damaged; it is shelled and sunk by *U-123*. *Sedgepool* is sunk by torpedoes. *Boekelo* and *Shekatika*, first torpedoed by *U-100*, are finished off by *U-123*.

16. Germans break off attacks to go after Convoy HX 79, which had caught up with SC 7. In total, eight different U-boats sink 20 ships and damage three. No U-boats are lost or damaged. Only 15 ships reach Britain, including the three damaged ones.

THE SLAUGHTER OF SC 7

Between 16 and 19 October 1940, a group of eight U-boats, led by some of the top-scoring German submarine commanders, attacked Convoy SC 7 and inflicted the heaviest loss to a single convoy during the war. No U-boats were sunk or even damaged in this action.

GERMAN FORCES
A. *U-38* (Type IX boat) (Heinrich Liebe)
B. *U-46* (Type VIIB) (Engelbert Endrass)
C. *U-48* (Type VIIB) (Heinrich Bleichrodt)
D. *U-99* (Type VIIB) (Otto Kretschmer)
E. *U-100* (Type VIIB) (Joachim Schepke)
F. *U-101* (Type VIIB) (Fritz Frauenheim)
G. *U-123* (Type IXB) (Karl-Heinz Moehle)
H. *U-124* (Type IXB) (Georg-Wilhelm Schulz)

ALLIED FORCES
1. Convoy SC 7 with 35 ships arranged into six columns
2. HMS *Bluebell* (Flower-class corvette)
3. HMS *Fowey* (Shoreham-class sloop)
4. HMS *Heartsease* (Flower-class corvette)
5. HMS *Leith* (Grimsby-class sloop)
6. HMS *Scarborough* (Hastings-class sloop)

Jim Laurier

THE CONDOR STRIKES, 26 OCTOBER 1940 (PP.64–65)

Beginning in 1940, German Fw 200 Condor long-range reconnaissance bombers from I/KG40 operated over the waters west of Britain **(1)**. On 26 October, a Condor flown by Bernhard Jope encountered the passenger liner *Empress of Britain* 70nm north-west of Ireland **(2)**. At 42,348 GRT, the *Empress of Britain* was Britain's second-largest ship and the tenth-largest merchant ship in the world. Jope spotted a very large ship through the clouds and changed course to make a low-level attack from astern. In the first attack run from about 650ft, he dropped a single 551lb bomb which hit the ship port side and started a fire. Jope made a wide turn to make another stern attack. Flying through what he described as stronger defensive fire than the first pass, he dropped another bomb, which missed. The next two passes were made from ahead of the target to avoid the heavy defensive fire from astern **(3)**. Altogether, four 551lb bombs were

dropped and two hit. When the Condor left the area, *Empress of Britain* was aflame and showed a slight list. Following the attack, the ship's captain ordered it to be abandoned, leaving only a skeleton crew aboard. This was accomplished, but Jope's message that the ship was still afloat prompted orders to *U-32* to proceed to the scene and finish off the huge liner. Under the command of Hans Jenisch, *U-32* arrived to find the liner under tow and under air and naval protection. After stalking the target for nearly 24 hours, Jenisch got into position to launch a total of three torpedoes, of which two hit. In the early hours of 28 October, *Empress of Britain* slipped under the waves, becoming the largest British ship lost during the war. This scene shows the liner under attack during Jope's third attack run. The Fw 200 is approaching the ship from ahead. Note that the ship is already on fire aft but is still under way **(4)**.

Atlantic for the remainder of the month. Kretschmer scored another major success on 3 November west of Ireland when he sank two auxiliary merchant cruisers totalling 30,000 GRT.

After the final tally was taken, October 1940 had become the most successful month thus far for the U-boats. In total, the U-boats sank a total of 63 ships (352,407 GRT), with the highlights being the two major convoy battles.

In the winter of 1940, the number of boats on patrol declined, but the Germans continued to score heavily against weakly defended convoys. In November, seven boats were deployed to the area west of the North Channel with another two farther to the west on weather duty. In the middle of the month, *U-137* sank three ships in outbound convoys. One of the convoys was targeted by ace boats *U-47* and *U-100*, without success. A Sunderland flying boat equipped with ASV Mark I radar was instrumental in this Allied success. This was the first incident of aerial radar being used to detect a U-boat and provided a portent of the impact of aircraft-mounted radar.

Outbound Convoy OB 244 came under attack from *U-103* on 21 November. After sinking two ships, the U-boat was driven off by a Flower-class corvette. Two days later, *U-123* found the same convoy as it was dispersing and sank four ships. At about the same time, *U-100* detected Convoy SC 11 with an escort of a single sloop and sank seven ships. Aside from Schepke in *U-100* sinking seven ships of 24,601 GRT, other boats with impressive scores during the months included *U-103* with eight ships of 43,651 GRT, and *U-123*'s six ships of 27,536 GRT. In return, *U-104* was sunk by a mine north-west of Ireland.

In the latter half of November and into December, only five boats were on patrol in the North Atlantic (another three were on weather duties). One of the submarines detected Convoy HX 90 just before the arrival of its escort group. Three boats were able to attack the undefended convoy on the night of 1/2 December. Surprisingly, the carnage was limited to five ships sunk and another four more torpedoed and damaged (one was later sunk by another U-boat). The next afternoon, a different U-boat found the convoy and sank two more ships. On 11/12 December, *U-96* sank four ships from Convoy HX 92. In addition to the convoy attacks, many independent ships were located and sunk. Losses during the month were heavy – 37 ships of 212,590 GRT.

Most Flower-class units served in the RN. Nine were given to the Free French Navy. *Aconit*, pictured here, established a fine war record from July 1941 until the end of the war. In addition to the RN and the Free French, nine other Allied navies operated Flower-class corvettes during the war, including the RCN and the USN. (Naval History and Heritage Command)

Merchant and U-boat losses, June 1940–March 1941

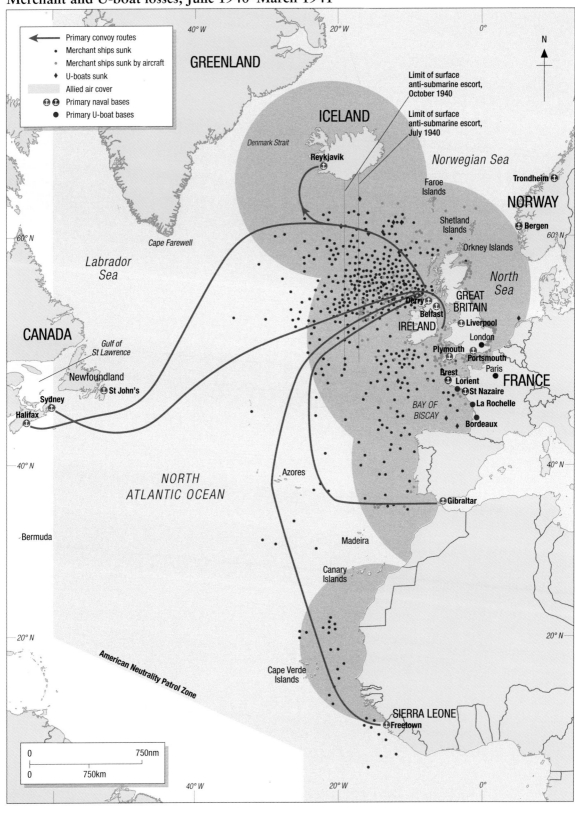

Primary convoy routes
Merchant ships sunk
Merchant ships sunk by aircraft
U-boats sunk
Allied air cover
Primary naval bases
Primary U-boat bases

GREENLAND

ICELAND

Denmark Strait

Reykjavik

Limit of surface
anti-submarine escort,
October 1940

Limit of surface
anti-submarine escort,
July 1940

Norwegian Sea

Trondheim

Faroe
Islands

NORWAY

Shetland
Islands

Bergen

Orkney Islands

Cape Farewell

Labrador
Sea

North
Sea

CANADA

Gulf of
St Lawrence

Newfoundland

St John's

Sydney

Halifax

Derry

Belfast

IRELAND

GREAT
BRITAIN

Liverpool

London

Plymouth

Portsmouth

Brest

Paris

Lorient

FRANCE

St Nazaire

La Rochelle

BAY OF
BISCAY

Bordeaux

NORTH
ATLANTIC OCEAN

Azores

Gibraltar

Bermuda

Madeira

Canary
Islands

American Neutrality Patrol Zone

Cape Verde
Islands

SIERRA LEONE

Freetown

0   750nm

0   750km

68

Dönitz kept the pressure on in other areas beyond the North Atlantic. Type IXB boat *U-65* deployed on 15 October and headed for a patrol area off West Africa. With the assistance of a supply ship, it conducted an extended deployment in the South Atlantic until early January. During this deployment, *U-65* sank eight ships of 47,785 GRT and damaged another.

As the U-boat crews enjoyed the Happy Time, there were signs that British defences were growing more effective. The numbers of escorts continued to rise as more corvettes entered service and destroyers were released from anti-invasion duties. In June–July, at the height of the escort shortage, even large convoys had only a single ASW escort. In November, the average escort rose to two ships. Beginning in early 1941, escorts received an important technological boost in the form of the Type 286 radar. It was fairly primitive: with no rotating antenna the escort had to manoeuvre to cover the target area. When it worked, ranges up to 20nm were recorded. Another technical improvement was the introduction of improved illumination rounds, which would make it easier to spot U-boats on the surface at night. Also in mid-1941, HF-DF systems were deployed on escorts. Given the volume of U-boat radio communications, this was an invaluable aid to provide U-boat locations in the vicinity of a convoy. The Germans thought that such a system could not be made small enough to fit aboard small escorts, so they made no attempt to reduce the volume of the radio traffic. Escorts also received radio-telephones, increasing their tactical coordination.

Most importantly, it was now painfully obvious that the effectiveness of the escorts rested primarily on better organization and training. In 1941, permanent escort groups were created. Every effort was made to keep the groups together even when they fell well below their full strength of eight ships. The second game changer was improved training. ASW training was moved from Portland to Western Approaches Command's new Anti-Submarine Training School at Tobermory on the Isle of Mull. Beginning on 1 July 1940, every new escort received one month of intensive ASW training. Following this, the ship joined its group for more training as part of the group. An ASW tactics school was also established at Derby House in Liverpool to train officers in an escort group in various tactical scenarios.

As the threat of invasion ebbed, Coastal Command began to shift its focus back to the Atlantic. After the fall of France, Coastal Command's priority was to watch the North Sea and English Channel for signs of a German invasion. Coastal Command's force level increased slowly, with better aircraft entering service. Given its long range and heavy payload, the Sunderland was particularly effective. It was the first aircraft to receive radar with the introduction of the ASV Mark I in the autumn of 1940. Against a submarine-sized target, the original set possessed only a 3–6nm detection range, depending on the aircraft's altitude. At the end of 1940, 25 Sunderlands and 24 Hudsons carried this radar. In late 1940, the more reliable Mark II entered service. Detection range was much better and by mid-1941 daytime attacks by aircraft on U-boats increased by 20 per cent. Night attacks were rendered more possible, but they were generally ineffective, since the radar had a minimum range of 1nm and in the final stage of the attack the attacking aircraft could not see its target. However, this was to be solved by the Leigh Light, a searchlight that lit up the submarines during the last seconds of the approach. In spring 1941, a modified depth charge reached service and replaced the ineffective anti-submarine bomb.

At the start of the war, the Coastal Command's most capable aircraft was the Short Sunderland flying boat patrol bomber. With its long endurance and bomb load of 2,000lb, it was a significant threat to U-boats. However, only 39 Mark I aircraft were in service in September 1939. In October 1940, 25 Sunderlands received radar. This is a Sunderland providing cover for a troop convoy which includes a battleship. (Stratford Archive)

With the replacement of the Anson with the Hudson, Coastal Command effectively closed the immediate areas of the North Channel to the U-boats by October. Sunderland patrols forced the Germans even farther out from the British Isles, in turn making the problem of finding convoys much more difficult. After the debacles of Convoys SC 7 and HX 79, Coastal Command changed its employment doctrine to flying in direct support of convoys. More than anything, it was Coastal Command's new weapons and tactics that brought the Happy Time to an end.

Losses to Allied Merchant Ships in Convoy, 1940

Convoy route	Ships in convoy	Lost in convoy	Lost as stragglers	Lost out of convoy
HX (Halifax to Britain)	3,424	48	33	24
SC (Sydney to Britain)	508	29	13	4
HG (Gibraltar to Britain)	1,718	4	5	2
OA/OB (outbound from Britain)	9,055	37	24	57
OG (Britain to Gibraltar)	2,197	6	3	0
SL (Sierra Leone to Britain)	1,502	7	14	1

For the entire year, 471 merchant ships were lost to U-boat attacks (2,186,158 GRT). In terms of ships, this was less than half the total (1,059) lost to all causes, but the majority of total tonnage lost (3,991,641). These were certainly significant losses, but they did not constitute a mortal threat

to Britain's or the Allies' war efforts. To compensate for losses, production of merchant ships in British yards totalled some 1 million tons and large amounts of neutral shipping were taken over by the British during the year.

At the start of the war, the RN was indecisive about whether to use escorts in submarine hunter groups or in direct convoy escorts. By the end of 1940, it was clear that convoys were effective both offensively and defensively. The bulk of U-boat losses were inflicted during their attacks on convoys, though the scale of these losses was still small. The case for the effectiveness of convoys against submarine attack was clear. Most merchant losses were incurred on ships not in convoy – of 456 merchants sunk by submarines during the year, only 102 were in convoy. Even during the Happy Time, 73 ships were sunk in convoy compared to 144 unescorted ships. Those ships in convoy simply suffered less. The critical HX convoys suffered only 2 per cent losses, HG convoys less than 1 per cent, and even the slow and vulnerable SC convoys lost just 6 per cent. Losses to outbound convoys were even less on a percentage basis.

In many ways, the Happy Time of July–October 1940 was the highwater mark for Dönitz's U-boats. The B-Dienst was operating at a high level. The absence of effective air patrols or convoy defences made it easy for the U-boats to attack their targets. But by winter, the increased range and effectiveness of Coastal Command patrol made it difficult to detect a convoy and then mass enough U-boats for a decisive attack before the convoy came under air cover. In December 1940, only a single convoy was located and attacked by U-boats.

The significant role of the RCN has been long overlooked in the Atlantic campaign. One of the few Canadian ships available at the start of the war was HMCS *Saguenay*, a River-class destroyer. In October 1940, it was transferred to serve as a convoy escort on the North Atlantic run. On 1 December 1940, *Saguenay* was torpedoed west of Ireland by the Italian submarine *Argo* while escorting Convoy HG 47. This was the first RCN ship damaged during the campaign. (Canadian Naval Heritage)

THE 1941 BATTLES

The first month of 1941 started with an exhibition of something close to a coordinated U-boat–Luftwaffe operation. Four boats were deployed west of the North Channel with another farther west on weather duty. With I/KG 40 and its Fw 200 Condors under Dönitz's operational control, German aircraft and submarines attempted joint operations with some degree of success. On 11 January, an outbound convoy was sighted by an Fw 200, but the U-boats were too far away to mount a concerted attack and the convoy lost only a single ship. Three days later, a U-boat sighted another outbound convoy and tried to vector in two Fw 200s without success. On 16 January, an Fw 200 detected another convoy. Though it was able to sink two ships with bombs, the U-boats were unable to attack the convoy, but they did dispatch nearby ships steaming independently. Convoy SC 19 was sighted by *U-93*, which attacked and sank three ships on 29 January. Two other boats called to the scene succeeded in sinking another ship each.

During this period, I/KG 40 recorded 15 ships sunk and three more damaged. Two other ships damaged by air attack were later sunk by submarines. The five deployed U-boats accounted for 12 ships. In one of their better performances, the three Italian submarines deployed to the west of Ireland sank a total of five ships. In total, January was a month of limited success with only 21 ships sunk by submarines in all areas for 126,782 GRT. During the month, only two convoys were attacked; the ships lost were mainly stragglers or ships from dispersed convoys. The Admiralty's Submarine Tracking Room was getting better at providing evasive routing.

From late January to mid-February, the number of boats deployed west of the North Channel was still limited. Farther to the west, Dönitz deployed another group of three Italian submarines. Although Convoy OB 279 was sighted on 3 February by *U-107*, it was only able to sink one ship in convoy and one straggler – no other boats were able to reach the convoy. Despite the lack of success against convoys, the seven deployed boats accounted for a total of 22 ships either steaming independently or straggling from their convoys. In addition, Italian submarine *Bianchi* sank three ships and damaged another. Fw 200s sent another three ships to the bottom.

In February, a convoy (HG 53 out of Gibraltar) came under combined German surface, air and submarine attack for the first time in the war. On 8 February, *U-37* sighted the convoy west of Cape St Vincent. The next day, the submarine attacked and sank two of the convoy's 16 ships. *U-37* maintained contact with the convoy and directed five Fw 200s against it on 9 February. These attacks accounted for another five ships. *U-37* mounted a second attack on 10 February and sank another ship. Still in contact with the convoy, *U-37* was able to bring heavy cruiser *Admiral Hipper* to the scene. Since the convoy dispersed, the cruiser was only able to find and sink a single straggler. In this joint operation, the Germans accounted for nine of HG 53's 16 ships.

Back in the North Atlantic, Convoy OB 287 was sighted by an Fw 200, which proceeded to sink two ships with bombs. In response, Dönitz ordered five U-boats and three Italian submarines to attack the convoy. None of the submarines was able to find the convoy, since the coordinates provided by the aircraft were incorrect. After *U-96* sank one of the ships previously damaged by aircraft, Dönitz called the operation off on 21 February. The next outbound convoy, OB 288, was also detected by aircraft south of Iceland. Fw 200s damaged two ships and gave Dönitz the opportunity to establish a patrol line with six U-boats and two Italian submarines. *U-73* briefly held contact before the convoy changed course to the north. Three U-boats were able to find and attack the convoy on the night of 23/24 February and sank three ships. On the morning of 24 February, the convoy scattered – seven more ships were sunk, one by Italian submarine *Bianchi*.

Next to come under attack was Convoy OB 289. *U-552* first sighted the convoy south-west of Ireland on 23 February, and Dönitz ordered three more boats to converge. During the night of 23/24 February, *U-97* sank three ships and damaged a tanker. Once the convoy dispersed, four other boats sank nine further ships, two from nearby Convoy HX 109. Prien arrived in the area and sighted OB 290 on 25 February. After the attacks on the two previous convoys, the British routed it well to the south to avoid the U-boat concentration. Attacking in the early morning hours of 26 February, Prien sank two ships and damaged two more. Five other boats (two Italian) were ordered to close on the convoy, but they failed to make contact. However, *U-47*'s beacons did succeed in directing six Fw 200s to the convoy on 26 February. In its single most successful attack of the campaign, I/KG 40 sank seven ships and damaged four more. Two stragglers from OB 290 were later sunk, one by Prien and one by *Bianchi*. Total Allied merchant losses in February amounted to 39 ships of 196,783 GRT. Interestingly, this was an excellent month for the Condors, with them accounting for another 27 ships sunk.

In March, Dönitz shifted his boats to the west to continue attacks against outbound convoys west of the North Channel. Convoy OB 292 was located by an Fw 200 on 2 March and lost a single ship to air attack. The British detected the presence of a line of U-boats and evaded attack by giving the convoy evasive steering orders. OB 293 was not as lucky. It was spotted on 6 March by Prien in *U-47*. Dönitz ordered four more boats to the area to form a wolfpack. The convoy's escort of three destroyers and two corvettes gave a good account of itself and turned the battle into a disaster for the U-boat force. On the night of 6/7 March, *U-70* was the first to attack and torpedoed two ships. Prien followed up with an attack by torpedoing a huge 20,000-ton whale factory ship. This was the ace's last success after 31 ships sunk. No further communication was heard from *U-47* – its loss remains unexplained. Kretschmer managed to get *U-99* inside the convoy and finished off the whale factory ship. He also dispatched one of the ships previously damaged by *U-70*. Making another attack, *U-70* torpedoed a Dutch tanker, but then it was rammed by the damaged ship. Two corvettes followed up with a depth charge attack that forced the boat to the surface where it was sunk. When *U-A* launched its attack, it torpedoed a freighter, but then it was surprised by destroyer *Wolverine* and depth charged. Though damaged, the boat was able to return to base. The final U-boat called to the scene failed to make an attack.

Further disaster befell the Germans during the next convoy encounter against HX 112. Escorting the large convoy of 41 ships was the 5th Escort Group of five destroyers and two corvettes with Commander Donald Macintyre making his first deployment as escort group commander. Lemp, now in command of *U-110*, spotted the convoy on 15 March south-east of Iceland. That night, he made two attacks but was driven off by the escorts

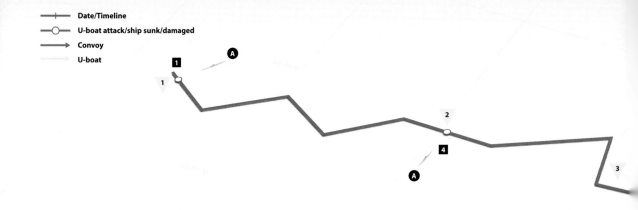

Legend:
- Date/Timeline
- U-boat attack/ship sunk/damaged
- Convoy
- U-boat

EVENTS

15/16 March

1. Convoy HX 112 is sighted by *U-110*. Four other boats (*U-99*, *U-100*, *U-37* and *U-74*) are ordered to head towards the convoy.

2. At 2230hrs, *U-110* torpedoes tanker *Erodona*. The ship is abandoned and breaks in two, but the bow is towed to Iceland and is later used to rebuild the ship. Two destroyers make an unsuccessful attempt to locate the submarine. *Volunteer* cannot relocate the convoy and is lost in the fog.

3. The 5th Escort Group is able to prevent any further attacks.

16/17 March

4. The U-boats track the convoy on the surface and prepare for additional attacks when night falls.

5. *U-99* penetrates the convoy from the north between two escorts and launches a near-perfect attack. Kretschmer sinks four ships (three tankers and a cargo ship) and damages a tanker in quick succession. After reloading, Kretschmer sinks another cargo ship. With his torpedoes expended, Kretschmer decides to withdraw.

6. At about 0048hrs on 17 March, *Walker* sights *U-100* on the surface trying to get into a position in front of the convoy. *Walker* attacks with ten depth charges after *U-100* dives. *Vanoc* also drops six depth charges.

7. At about 0300hrs, *U-100* surfaces and is spotted by destroyer *Vanoc*. The destroyer rams *U-100*; Schepke is killed on his bridge and the submarine goes down taking 38 of the 44 crewmen.

8. At 0337hrs, *U-99* nearly collides with a destroyer while making its escape. Kretschmer dives his boat but is picked up by sonar on *Walker*. The destroyer launches a depth-charge attack and inflicts severe damage on *U-99*. Kretschmer is forced to surface and comes under fire from the two destroyers. Kretschmer and 39 of his crew are pulled from the water by the British.

9 No further attacks are launched on Convoy HX 112.

DEATH OF THE ACES

On the night of 16/17 March 1941, a group of U-boats closed in on Convoy HX 112. German expectations of an easy victory were derailed when an experienced Royal Navy escort group conducted a series of effective counter-attacks. In a shattering blow to the U-boat arm, *U-99* and *U-100* were sunk and aces Otto Kretschmer and Joachim Schepke lost.

GERMAN FORCES
A. *U-110* (Type IXB) (Fritz-Julius Lemp)
B. *U-99* (Type VIIB) (Otto Kretschmer)
C. *U-100* (Type VIIB) (Joachim Schepke)
D. *U-37* (Type IXA) (Asmus Nicolai Clausen)
E. *U-74* (Type VIIB) (Eitel-Friedrich Kentrat)

ALLIED FORCES
1. Convoy HX 112 with 41 ships
2. HMS *Walker* (W-class destroyer)
3. HMS *Vanoc* (V-class destroyer)
4. HMS *Volunteer* (modified W-class destroyer)
5. HMS *Sardonyx* (S-class destroyer)
6. HMS *Scimitar* (S-class destroyer)
7. HMS *Bluebell* (Flower-class corvette)
8. HMS *Hydrangea* (Flower-class corvette)

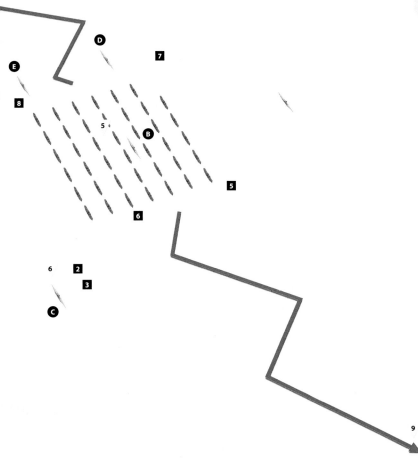

HMS *Vanoc*, a V-class destroyer commissioned in 1917, is shown here in its original World War II configuration. As part of the 5th Escort Group, it played a major role during the defence of Convoy HX 112 in March 1941 when two U-boats were sunk in exchange for the loss of five merchant ships. (Stratford Archive)

after torpedoing a single ship. The next day, *U-37* and Schepke's *U-100* joined the battle, but they were also driven away. Kretschmer in *U-99* arrived during the night of 16 March. He boldly slipped inside the convoy on the surface and sank five ships in quick succession and damaged another. With no torpedoes remaining, Kretschmer submerged to make his escape. *U-99* was detected by sonar and attacked by a very accurate depth charge pattern from destroyer *Walker*. The badly damaged boat was forced to the surface where Kretschmer ordered it to be scuttled. He and 39 other crewmen survived the action and were taken prisoner. When Schepke attempted to penetrate the convoy, he was detected by radar on destroyer *Vanoc*. The destroyer proceeded to ram and then depth charge *U-100*. Schepke was not among the six survivors fished out of the water by the escorts. The defence of Convoys HX 112 and OB 293, the loss of two submarine aces and the capture of a third within two weeks was a tremendous blow to the U-boat force. The first successful use of the Type 286 radar by an escort also marked an important point in the campaign.

For the remainder of March, the Germans were unsuccessful in massing against a convoy. At the end of the month, six boats operated west of the North Channel. Although they had the assistance of I/KG 40, Dönitz was not able to mass more than two boats against a convoy. Nevertheless, several boats sank between two and five ships during the period, primarily against ships steaming independently. For the month, total losses came to 41 ships of 243,020 GRT.

OPERATIONS IN THE SOUTH ATLANTIC

Dönitz understood from his previous foray into the South Atlantic that the area was lightly defended. To stretch British defences even further, he planned the first wolfpack operation in the Freetown area. Three boats were selected – U-105, U-106 and U-124, all Type IXBs. On their southward transit, all three refuelled from a German tanker in Las Palmas in the Canary Islands.

Dönitz ordered U-105 and U-124 to support battleships *Gneisenau* and *Scharnhorst*, which had spotted Convoy SL 67 north-east of the Cape Verde Islands. The convoy was escorted by battleship *Malaya*, which was enough to deter the German capital ships. On the night of 7/8 March, the submarines attacked and sank five ships, but they failed to sight the battleship.

Convoy SL 68 was sighted by U-106 east of the Cape Verde Islands on 15 March, and called in U-105. Over the course of the next seven days, U-105 sank five ships and U-106 two, while also damaging *Malaya*. The single torpedo hit forced the battleship into repairs in the United States for four months. Meanwhile, U-124 operated for four weeks off Freetown, during which time it sank seven ships before departing on 20 April after expending all its torpedoes.

U-105 and U-106 remained on station after refuelling from supply ships and were joined by a second wave of five U-boats and two Italian submarines. By the time they had concluded their deployments, U-105 had sunk 12 ships (71,450 GRT) and U-106 eight (plus damaging *Malaya*). Four of the U-boats in the second wave had also scored heavily. Foremost was U-107 under Günter Hessler (Dönitz's son-in-law, and he made Hessler a U-boat commander although he had never served on a submarine), which sank 14 ships (86,699 GRT), marking this as the most successful patrol by a U-boat during the entire war. In addition, U-103 sank 12 ships, U-38 eight and U-69 another five. The second-wave group was forced to curtail its deployment after the supply ships were sunk by British forces.

One of the returning boats, U-69, was joined by two of the first-wave boats, U-66 and U-123, and mounted a series of attacks against Convoy SL 78 west of the Canary Islands beginning on 27 June. In total, eight ships were sunk.

LULL IN THE NORTH ATLANTIC

Few convoys in the North Atlantic were attacked or even detected during April. Operations by Fw 200s continued but failed to produce results. Late in the month, Convoy HX 121 was sighted by a U-boat west of the North Channel and Dönitz ordered five more boats into position to attack. Four boats made contact, but they managed to sink just four ships. In exchange, U-65 was sunk by the destroyer *Douglas*. Eleven boats recorded the sinking of 14 ships in the North Atlantic during the period. However, when the successes of all boats from all areas are added up, Allied merchant losses rose to 43 ships of 249,375 GRT.

In the first half of May, Dönitz's attempts to attack convoys in the North Atlantic met with more frustration. The WAC began to route convoys farther to the north to benefit from the protection of escorts and aircraft operating from Iceland. After three unsuccessful attempts to attack a convoy, Dönitz

On its second patrol, Type IXB boat *U-110* was part of the pack converging on Convoy OB 318. After sinking two ships, escorts depth charged *U-110* and forced it to the surface. The crew abandoned ship before ensuring that the boat was going to sink. This incredible oversight gave a boarding party from the destroyer *Bulldog* the opportunity to strip the boat of a treasure trove of cryptologic material. (Royal Navy, now in the public domain)

changed tactics. Aggressive patrolling by Coastal Command made operations in the Eastern Atlantic east of 20 degrees west longitude untenable. On 8 May, he ordered his boats more to the south-west of Iceland, sent the Italian boats to their own operational area away from the U-boats and stopped direct coordinated operations with I/KG 40. Several convoys were spotted on 7–8 May, but all were well defended. Convoy OB 318 was attacked by *U-94* south of Iceland and two ships were lost, but the 3rd Escort Group damaged the offender. The following day, parts of the same escort group reinforced the escorts of HX 123. On the night of 8 May, Lemp on *U-110* spotted the convoy and launched an attack that sank two ships. However, corvette *Aubrietia* forced Lemp's boat to the surface with a well-placed depth charge barrage. Once on the surface, the boat was subjected to a barrage of gunfire that killed Lemp. As the remaining crewmen slipped into the sea, a boarding party from destroyer *Bulldog* seized the boat with its Enigma machine and code materials. *Bulldog* took *U-110* in tow, but it sank on 11 May on the way to Iceland. Convoy HX 123 was subjected to additional attacks that sank four more ships and damaged another. In exchange, another U-boat was damaged by depth charges.

Dönitz formed eight boats into the 'West' group and deployed south-south-east of Cape Farewell in southern Greenland in mid-May. On 19 May, one of the boats, *U-94*, spotted Convoy HX 126, launched its attack and sank two ships. The next day, two more ships were sunk by *U-556*. The other West boats also found the convoy, but they were unable to inflict further damage; one of them was damaged by depth charges from an escort. During the course of its transit, 33 merchant ships were part of HX 126. Twelve of these were sunk while it was unescorted in the initial part of its transit or after it dispersed after reaching coastal waters near Britain. For the British, this was another debacle and prompted the institution of continuous anti-submarine coverage for North Atlantic convoys. On 25 May, the same boats were formed into a patrol line in support of the battleship *Bismarck*. The effort was unsuccessful, and the battleship was sunk by British forces on 27 May. In May, merchant losses to Axis submarines rose to 58 ships of 325,492 GRT. However, more than half of these were lost around Freetown as a result of Dönitz's efforts to open a new front in the South Atlantic.

As Allied shipping losses remained high during May, Dönitz lacked the insight to understand that the Germans were losing the Atlantic campaign. British evasive routing of convoys made it increasingly hard for the U-boats to find them. In May, only a single convoy was attacked (HX 126) and it was located at 41 degrees west longitude, south of Greenland – the farthest point to the west a convoy had been attacked. The Germans were being pushed farther and farther out into the Atlantic. Other than the success against HX 126, convoy attacks were mounted by single U-boats that stumbled onto a convoy. HX 126 was the last convoy to undergo a significant attack for three months. Another factor that limited Dönitz's prospects was when, on 18 June, the British changed the top speed of ships required to convoy from 13 to 15 kts. This had the effect of limiting the number of ships steaming independently; losses of such ships went from an average of 35 per month to just 12.

By the start of June, Dönitz formed another West group of six boats. Ten more boats joined West by 20 June. Despite this large concentration, no convoys were found or attacked. However, the Germans continued to feast on ships steaming independently. Eleven boats sank 27 such ships during the month. However, the lack of overall success prompted Dönitz to assess that the British were successfully re-routing convoys, so he broke the West group up to cover the Central Atlantic. *U-203* detected Convoy HX 133 south of Greenland on 23 June. That night, the U-boat sank one ship before it lost contact with the convoy. The next day, the same boat sighted Convoy OB 336 headed west. The boat attacked this new target and sank another ship. Four more boats were ordered to attack OB 336, but they were only able to sink two additional ships. Six more boats shadowed the convoy but failed to launch attacks. HX 133 came under attack again beginning on 26 June from three more boats; one managed to sink two ships, but three Flower-class corvettes sank another U-boat to the east of the convoy. The battle continued on 29 June when *U-651* sank another ship, but in turn it was sunk by five escorts. Although Convoy HX 133 was spotted later in the day by an Fw 200, no further submarine attacks were possible. This convoy battle demonstrated the growing power of the escorts. Dönitz committed a total of ten boats against the convoy. Initially, it was protected by four escorts. The WAC reinforced the escort with two more escort groups until 13 escorts were involved in defence of the convoy. In total, this convoy battle cost the British 11 ships (57,215 GRT) in exchange for two U-boats.

Beginning its career as *U-570*, and ending it as HMS *Graph*, this was the only U-boat to see active service on both sides in the Atlantic campaign. The Type VIIC boat was captured on 27 August 1941 when the inexperienced captain and crew surrendered to a Hudson bomber. In RN service, as in this view, it conducted three patrols before being relegated to training duties. (Naval History and Heritage Command)

Allied efforts in the Atlantic were beginning to pay off. In spite of the greater number of U-boats at sea, shipping losses dropped. In the Atlantic, 22 ships of 94,209 GRT were lost in July and 23 ships of 80,310 GRT in August. Not until September did another major attack occur on an Atlantic convoy.

Dönitz reacted to the new situation in July by concentrating 15 boats in the waters between Ireland and Iceland. Despite I/KG 40 reporting a convoy, two patrol lines were unsuccessful in finding any convoys. This failure was largely due to the efforts of Coastal Command, which was patrolling the entire area. During August, 18 attacks were recorded by aircraft against U-boats.

Over the next three months, only four convoys were attacked in the North Atlantic. In August, Dönitz massed 20 boats south-west of Iceland. Now able to decode U-boat traffic in only a few hours, the Submarine Tracking Room possessed an unprecedented level of insight into U-boat dispositions. On 22 August, six convoys were diverted to the north. As a result, none was attacked. During the course of German attempts to attack Convoy HX 145, a Coastal Command Hudson attacked and damaged *U-570* on 27 August. Chlorine gas from battery acid mixed with seawater panicked the inexperienced crew and the boat's equally inexperienced commander surrendered to the bomber circling overhead. The following day, after numerous RN escorts arrived on the scene, they took off the crew, and towed the boat to Iceland. It later entered RN service as HMS *Graph*.

In late August, Dönitz assembled a pack of 14 boats south-west of Iceland. The *Markgraf* pack was foiled by the Submarine Tracking Room's continuing excellence in diverting convoys out of harm's way. On 1 September, the five convoys in the danger area were all routed to the north to avoid attack. On 6 September, Dönitz changed tactics and ordered Markgraf to cover a wider area. The British decoded these orders and ordered the two nearest convoys to the south to avoid attack. Heavy weather in the area made this impossible, so the convoys were instead directed to hug the coast of Greenland. Convoy SC 42, escorted by the RCN's 24th Escort Group with one destroyer and three corvettes, was spotted by a U-boat on 9 September near Cape Farewell.

SC 42 was a typical North Atlantic convoy of the period, and its fate is illustrative. It departed Sydney, Cape Breton Island, on 30 August with 64 merchants escorted by an RCN group of one destroyer and three corvettes. It took a northerly route and on 6 August was near Cape Farewell in Greenland. At this point, the Submarine Tracking Room determined that a U-boat pack was gathering to attack, so the convoy was ordered to head even farther north to hug the coast of Greenland. The first U-boat was spotted on the morning of 9 September by a straggler just astern of the convoy. That evening, the convoy made an evasive manoeuvre, but the massive amount of smoke from the merchants, visible for 30nm, had already brought U-boats to the scene. Escort Group 24 received another two corvettes as reinforcements, but the odds were in favour of the Germans, with a dozen U-boats facing five largely untrained Canadian corvettes and a destroyer, all without radar. At 2130hrs, the attacks began, and the first ships went down. Between dusk and midnight, seven more ships were sunk, some by U-boats attacking from within the convoy. Of the 17 U-boats Dönitz sent toward the convoy, at least eight attacked the convoy during the night. Two more ships were lost later in the night. The outnumbered escorts were unable to defend the convoy. The destroyer detected and tried to engage a surfaced U-boat amid the columns of the convoy with no luck, and later three more escorts gained contact on a submerged U-boat and began an attack. The U-boat survived, since the escorts could not leave the convoy unprotected to mount a sustained attack. The next night, the attacks resumed, and five more ships went down. The escort was reinforced with two more corvettes, which accounted for *U-501*. The carnage looked ready to resume on the night of 11 September, even after a fresh escort group with five ships arrived from Iceland and sank *U-207*. Only the arrival of heavy fog around the convoy prevented another night of death and destruction.

The fate of Convoy SC 42 showed that if the Germans were allowed to mass on a convoy, even a well defended one, the results were deadly. In total, SC 42 suffered 16 ships lost and a tanker damaged. In exchange, two U-boats were lost.

During the period when SC 42 suffered heavy losses, two other wolfpacks formed on 1 September met with only frustration. The packs were formed west and south-west of Iceland; despite occasional sightings from U-boats and aircraft, Dönitz was unable to mass his boats against a convoy even when the two packs were formed into one to pursue OG 73, which had been sighted on three occasions.

ACTION IN THE CENTRAL ATLANTIC

With the British successfully diverting convoys around the mass of U-boats south of Iceland, much of the action during the summer of 1941 shifted to the south against the Britain–Gibraltar route. Here the Germans had better cueing information on convoy movements. Using B-Dienst information, reports from Axis agents watching Gibraltar and reconnaissance information from I/KG 40, the Germans were able to mass on several convoys. B-Dienst gained information on the location of Convoys OG 69 and SL 80 on 24 July. Fourteen U-boats were sent to attack them, supported by Condors, which gained contact on both the next day. Contact on Convoy SL 80 could not be maintained, but Dönitz was able to bring seven U-boats and three Italian boats against OG 69 beginning on 26 July. Over the next three days, seven ships were sunk for no Axis losses.

In early August, Convoy SL 81 was tracked by B-Dienst and then detected by a U-boat west of Ireland. By 3 August, ten U-boats had gathered around the convoy. Despite the presence of a strong escort (three destroyers, eight corvettes and a CAM [catapult aircraft merchant] ship), the Germans inflicted heavy losses. The opening round on 3 August went well for the escort, with a Hurricane fighter from the CAM shooting down a Condor and the escort sinking a U-boat and protecting the convoy from attack that night. The next day developed in favour of the Germans with two Condors sinking one merchant and that night four U-boats sank five more merchants after getting inside the convoy.

Convoys HG 68 and HG 69 got through unscathed, but on 17 August, OG 71 was detected by a Condor west of Ireland. Dönitz sent eight boats toward the convoy and on the night of 18/19 August, three of them were able to launch attacks and sink a Norwegian escort and three merchants. The 5th Escort Group drove off the nearby boats on 19 August and was reinforced by three destroyers over the next two days. With the aid of a Condor report,

Merchant and U-boat losses, April–December 1941

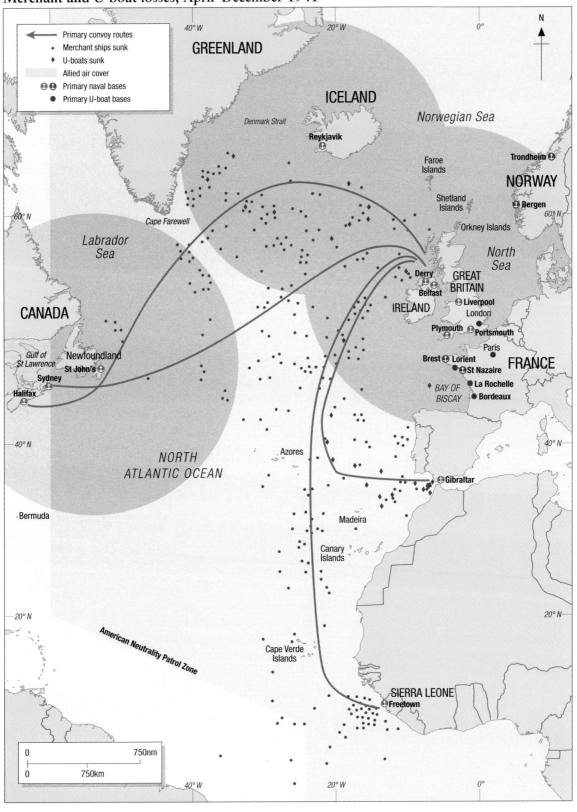

Legend:
- ← Primary convoy routes
- · Merchant ships sunk
- ♦ U-boats sunk
- Allied air cover
- ⊕ Primary naval bases
- ● Primary U-boat bases

GREENLAND

ICELAND

Denmark Strait

Reykjavik

Norwegian Sea

Faroe Islands

Shetland Islands

Orkney Islands

Trondheim

NORWAY

Bergen

North Sea

Cape Farewell

Labrador Sea

60° N

Derry
Belfast

GREAT BRITAIN

IRELAND

Liverpool
London

CANADA

Newfoundland

Gulf of St Lawrence
St John's

Sydney

Halifax

Plymouth
Portsmouth

Paris

Brest
Lorient
St Nazaire

FRANCE

La Rochelle
Bordeaux

BAY OF BISCAY

40° N

NORTH ATLANTIC OCEAN

Azores

Gibraltar

Bermuda

Madeira

Canary Islands

20° N

American Neutrality Patrol Zone

Cape Verde Islands

SIERRA LEONE
Freetown

0 ——— 750nm
0 ——— 750km

40° W   20° W   0°

the U-boats were able to resume attacks on 22 August. This time, a British corvette and five more ships were sunk. For a loss of ten ships and two escorts, the British were unable to sink a single U-boat.

GERMAN SUCCESS IN THE NORTH ATLANTIC

After months of frustration, in September, Dönitz's efforts in the North Atlantic paid off. In total during that month, Allied shipping losses rose again, this time to 53 ships of 202,820 GRT. This was primarily the result of attacks on four convoys. Two of these were slow convoys headed for Britain. Both were located south of Greenland giving Dönitz time to mass on them.

The fate of Convoy SC 42 has already been described (see page 80 onwards). SC 44 was also escorted by an RCN escort group. On 20 September, for the first time, American destroyers were dispatched to reinforce a convoy when it came under attack. However, they arrived too late to make a difference. Convoy SC 44 came under attack from five U-boats east of Cape Farewell; four ships and a corvette were sunk, with no German losses. A total of 20 merchants and an escort were lost in the two convoys. In return, only two U-boats were sunk.

The other two convoys heavily attacked during the month were SL 87 and HG 73. Convoy SL 87 was composed of 11 merchants and four escorts. Seven merchants were sunk. HG 73 was spotted by an Fw 200 off Cape St Vincent and Dönitz was able to assemble a pack of U-boats. Convoys steaming from Gibraltar were especially vulnerable to detection from the

Flower-class corvette HMCS *Lévis* was laid down in a Canadian shipyard and commissioned into RCN service in May 1941. The following month it joined the Newfoundland Escort Force. On 19 September, as part of the 19th Escort Group escorting convoy SC 44, it was torpedoed by *U-74* east of Cape Farewell, Greenland. The corvette foundered the following day, becoming the first Canadian Flower-class corvette to be sunk. (Canadian Naval Heritage) air and to air attack, since the I/KG 40's base at Bordeaux was so close and the convoy route was in range for its entire time. HG convoys enjoyed no air cover.

THE MEDITERRANEAN WESTERN APPROACHES DIVERSION

Beginning in September 1941, the situation in the Mediterranean prompted Hitler to order submarines from the Atlantic into the area. The first group of six boats entered the Mediterranean successfully in late September and early October. A second group of four boats followed on 11 November, but only three boats survived the passage. A third group of five boats passed through the Strait of Gibraltar during the last part of November. During December, 17 U-boats attempted the passage, but two were sunk and four were severely damaged and returned to France. These submarines fared poorly as the British had ascertained the redeployment and had reinforced patrols in the area. In addition to the boats sent into the Mediterranean, more boats were deployed in the approaches west of Gibraltar to attack reinforcements from Britain that the Germans expected to pass through the area.

The concentration of U-boats in the Western Approaches to Gibraltar led to several major convoy battles. Since the area was often subjected to Fw 200 attack, the British deployed their first auxiliary carrier (later known as escort carriers) to counter the threat and strengthen the escort. Named *Audacity*, the ship was a captured German merchant which was converted to hold a flight deck that could carry six fighters. While escorting Convoy OG 74, its fighters shot down a Condor when the convoy came under attack on 20–21 September. OG 74 was under the protection of Commander Walker's 36th Escort Group. Only two ships were sunk by U-boats on the night of 20 September before they were driven off by Walker's group. Three more stragglers were sunk.

HMS *Audacity* was the first RN escort carrier to see action in the Atlantic campaign. To get aircraft to sea, the Admiralty decided to convert several merchant ships into auxiliary carriers. *Audacity* was a basic conversion of the captured German cargo ship *Hannover*. The new carrier was commissioned on 17 June 1941; it could carry six fighters. Assigned to escort convoys coming to and from Gibraltar, it was sunk on its fourth mission on 14 December 1941. (Naval History and Heritage Command)

On 23 September, Dönitz shifted his boats to attack Convoy HG 73. Despite the very strong escort of one destroyer, two sloops, eight corvettes and a CAM ship, the Germans again scored heavily. Nine ships were sunk over the course of 25/26 September in a series of night attacks. Again, no U-boats were sunk. In October, Convoy OG 75 was spotted by Condors but was not attacked and HG 75 lost only four ships after Dönitz made a major effort to attack it.

The Admiralty held back the next convoy until a much stronger escort could be assembled. The next convoy, HG 76 with 32 ships, was protected by the 36th Escort Group under Commander Walker. His strengthened Escort Group included three destroyers, two sloops, seven corvettes and *Audacity*. On 14 December, the convoy of 32 ships departed Gibraltar. The battle opened the next day when an Australian destroyer sank *U-127*. On 16 December, the convoy was detected by an Fw 200 – Dönitz now had the information he needed to order the *Seeräuber* wolfpack of five U-boats, reinforced by five more, to converge on the convoy.

In a pitched battle over four days and nights, German aircraft and submarines attacked the convoy. Four more U-boats were destroyed – *U-131* to surface escorts and fighters from *Audacity*, and *U-434*, *U-574* and *U-567* to escorts (with Walker's flagship, the sloop *Stork*, accounting for *U-574*). Two Condors were lost to fighter attack. In return, the British also suffered heavily. Only two merchants were sunk, but a destroyer was sunk by torpedoes, and *Stork* was damaged when it rammed *U-574*. Dönitz ordered his U-boats to prioritize the destruction of the carrier, and on 21 September, it was dispatched by torpedoes from *U-751*. The ferocity of the convoy's defence and the scale of its losses forced Dönitz to break off the action on 23 September. In the first convoy action of the war against a convoy defended by an aircraft carrier, the U-boats were badly beaten.

Dönitz's shift to the Mediterranean and its Western Approaches had a dramatic impact on the Atlantic campaign. Already in October, losses to U-boats fell to 32 ships of 156,554 GRT as the boats made their way south into the Mediterranean. One of the few convoys attacked that month was SC 48, which was routed through the North Atlantic under heavy escort and then reinforced by five RN and USN destroyers and another RN corvette. Beginning on 17 October, three ships were lost before the reinforcements arrived, and another six after their arrival. USN destroyer *Kearney* was torpedoed and damaged in this battle, but was towed to Iceland and survived. This was the first USN ship damaged by enemy action in the war.

In the middle of the month, Dönitz formed the *Breslau* pack with six German and three Italian boats. One of these detected HG 75 on 23 October. That night, two of the German boats were able to launch attacks, sinking three ships and an escorting destroyer. Subsequent attacks against the convoy were unsuccessful.

Although the focus of U-boat operations shifted to the Mediterranean approaches, Dönitz tried to maintain pressure in the North Atlantic. After the successful operation against Convoy SC 48, Dönitz formed seven boats into pack *Reissewolf* and nine more into *Schlagetot*. Both were deployed west of Ireland but achieved little. Convoy SL 89 was spotted by a U-boat on 20 October and the convoy lost three ships to submarine attack the following day. By 23 October, the escort had driven away the submarines near the convoy. Reissewolf was unable to achieve anything else when

Watch officers aboard an escort keep watch for U-boats in this scene from October 1941. Without radar, visual observation was the only method to locate incoming threats. At night, with decks awash, even a surfaced boat was very difficult to spot. (Royal Navy, now in the public domain)

the Submarine Tracking Room diverted convoys around the pack. On 27 October, one Reissewolf boat spotted ON 28 and the pack was ordered to converge. Between 28 and 30 October, five boats tried to attack the convoy, but they were driven off by the five escorting USN destroyers after damaging a USN oiler. The next convoys, HX 156 and SC 51, were rerouted to the south to avoid Reissewolf. Convoy ON 30 was also sent to the south after being handed over to a USN escort and avoided attack.

During the last two months of the year, U-boat activity was greatly reduced as the full impact of the redeployment of German submarines to the Mediterranean took effect. In November, a mere 13 ships of 62,196 GRT were lost. One of the few convoys that came under attack was SC 52, detected south of Cape Race, Newfoundland. This was the farthest point west that a convoy had been detected. So fearful was the Admiralty that the RCN escort group could not provide adequate protection for the slow convoy, it was sent back to Nova Scotia – the only time during the war when a convoy was sent back by the threat of German attack. On their way back, four ships were sunk by U-boats and another two were lost due to grounding.

In December, convoys were running through the North Atlantic almost undisturbed. At one point, only three boats were on patrol in the rough waters of the North Atlantic. Only by chance, *U-130* encountered SC 57 on 10 December and sank three ships. This was the only success during the month against a North Atlantic convoy. In December, only nine ships were sunk in the Atlantic of 45,931 GRT, though total losses to U-boats in all areas were 26 ships of 124,070 GRT. During the last month of 1941, 28 U-boats were either in the Mediterranean or earmarked for transfer there. By 8 December, only 27 boats were available for the entire Atlantic.

Due to a lack of resources, Dönitz was unable to keep the pressure up in the South Atlantic. In May, 30 Allied ships were sunk in the area. For several reasons, losses dropped dramatically; in June only five ships were sunk, in the next two months only two and in September none. In the final three months of the year, only six ships were lost. This was due to Dönitz sending fewer boats to the area, and this was reduced by successful British efforts to sink German supply ships used to support U-boats in these distant waters. In addition, whenever possible, merchant ships were routed out of the areas off the West African coast and air and escort patrols in the area were strengthened.

THE ITALIAN CONNECTION

Italy entered the war in June 1940 on the side of the Axis. At the start of the war, the Italian Navy boasted a total of 115 submarines of which 84 were operational. Most were suited only for operations in the Mediterranean, but a large number were capable of open ocean operations in the Atlantic. Italian submarines were inferior to German units and Italian submarine captains were less aggressive than their German counterparts. In a portent of things

to come, between 5 June and 13 July, two Italian submarines departed the Mediterranean and operated in the Central Atlantic. Neither boat recorded any success before returning to their base in the Mediterranean.

On 24 July, the Italians offered to assist the Germans in attacking British commerce in the Atlantic. Dönitz accepted the offer and Bordeaux was offered to the Italians as a base (later codenamed BETASOM by the Italians). An Italian officer joined Dönitz's staff to coordinate operations. By November, 26 submarines were assigned to BETASOM, with the eventual total reaching 28 Italian submarines from the Mediterranean and four from the Italian Red Sea Flotilla based in Massawa, Eritrea. The addition of 32 submarines appeared to hold great potential in a period when Dönitz was struggling with an inadequate number of U-boats.

The initial groups of Italian submarines departed the Mediterranean, operated near the Azores and then proceeded to Bordeaux. Dönitz's first idea for the Italians was to use them in coordination with his own U-boats. The first effort at joint operations was made in October–November 1940 when Dönitz sent the Italian boats to operating areas to the west and south-west of the German boats off the North Channel. Dönitz placed the Italians out of British air range and in a position where he hoped they could provide detection of approaching convoys. This coordinated operation ended in failure; the Italians did not find any new convoys nor did they attack the convoys previously located by the Germans. Accordingly, on 5 December, Dönitz called off the operation and redeployed the Italians to look for individual merchant ships south and west of the German patrol areas.

On 18 February 1941, Dönitz mounted another attempt at coordinated operations with the Italians. He deployed the Italian boats to extend the area of coverage south of Iceland. By 5 May, Dönitz recognized that this attempt was also a failure. From this point, the Italians were only assigned independent operations during which they enjoyed some success. On 26 May,

Although less aggressively handled then their German counterparts, Italian submarines played an important though forgotten role in the Atlantic campaign. Those sent to the Atlantic were larger than their German counterparts. This is the Calvi-class submarine *Giuseppe Finzi* seen from an American merchant ship on 20 July 1941. This was one of the more successful Italian boats, sinking five merchant ships in its nine patrols. (Naval History and Heritage Command) seven Italian boats were deployed west of Gibraltar to attack convoys. Against Convoy OG 63, two Italian submarines sank two merchant ships on 5 and 6 June. The Italians claimed other hits, but no additional ships were hit. On 12 June, an Italian submarine spotted Convoy SL 76 east of the Azores. In an attack the following day, *Brin* sank two ships.

By any measure, Italian submarines operating in the Atlantic were less effective than German ones. After an uncertain start, the performance of the Italians improved in 1941 when younger captains were assigned to the Italian boats, German training was provided to Italian crews and technical refinements, including the reduction of the large sails on Italian boats, were undertaken. The Italians gradually became more familiar with the harsh operating conditions in the Atlantic. When losses of Italian submarines in the Mediterranean increased, 11 BETASOM boats returned to the Mediterranean. Despite these difficulties, BETASOM boats accounted for 109 Allied merchants (593,864 GRT) before the last seven Italian boats at Bordeaux were converted into transports in 1943.

THE SITUATION AT THE END OF 1941

From the end of the Happy Time until the end of 1941, Britain's fortunes in the Atlantic improved. Merchant losses were still heavy, but they were not sufficient to threaten Britain's merchant lifelines. From 1 April until the end of the year, shipping losses to Axis submarines amounted to 328 ships of 1,576,000 GRT. Of these, 206 ships were not sailing in convoy. Losses were dramatically reduced by evasive routing of convoys in the North Atlantic throughout the period, and in the South Atlantic during the last months of 1941. Evasive routing using intelligence derived from Ultra probably prevented the destruction of at least 300 ships alone in 1941.

In convoy encounters, the better trained and organized escorts were beginning to exact a growing toll on U-boats. The ratio of losses of merchants lost in convoy to U-boats destroyed was approximately 6:1, a rate that Dönitz could not afford. Where available, aircraft made a huge difference in the battle against the U-boats. Within 400nm of a Coastal Command base, U-boat operations were limited and therefore shipping losses rare. Between 400nm to 600nm from a Coastal Command base, fewer aircraft had the range to operate and merchant losses were correspondingly higher. Beyond 600nm, the U-boats did not have to worry about British aircraft – this is where the Germans increasingly concentrated their operations and where merchant losses were the heaviest.

German losses in 1941 totalled 28 U-boats, and of these 20 were lost at the hands of convoy escorts. New construction surpassed losses, so by the end of 1941, the force was up to 86 operational boats with another 150 involved in training or on trials. Allocation of the available operational boats was driven by other considerations besides the best way to implement Dönitz's tonnage war. During the last half of 1941, the Mediterranean theatre absorbed a huge part of the operational U-boat force – 15 were moved into the Mediterranean with another 35 allocated to move there or to be stationed in the Western Approaches to Gibraltar to cut off reinforcements the Germans believed were headed into the Mediterranean. This left a mere 36 boats for operations in the rest of the Atlantic. To make matters worse, in December, Dönitz was ordered to send six boats to patrol off Norway in response to Hitler's fears that the British were about to invade.

For Dönitz, the number of boats at sea was gradually increasing. The average number of boats at sea was 24 in May, rising to 36 in August, and then to 38 in November. From July to October 1941, the overall number of operational U-boats rose from 65 to 80. Production also ramped up over this period and averaged almost 18 boats per month. However, in terms of effectiveness, U-boats were dramatically decreasing. The average tonnage sunk daily by a U-boat in November 1941 was 66. This compared poorly with the wartime peak of 976 recorded in October 1940.

Through a combination of German submarine deployments to the Mediterranean and the focus on attacking convoys to and from Gibraltar, Dönitz was forced to virtually abandon the North Atlantic in late autumn 1941 until the end of the year. Dönitz's strategy of expanding the tonnage war was minimally effective, again due to expanded British defences and evasive routing. At the end of the year, the focus was on attacking convoys to and from Gibraltar, but this lacked the prospect of inflicting heavy losses on Allied shipping.

Probably the most important event of World War II was the Japanese attack on the USN's Pacific Fleet in Pearl Harbor. As a result, the US entered the war, and the nature of the entire war was transformed. This included the Atlantic campaign where the U-boats now faced the combined strength of the RN and much of the USN. The United States's entry into the war also presented a huge opportunity to Dönitz, and it was not one he missed. Twelve U-boats were preparing to mount an offensive off the east coast of the US. The disaster that followed was arguably a greater defeat than that of Pearl Harbor.

AFTERMATH

The first six months of the Atlantic campaign were only a skirmish. Following the Norwegian campaign, the Germans again turned their attention to cutting off British trade. In June 1940, France surrendered. This changed the entire complexion of the campaign as the U-boats then had bases from Norway down through France. This gave the Germans a series of naval and air bases which directly threatened Britain. From the spring of 1940 until the spring of 1941, Britain was under the greatest threat of a German blockade.

However, the Germans lacked the plans and the assets to take advantage of this situation. Instead of mounting pointless terror raids against British cities, a concerted campaign against British ports would have been more impactful. In terms of naval resources, the Germans lacked the means to launch crippling attacks against British shipping. German surface raiders were not numerous enough to provide decisive results, and the operations of the Kriegsmarine's heavy surface units, though spectacular when used against shipping, amounted to little more than pinpricks.

Had the Germans given the highest priority to U-boat construction at the outset of war, decisive results might have been possible. Instead, this priority was only assigned in July 1940, which meant that new boats did not arrive in greater numbers until the middle of 1941. It also meant that the British had almost a full year to ramp up escort production. The delay in the increase of U-boat construction until after the British dramatically increased escort production was one of the main reasons the U-boat offensive against Britain was defeated.

With the limited number of boats available, Dönitz realized only minor success in the opening months of the campaign. By May 1940, sinkings from U-boat attacks in the Atlantic totalled 148 ships of 678,130 GRTs. Even when additional shipping losses were added from mines and smaller U-boats in the inshore waters off Britain, the total attrition of shipping in no way posed a serious threat to Britain and its war effort. Compared to the losses caused by surface ships and mines, it was readily apparent to both the British and the Germans that U-boats posed the main threat to shipping. In 1939, the British merchant fleet reached 17,984,000 GRT. Given this, the scale of losses to date was insignificant. At this point, Allied construction of new ships was covering losses.

The U-boat threat grew in the second part of 1940. During the so-called Happy Time, U-boats accounted for an average of eight ships per month/per boat. A combination of little British intelligence on U-boats, inadequate air cover, few escorts and rudimentary tactics and training made this possible.

Only the fact that there were fewer than 30 U-boats at sea during this period saved the Allies from suffering truly crippling losses. However, this success was fleeting – by February 1941, the monthly average was down to two ships per month/per boat. From this point, Dönitz was forced to rely on mass attacks against convoys instead of relying on a small number of excellent commanders decimating poorly guarded convoys. In this book, and in every other account of the battle, only the convoys that came under attack are mentioned. The vast majority of convoys were not subjected to attack and thus their safe passages go unmentioned. This is borne out by the numbers. Between 1 January and 30 June 1941, 37 HX convoys set out for Britain with 1,413 ships. Of these, only 30 ships were lost – a loss rate of just over 2 per cent. Of the 91 HX convoys from late 1940 until the end of 1941, 79 were not attacked and did not suffer any losses. Even the slow 18 SC convoys suffered little – only 11 of 576 ships were lost, about the same rate of loss. Overall, from SC 8 until SC 62 at the end of 1941, 46 of 56 convoys suffered no losses at all. For the 19 SL convoys, 26 of 750 ships were sunk (over 3 per cent loss). Of the 340 ships in HG convoys, 10 were lost (3 per cent). Losses to westbound convoys were always lower. A total of 109 OB and OG convoys transited during this period; of the 3,307 ships, 33 were sunk for a loss rate of less than 1 per cent.

During the final six months of 1941, the Allies successfully defended their North Atlantic convoys. Escorts for HX convoys were the most successful – of 1,560 ships in 31 convoys, only two were damaged. As had been the case since their inception, the slow SC convoys were the most vulnerable. Of the 1,187 ships in 27 such convoys, 35 were lost. Even this represented only a 3 per cent loss rate. On a smaller scale, the 17 SL convoys suffered a proportionately greater loss rate of 4 per cent (15 ships sunk out of 359).

Losses to outbound convoys in the North Atlantic were historically lower, and this remained true in the second half of 1941. Of the 2,537 ships steaming in 60 OB and ON convoys, a mere three were sunk. Proportionally, the highest losses were suffered by the HG and OG convoys. In 11 such convoys with 509 ships, 32 were lost (just over 6 per cent). Finally, on 15 OS convoys, with 574 merchants, only eight were lost.

Although worldwide losses of merchant ships in 1941 added up to 1,299 ships (of which 833 were British), new construction in Britain and the addition of foreign-flagged ships meant that there was a net tonnage gain in Britain's merchant fleet over the second half of 1941 of 249,000 GRT. At the end of 1941, the size of Britain's merchant fleet was larger than it had been at the start of the war. Including British flag ships and foreign flag ships under British control, 3,616 ships were available of some 20,693,000 GRT. This fleet was able to import 44,586,000 GRT into Britain in 1941. Although lower than pre-war levels, and low enough to force the rationing of some items, this was sufficient to meet basic requirements. Germany's plan to blockade Britain was failing.

By mid-November 1941, virtually all German naval operations in the North Atlantic ceased. The Allies used the second half of the respite in 1941 to good effect by reinforcing defences in the North Atlantic, which was always the most important area of the Atlantic campaign. By the end of 1941, the British appeared on the verge of victory. In December of that year, the US entered the war, making Britain's long-term prospects excellent. Now the U-boats were facing the combined resources of the two largest maritime powers on the planet.

WERE THE ALLIES ON THE VERGE OF VICTORY AT THE END OF 1941?

Books on the Atlantic campaign focus on the operations and losses caused by U-boats and often fail to give the RN a similar degree of attention. After an uneven beginning, by the end of 1941, the RN (with the often-overlooked assistance of the RCN and the USN) had forced Dönitz onto the back foot and looked ready to throttle the U-boat offensive. In June 1941, the RN and the RCN had grown exponentially since the start of the war – 248 destroyers and escort destroyers were in service with another 157 under construction; 99 corvettes were in service, with another 44 under construction in Britain and 52 in Canada. The very successful sloops (and similar US Coast Guard cutters given to the British) totalled 48 in service with three more being built. Coastal waters were covered by 300 ASW trawlers with 47 more under construction.

Not only were the numbers of escorts much greater than at the start of the war, but they were more effective. Permanent escort groups were showing their worth. Training and leadership in the escort groups were all much improved. In addition, tactical improvements made the escorts more deadly. Radio–telephone communications provided a much quicker response to U-boat attack. The switch from five to ten depth charge

At the start of the war, Coastal Command was unable to find or attack U-boats. These problems were not overcome until late 1941, making the waters of the Atlantic within range of British aircraft a much more dangerous place for German submarines. This is an Armstrong Whitworth Whitley Mark VII bomber, converted into a maritime patrol aircraft, conducting an attack on a surfaced U-boat on 1 December 1941. A total of 146 Whitley Mark VIIs saw service in four Coastal Command squadrons. (Naval History and Heritage Command)

patterns made it more likely that a U-boat would be sent to the bottom of the ocean.

Equally important as the growth of the escort force was Coastal Command's turnaround from the start of the war. This was evident by mid-1941. Operating from bases in Britain and Iceland, it had some 200 aircraft patrolling at farther distances. These included 80 Hudsons, 36 Catalinas and 10 Liberators. In addition, Sunderlands, Wellingtons and old Whitleys were still in service. This force flew missions 700nm from Britain and 400nm from Iceland, while the RCAF monitored waters out to 600nm from Canada. This left an air gap of 300nm in the mid-Atlantic. From July 1941, it took 18 months to close it. It became the centre of operations in 1942 and for the first half of 1943.

For the British, the way ahead for 1942 appeared clear. Convoys were the best method of protecting shipping, and by massing escorts and aircraft for their protection, U-boats were increasingly at risk. If escort carriers and long-range aircraft could enter the battle in significant numbers, the defence of convoys would be greatly strengthened.

With an avalanche of British and Canadian-built escorts reaching service, and an expanded Coastal Command, all underpinned by an excellent intelligence network, the odds against the U-boats were increasing. Britain was no longer fighting alone. Since May 1941, the US had been an ally of Britain giving it enormous resources in the form of Lend-Lease and even escorting convoys in huge swathes of the Atlantic. In December 1941, with the US in the war on a formal basis, it became impossible for the Germans to achieve victory in the Atlantic.

Dönitz's prospects for 1942 did not look promising. The favourable trend he did have was increased U-boat production that by 1942 would provide him with the 300 boats he stated in 1939 were necessary to win the campaign in the Atlantic. With this number of submarines, he might have the capability to find convoys and mass enough U-boats against them to overwhelm their defences. Before this theory could be tested, the American entry into the war provided Dönitz with an opportunity that he was quick to seize. A second Happy Time was on the horizon.

USS *Reuben James* was a Clemson-class destroyer commissioned in 1920. Many of these dated ships were still in commission in 1941. As part of the escort of Convoy HX 156, it was torpedoed by *U-552*. The resulting explosion of the forward magazine broke off the ship's bow. After only a few minutes, the stern section also sank. Of the crew of 144, only 44 survived. (Naval History and Heritage Command)

FURTHER READING

Books on the Atlantic campaign abound, ranging from overviews to focused works on specific battles, platforms or technologies. These are among the most useful and are recommended for further reading.

Blair, Clay, *Hitler's U-boat War, The Hunters, 1939–1942*, Random House, New York (1996)

Blair, Clay, *Hitler's U-boat War, The Hunted, 1942–1945*, Random House, New York (1998)

Brown, David K., *Atlantic Escorts*, Naval Institute Press, Annapolis (2007)

Dimbleby, Jonathan, *The Battle of the Atlantic*, Oxford University Press, Oxford (2016)

Dönitz, Karl, *Memoirs Ten Years and Twenty Days*, Naval Institute Press, Annapolis (1990)

Good, Timothy S., *The Allied Air Campaign Against Hitler's U-boats*, Frontline Books, Yorkshire (2021)

Hague, Arnold, *The Allied Convoy System 1939–1945*, Naval Institute Press, Annapolis (2000)

Haskell, W.A., *Shadows on the Horizon: The Battle of Convoy HX-233*, Naval Institute Press, Annapolis (1998)

Haslop, Dennis, *Britain, Germany and the Battle of the Atlantic*, Bloomsbury, London (2013)

Howarth, Stephen & Law, Derek (eds), *The Battle of the Atlantic 1939–1945*, Greenhill Books, London (1994)

Milner, Marc, *Battle of the Atlantic*, Tempus, Stroud (2003)

Ministry of Defence (Navy), *The U-boat War in the Atlantic 1939–1945*, HMSO, London (1989)

Möller, Eberhard & Brack, Werner, *The Encyclopedia of U-boats: From 1904 to the Present Day*, Greenhill Books, London (2004)

Morgan, Daniel, & Taylor, Bruce, *U-boat Attack Logs*, Seaforth Publishing, Barnsley (2011)

Niestle, Axel, *German U-boat Losses During World War II*, Naval Institute Press, Annapolis (1998)

Raeder, Erich, *My Life*, Naval Institute Press, Annapolis (1960)

Rohwer, Jürgen, *Chronology of the War at Sea 1939–1945*, Naval Institute Press, Annapolis (2005)

Roskill, S.W., *The War at Sea 1939–1945, Volume I: The Defensive*, HMSO, London (1962)

Showell, Jak P. Mallmann, *The German Navy in World War Two*, Naval Institute Press, Annapolis (1979)

Smith, William, *Churchill's Atlantic Convoys*, Pen & Sword Maritime, Yorkshire (2023)

Stegeman, Bernd, et al., *Germany and World War II, Volume II*, Oxford University Press, New York (1991)

Terraine, John, *The U-boat Wars 1916–45*, G.P. Putnam & Sons, New York (1989)

Walter, Brian E., *The Longest Campaign*, Casemate, Havertown, PA (2020)

Wynn, Kenneth, *U-boat Operations of World War II Volume 1: Career Histories, U1–U510*, Naval Institute Press, Annapolis (1997)

Wynn, Kenneth, *U-boat Operations of World War II Volume 1: Career Histories, U511–UIT25*, Naval Institute Press, Annapolis (1998)

www.uboat.net

INDEX

Figures in **bold** refer to illustrations.

TANK AND CREW UNIFORMS SINCE 1916

MARTIN WINDROW

with colour illustrations by
GERRY EMBLETON

squadron/signal publications

ISBN 0-89747-103-2

DEDICATION

This book is dedicated to Mumble, without whose
unflagging interest it could have been written in
half the time. *You* try turning out deathless prose
with an owl riding your typewriter carriage backwards and forwards . . .

Key to cover illustrations. Front, colour *Captain of the
Italian Social Republican Armoured Group* Leonessa,
*1944, wearing the black uniform which was so clearly
modelled on the German pattern (Gerry Embleton).*
Front photograph *A typical group of British AFV crewmen
in Burma; a Priest self-propelled howitzer crew of 18
Field Regiment, Royal Artillery, in January 1945, wearing
little more than jungle green slacks and bush hats (Imperial War Museum).* **Back, upper** *Czech Army T-34/85
crew, circa 1953, in earth-brown overalls and brown
leather Soviet-style helmets. The 2nd Lieutenant standing
at the rear has Russian-style shoulder boards and a Sam
Browne; all wear an enamel badge on the right breast,
probably a proficiency award (Zdenek Bryna).* **Back,
lower** *Crewman 'pulling through' the 75 mm main armament of an M3 medium tank of the US 1st Armored
Division in Tunisia, 1943. He wears the steel helmet, the
'tanker's jacket' or windcheater, and one-piece light OD
herringbone twill overalls (Imperial War Museum).*

Printed in Great Britain.

CONTENTS

INTRODUCTION

This book came to be written for the best possible reason: I needed it on my own reference shelves, and since nobody else had written it I had to to it myself.

The majority of potential readers will probably be found among the thousands of scale modellers of armoured fighting vehicles (AFVs) who have so transformed the modelling scene in the last ten years. In my personal view, the inclusion of an animated and accurately finished commander figure adds a great deal to the appeal of a scale model tank; it gives it a sense of proportion, of period, and of nationality. Apart from models associated with AFVs, the field of armoured crew uniforms offers the single figure modeller many attractive and unusual subjects.

Keeping the practical requirements of the modeller firmly in mind, I have limited the scope of this book in various ways. I have kept the interwar and postwar sections short, to allow the maximum possible space for the 1939-45 period, which is unquestionably the most popular. I have dealt only with ranks from Private to Colonel, and only with those orders of dress and protective outfits normally to be seen on the battlefield, worn by personnel when serving with AFVs in the front line. I have concentrated on battle tank regiments at the expense of other types of armour, while making an exception of the very colourful and varied outfits worn by German self-propelled artillerymen in the Second World War.

For space reasons, again, I have been forced to exclude from Gerry Embleton's superb colour plates many interesting uniforms; in most cases I have been obliged to avoid duplication, and colour and monochrome illustrations of the same subjects will not be found often between these covers. Subjects such as cap badges of cavalry units in armies with a jealously-guarded regimental tradition are naturally too broad for a book of this size; representative examples are given, and readers are advised to follow up the details in standard reference works. To avoid devoting precious colour space to repetition of items adequately covered in the photographs, I have crammed several colour plates with heads and torsos – where most insignia are worn, and which are generally visible in a tank turret – and left the legs for the text descriptions and photographs.

I have stuck largely to everyday language when describing colours; the variations are so wide within any regulation issue of uniform that it is pointless – as well as pompous – to get bogged down in attempts at pseudo-academic exactitude. Some shades – eg, German field grey or French horizon blue – need no further qualification. American 'olive drab' can mean anything from dark brown to light grey-green, and I have qualified the phrase in most cases. Readers new to this area of interest should remember that to an American, 'khaki' is a light sandy shade, and to an Englishman it is a nasty brown with mustard yellow overtones. I have used the word in its national context in most cases; the British meaning may be understood by the use of 'khaki' in all British sections and most European ones.

In order to keep some sort of physical balance between the lengths of Parts 2 and 3, I have described under the interwar headings various national uniforms which continued in use during the Second World War but which were introduced before 1939. This is the explanation for those Second World War sections which at first sight appear oddly neglected.

A book of this size cannot hope to be comprehensive, and I am all too aware that there are many gaps – and probably a certain number of straightforward mistakes. Readers who spot holes they can fill from their files are invited – begged, even! – to write to me, preferably with first-hand descriptions and, wherever possible, photographs. All will be returned quickly and gratefully.

I hope the reader will get as much pleasure from using this book as I had in compiling it. This task would have been quite impossible without the patience and generosity of many people, some old friends and some new. I am happy to record my gratitude to the following, in particular: Andrew Biwandi, Zdenek Bryna, Mike Chappell, Geoff Cornish, Paul Cross, Brian L. Davis, Gerry Embleton, Will Fowler, J. B. Haigh, R. G. Harris, Philip Katcher, Gustav Krupa, Patrick Leeson, Furio Lorenzetti, Mark MacLaughlin, Bob Marrion, Charles Milassin de Csiky, Bryan Perrett, Major General C. E. Pert, CB, DSO, Bruce Quarrie, Guido Rosignoli, Mike Roffe, Mike Ross, Richard Ross, John Sandars, Willem Steenkamp, Hans Rudolf von Stein, H. Travis, Sergeant Les Watling, John and Robert Wilkinson-Latham, Dick Windrow, Terry Wise, J. Woodroffe and Steven Zaloga.

THE FIRST WORLD WAR

Great Britain

Britain's fledgling tank corps was designated 'Heavy Section, Machine Gun Corps' in May 1916, a move which marked the first period of operational capability. It was divided into six companies, lettered 'A' to 'F', each company comprising four sections, each having three Male and three Female tanks and one spare tank. The theory was that the six tanks would operate in sub-sections of two; the gun-armed Males would destroy wire and machine-gun nests, while the machine-gun-armed Females would discourage the enemy infantry. (In practice, of course, this fine distinction broke down due to the enemy's unsporting failure to join battle in neatly balanced parties of infantry and machine-gunners.) Each tank crew was made up of an officer, an NCO and six enlisted men.

In November 1916 the 'Heavy Section' became the 'Heavy Branch', and that winter the original companies were expanded into lettered battalions. In January 1917 came the first authorisation for coloured shoulder tallies as battalion distinctions (see below); and in May 1917 the white cloth tank arm badge was instituted, both moves being designed to foster ésprit de corps in an organisation whose officers and men were drawn from many different

1916: the tan leather helmet used by the first operational British tank crews, and the drab grey-blue or khaki overall, complete with rank chevrons. The netting is anti-grenade wire, covering the top of the tank over a framework of stanchions and wire stays (Imperial War Museum).

This young private wears the Machine Gun Corps cap badge, the shoulder title 'H/MGC' for 'Heavy Branch', and the white tank arm badge. Since the badge was introduced in May 1917, and the Tank Corps took over from the MGC in July of that year, the photo may be dated with confidence to between those two months (J. Woodroffe).

sources. In July 1917 the organisation was at last renamed 'Tank Corps', and acquired its own tank cap badge. Expansion continued and, by the time the tanks made their mark at Cambrai in November 1917, 'G', 'H' and 'I' Battalions had been added to the rolls. In 1918 the lettered battalions were numbered; and by the time of the Armistice, with the incorporation of several armoured car units, the Corps had 26 battalions and several support and workshop units.

The basic service dress of the enlisted ranks was the 1902-1913 khaki serge uniform common to all branches of the Army. There was a peaked, flat-topped khaki cloth cap with a brown leather chin-strap and a stiffened peak and crown. In the field a soft-topped version with earflaps which were worn buttoned up over the crown, termed a 'trench cap', was popular. The single-breasted tunic had five brass buttons down the front closure, a fall collar, plain shoulder straps, two reinforced areas on the fronts of the shoulders, two rear vents, and four pockets. The breast pockets were of patch type, box-pleated, with buttoned rectangular flaps, and the skirt pockets were concealed but had external buttoned flaps. Straight khaki trousers were gathered below the knee into khaki puttees, and black ankle boots were worn.

In 1916-17 the majority of the enlisted ranks wore Machine Gun Corps cap badges – crossed Vickers machine-gun barrels, crowned, in bronze – and the Corps' shoulder titles at the end of the shoulder strap – 'MGC', and later 'H' over 'MGC' for 'Heavy Branch'. Some NCOs may have retained the insignia of previous affiliations, but by early 1917 this would have been unusual. The coloured shoulder flashes authorised in January 1917 were worn in different ways, often as slip-ons covering the outer half of the shoulder strap, but sometimes as patches sewn to the upper surface of the straps only. (A complete listing accompanies this chapter.) Colour coding was sometimes even more flamboyant, and Haswell Miller shows a Sergeant of 'D' Battalion with his helmet painted blue all over. Flashes painted on the sides of the steel helmet seem to have been common.

The white cloth tank badge authorised in May 1917 was worn on the upper right arm, above any rank chevrons, and was awarded on completion of training. The new cap badge of the Tank Corps, worn from July 1917, was a crowned wreath with a stylised three-quarter front view of a tank between upper and lower scrolls reading 'Tank' and 'Corps' in capitals. After an action in July 1918 the 9th Battalion was authorised to wear the badge of the French 3rd Division on the left shoulder, and was awarded the *Croix de Guerre avec Palmes*.

Shorts were quite commonly worn in hot weather on the Western Front; this Tank Corps officer, whose lack of cuff ranking suggests that he may have been a Guards officer before joining the Corps, wears shorts, puttees, a soft-topped service cap and an extremely beaten-up service dress tunic. In the original print one can make out coloured tallies on the shoulder straps, and two gold wound stripes set vertically on the left forearm. Note leather equipment set, and gas mask satchel. Several bulky items are stowed in the bellows skirt pockets of the tunic (Imperial War Museum).

Normal personal equipment worn with the vehicles was the brown leather 1916 set, comprising a belt with a brass snake buckle, with or without shoulder braces; a revolver holster, usually with lanyard to the neck, and a small cartridge pouch. The holster was worn butt forwards on the left. The gas mask satchel, in grey-green canvas webbing, was usually worn round the neck hanging on the chest, sometimes held in to the body by a string passing from D-rings on the satchel round behind the body.

Officers wore their 'regimentals' in 1916, and these presented a pretty motley appearance, as regimental cap and collar insignia and peculiarities such as Scots doublet tunics, Rifle buttons, Fusilier flashes and cavalry affectations of various kinds were widely observed. By 1917 increasing numbers of junior officers were being commissioned from the Machine Gun Corps Cadet Battalion, wearing MGC insignia on the standard service dress, but more senior officers would have retained regimental items until the formation of the Tank Corps at least and, in some cases, until 1918. The officers' tunic was of dark khaki barathea, single-breasted with five brass buttons, an open stepped collar, plain shoulder straps, box-pleated patch breast pockets with buttoned three-point flaps, and large unpleated bellows skirt pockets with rectangular buttoned flaps. The tunic was worn either with khaki trousers, or pale Bedford cord riding breeches; with brown riding boots, or brown laced ankle boots and long leather gaiters, or puttees. A light khaki shirt and tie, and a khaki service dress cap completed the uniform. The cap was often of the soft-topped 'trench' variety, with or without earflaps fixed up round the band. Ranking was normally worn on the cuffs in the form of lines of brown and white herringbone tape round the cuff, and devices sewn to a false cuff flap edged with the same tape; see diagram accompanying this chapter. It was occasionally seen on the shoulder straps instead, although this was limited to Guards officers officially. Equipment included the Sam Browne belt with pistol, a map case, binoculars, and almost invariably, an ashplant walking stick.

Above *Tank Corps cap badge, worn – officially – from July 28 1917 to October 17 1923; and example of British officer's cuff ranking, here the two stripes and three pips of a Captain. The cuff flap was butted up to the front seam of the sleeve.*

NCOs wore the normal rank chevron sequence on their tunic sleeves – one, two or three brown and white herringbone tape chevrons, point down, for Lance-Corporal, Corporal and Sergeant; a crown above three chevrons for Staff or Colour Sergeant; and warrant badges on each forearm for Sergeant-Majors. Service chevrons might be seen on the

Below left and below *The inner and outer surfaces of the steel, leather and chain mail face mask worn by some early British tank crews. German machine-gun ammunition Type 'K' was capable of penetrating the armour and even non-armour piercing rounds, at close range and in great concentration, sent showers of lead fragments into the various slots and ports (Imperial War Museum).*

right forearms of enlisted men, in the form of small blue thread chevrons, each representing six months' service overseas. Vertical gold braid stripes about two inches long might be observed above the left cuff, centred on the sleeve; each indicated a wound in action.

The overalls worn in the tanks seem to have been simple one-piece 'boiler suits' of denim material, without visible pockets apart from two conventional 'slash' pockets in the 'trousers', and with a very small stand collar. A display in the Imperial War Museum, London, states that in 1916 these overalls were light blue. A primitive leather crash helmet was issued in 1916, and was certainly worn to some extent, as it appears in contemporary photos. Of Teutonic shape, rather like a medieval knight's *salade*, it was constructed of pieces of tan brown leather riveted together along overlapped edges. It had very little padding, and it is hard to see how it could offer much protection from the knocks which were inevitable in a lurching tank crammed with guns, an unprotected engine and seven men. Apparently its Germanic shape was a danger, and some 'unhorsed' tank crews were fired upon by their own infantry; doubtless the pale blue overalls, faded to greyish, helped the impression.

Very dark blue or black denims seem, again from photographic evidence, to have been worn when

A British tank crew parading in Germany shortly after the Armistice, wearing khaki service caps and brown overalls, and full sets of leather equipment complete with shoulder braces (R. G. Harris).

working on the vehicles by mechanics, etc; but by the major expansion of 1917 a drab lightish brown or tan overall seems to have been the norm for wearing in the vehicle in the front line. A very common combination seen in photos is the steel helmet; the service dress tunic worn over the top part of the overall, with 1916 leather equipment and gas mask; and the legs of the overall emerging under the tunic and falling loose to the ankle, covering the khaki trousers and puttees. In warm weather one sees photos of tank crewmen wearing khaki shorts, puttees and boots, and either the collarless 'greyback' shirt or the khaki tunic. The padded leather, steel and chain mail face mask illustrated in accompanying photos was a common sense device for tank crewmen of all nations, given that there were many unguarded moving parts, and that bullet-splash was a major hazard of combat. The Germans used armour-piercing machine-gun ammunition, and everybody tended to concentrate small arms fire on the vision slits of a tank, so that fragments of lead constantly sprayed into the gunners' faces. How widely it was used in practice is less certain; the sense of confinement and the loss of all-round vision in an already confined and dimly lit tank may well have seemed too irritating a price to pay for protection.

By one of the quirks of illogic dear to all military organisations, the most prominent users of armoured cars – at least until the final year of the war – were sailors of the Royal Navy! In the French Channel ports during the first year of the war these crews seem to have worn regulation naval landing party rig, complete with brown leather equipment.

Group of British tank men examining German anti-tank rifle, 1918. They display many characteristic details. Three, standing, wear khaki service dress tunics over overalls; one, second from left, wears overalls alone – the glossy look seems to come from oil-stains, as it is not noticeable over the whole suit. A two-colour battalion flash is clearly visible on the shoulder straps of some of these men, as is the tank badge (left). Interestingly, the young Second Lieutenant, crouching, wears neither. He has shorts in place of breeches, and a steel and mail face-mask pushed up on his forehead (Imperial War Museum).

Later the Army's khaki service dress was taken over, with some RN insignia, and apparently the brown leather equipment was retained.

Those crews of the Royal Naval Air Service Armoured Car Division (!) who travelled an incredible road through the Near East to Russia, to support the Russians and Rumanians against Austrians, Turks, Kurds and finally Bolsheviks, wore normal khaki with the following amendments. The officers wore the RN cap badge, the Petty Officers (the lowest rank in the unit) a horizontal oval bronze badge with a crown above the centre, bearing 'R.N.A.S.' above a right-facing armoured car above a short foliate spray. 'Collar dogs' seem to have been worn from time to time by all ranks, and were in the shape of a bronze armoured car facing right as viewed. Ranking was naval, but officers wore both RN and Army ranking on their service tunics (see Colour Plate 1). Officers had a No 1 uniform of white-topped naval cap, blue naval jacket with gold insignia, khaki breeches and top-boots or ankle boots with puttees.

Tank Corps shoulder tally colours, 1918

'A' Coy, later 'A' Bn, later	1 Bn	– red
'B' Coy, later 'A' Bn, later	2 Bn	– yellow
'C' Coy, later 'A' Bn, later	3 Bn	– green
'D' Coy, later 'A' Bn, later	4 Bn	– blue (light – dark from 1922)
'E' Coy, later 'A' Bn, later	5 Bn	– red/light blue
'F' Coy, later 'A' Bn, later	6 Bn	– red/yellow
'G' Bn, later	7 Bn	– red/green
'H' Bn, later	8 Bn	– red/dark blue
'I' Bn, later	9 Bn	– red/brown
'J' Bn, later	10 Bn	– red/white
'K' Bn, later	11 Bn	– red/black
'L' Bn, later	12 Bn	– red/purple
13 Bn	– green/black	
14 Bn	– green/purple	
15 Bn	– green/yellow	
16 Bn	– black/yellow/black	
17 Bn	– green/white	
18 Bn	– green/dark blue	
19 Bn	– red/white/red	
20 Bn	– red/yellow/red	
21 Bn	– red/black/red	
22 Bn	– red/green/red	
23 Bn	– red/blue/red	
24 Bn	– green/yellow/green	
25 Bn	– green/black/green	
26 Bn	– green/white/green	
Tank Carrier Coys	– green/brown	
Gun Carrier Coys	– blue/white/blue	
Central Workshops	– purple	
Advanced Workshops	– purple/yellow/purple	
Central Stores	– purple/white	
Tank Field Bn (Salvage Coy) – 4 rows of 8 black/white checks		
2 Salvage Coy	– ditto, red/white	

France

The French tank arm was initially formed as a branch of the artillery – *Artillerie Spéciale*. Thus the early units of Schneider and St Chamond heavy gun-carrier tanks were organised in batteries, groups and *groupements* in the artillery fashion. A battery had four tanks, and corresponded to a platoon; a group had four batteries and corresponded to a company; a *groupement* comprised two or more groups, and corresponded to a battalion. It was with this organisation that the Schneider and St Chamond went into battle for the first time, on April 16 1917 at Chemin des Dames and at Laffaux Mill on May 5 1917, respectively.

The crews wore standard horizon blue service dress. For enlisted men this had a single-breasted tunic with seven blue-painted buttons down the front from throat to waist; a standing collar with rounded top inner corners; no chest pockets, but internal skirt pockets with straight, external flaps with concealed buttons. The cuffs were plain, as were the shoulders. The tunic was worn with baggy semi-breeches or pantaloons, confined in puttees from the knee down, and brown laced ankle boots.

The collar bore patches, corresponding in shape to the 'front' two inches or so of the collar on each side, cut with a double-scallop rear vertical edge. These were scarlet, with the numbers of the soldier's original artillery unit in blue, green or white depending upon the type of regiment, and two lines of the same colour piping following the rear edge. In 1915, when the horizon blue uniform first appeared, the trouser seams were piped in scarlet, but this would have been less commonly seen in 1917-18. Enlisted men wore ranking in the form of 35 mm-long diagonal stripes of red wool or gold lace on the outer face of each cuff: one and two red bars for Privates First Class and Corporals, one and two gold bars for Sergeants and Senior Sergeants. The headgear was various. In action the blue-painted Adrian steel helmet, with its front embossed with an artillery badge of crossed cannons and a shell, was normal. Two kinds of cloth headgear were worn, apparently indiscriminately: a horizon blue sidecap with tall 'peaks' and a deep turn-up, and a low, soft horizon blue-covered képi with a round black peak and black chinstrap. No insignia were worn on these.

Officers wore a variety of personally-purchased horizon blue tunics, with breeches often piped scarlet. Tunic details seem to have varied widely in such matters as shape of collar (stand, stiff stand-and-fall, broad fall type); pockets (two or four, pleated or unpleated, buttons visible or concealed); and shoulder straps (usual, but not invariable). The most one can say is that they all seem to have been crotch-length, cut generously in the skirt, had one row of about six gilt buttons, and had a plain round false cuff. Collar patches were frequently not worn. Ranking was worn on the outside of the cuff in the form of 35 mm lengths of horizontal gold lace, from one to five identifying ranks, with five in alternate strips of gold-silver-gold-silver-gold marking a full Colonel. These ranking strips were repeated *en chevron* on the front of the sidecap crown when worn by officers, and as horizontal bars on the front of the horizon blue-covered képi. When the uncovered officers' képi was worn it was midnight blue with a red top. Gold lace decorated the top in a quatrefoil knot, and thin lines of gold lace surrounded the top part of the vertical surface, the number corresponding to the rank; short lengths of vertical lace passed from these over the top edge at front, back and sides, and

'Teddy', a French St Chamond photographed in 1917. The crew wear horizon blue uniforms, and four different headgears: the blue sidecap or bonnet de police, the blue-képi, the small civilian beret, and the Adrian helmet. On the original print the officer can be seen to wear the two short lace bars of a First Lieutenant on his sleeve (Imperial War Museum).

the front was decorated with a gold unit number and a gold false chinstrap. Warrant Officers wore basically the same uniforms as junior officers, but with a single rank lace broken with red. Officers wore puttees and ankle boots; long buckled brown leather gaiters and ankle boots; or brown leather boots laced from instep to knee, to taste. Brown leather belts with brass frame buckles had one prong for enlisted ranks, two for officers; the latter were of Sam Browne type, with a shoulder belt. The brown holster of the Ruby automatic or 1892 revolver was of a broad, triangular shape with a deep flap and bellows sides.

A very popular headgear among tank officers and men from 1917 onwards, although an unofficial one, was the black or midnight blue beret. This was worn to personal taste, without insignia. Being a civilian item it varied a lot in size, but was usually small.

In the vehicle the main protective clothing worn by all crewmen was the thigh-length black leather vehicle driver's coat, with a deep fall collar in black cloth. This had two rows of four black buttons, and prominent vertical and horizontal seams. Officers wore conventional cuff ranking on the sleeves of

Above *Excellent study of a French Schneider crew; all wear Adrian helmets with the artillery's crossed cannons and shell badge. Among this group can be seen the loose dark blue overall trousers (two men at right); the dagger (left, and centre pair); puttees and horizon blue trousers (centre pair); and long buckled gaiters (two men at left) worn by officers and NCOs. Both these two have rank bars just visible on the cuffs of their leather coats (Imperial War Museum).*

this coat. It is illustrated on Colour Plate 1 and in the accompanying photos. No collar patches seem to have been worn. This coat was worn either over the horizon blue service dress, or over a set of dark blue one-piece working overalls of denim material. When in action the minimum of personal equipment was worn; normally it was limited to a belt and holster, a gas mask canister, and sometimes a haversack of unbleached canvas slung around the body. Fighting daggers were also worn on the belt in the last year of the war.

The appearance of the Renault light tank and its baptism of fire at Ploisy-Chazelle on May 31 1918 saw the birth of a truly separate tank arm. The Renault was first issued to the newly-raised 501st Regiment of Combat Tanks, with three battalions; other regiments in this numbering sequence were raised during 1918. The new branch was mainly distinguishable by the branch colour of its insignia, which was grass green instead of artillery red. Collar patches were horizon blue with green regimental numbers and green rear edge piping, and enlisted rank stripes were green; metallic rank lace was silver. Some examples of green

Left *French St Chamond crew 'in the office', 1917; all wear blue-painted Adrian helmets and black leather vehicle-driver's coats. The nearest has a pistol holster and a gas mask canister slung round his body on crossstraps.*

trouser piping were observed, but it was not a universal practice.

From October 1917 a badge for tank crews was gradually introduced; it is logical to guess that this may have been worn only by those Assault Artillery units operating the heavy gun-carrier tanks under the old system, as such an insignia would perhaps have been superfluous in the *régiments de chars de combat?* It was in the form of crossed cannons with a knight's helm superimposed on the junction, facing left, and was worn in red on the upper left sleeve.

A metal badge had been worn since early 1917 by some officers and men of the *Artillerie Spéciale*, pinned to the right breast; its use seems to have been only semi-official, at best. It was in the form of a circular, open silver wreath, with a gold salamander (lizard) rampant to the right (later, left) breathing flames back over its shoulder. At the bottom of the wreath was a shield bearing an entwined 'AS' cypher.

Germany

Since Germany was forced to react hurriedly to the British initiative in tank warfare, it is hardly surprising that no German tank arm with a truly independent identity was founded before the Armistice. The Commander of Heavy Combat Vehicles was responsible directly to Army Supreme HQ; but through the obvious necessity of drawing many of the essential technical personnel from the Motor Transport branch of the Communications troops, the tank *Abteilungen* were generally considered to be part of the *Kraftfahrtruppen*.

Initially at least, a definite link existed between the infant tank units and the assault troops; though exactly what was the nature and extent of that link seems to have been lost in the turmoil of two German defeats, civil disturbance and foreign occupation over the past 60 years.

The assault troops apparently owed their birth, or at least their expansion, to one Major Ulrich Rohr. At the time of Verdun, special raiding squads of *Sturmtruppen* were formed to break the stalemate which artillery, massive wire entanglements and machine-guns had imposed on conventional forces.

These 'commandos' were so successful that assault companies were attached to infantry divisions in the front line; and by 1918 no less than 18 fully-fledged assault battalions had been formed and attached to German Armies, each with its integral elements of light artillery, machine-guns, trench mortars and flame-throwers in addition to infantry assault companies. The 5th *Sturmbataillon* was named after Major Rohr, and was attached to the German 5th Army. It was this unit which demonstrated the new A7V heavy tank before the Kaiser on February 27 1918. On March 21, *Abteilung Nr 1* went into action at St Quentin with its five A7Vs, in support of an assault battalion.

Initially the tank detachments were termed *Sturm-Panzerkraftwagen-Abteilungen;* the first two were set up in September 1917, and five more in December 1917. Another minor clue to the relationship between tank and assault units is the similarity, in certain respects, of their uniforms. Both assault infantry and tank crews wore tunics and trousers reinforced with leather at knees and elbows, and tank crews carried fighting knives like the trench raiders. If we put all these small facts together some kind of official link becomes clear; but more than that, the author has been unable to discover. Is it permissible to speculate that at first it was intended to entrust tank warfare solely to the assault troops, but that the scope of the technical effort involved put paid to the plan?

By the end of the war the following units had been activated; note that British sources usually identify them by the numbers 1 to 9 in sequence, but that the numbers quoted in the table at the foot of the page are from German sources.

The author has been unable to confirm when the title changed from its original form of Assault Armoured Vehicle Detachment to the form quoted here, Heavy Combat Vehicle Detachment.

Each detachment fielded five vehicles. Its establishment was one Captain, five Subalterns and either 170 or 134 enlisted men, the greater number for the A7V units, the smaller for units of British tanks. This was broken down into 81 drivers, 48 machine-gunners, 22 artillery personnel, 12 signal-

Unit	Base	Equipment
Schwere Kampfwagen-Abteilung Nr 1	Marchienne au Pont	A7V
Schwere Kampfwagen-Abteilung Nr 2	Marchienne au Pont	A7V
Schwere Kampfwagen-Abteilung Nr 3	Marchienne au Pont	A7V
Schwere Kampfwagen-Abteilung Nr 11	Roux, near Charleroi	British captures
Schwere Kampfwagen-Abteilung Nr 12	Roux, near Charleroi	British captures
Schwere Kampfwagen-Abteilung Nr 13 (Bavarian)	Roux, near Charleroi	British captures
Schwere Kampfwagen-Abteilung Nr 14	Roux, near Charleroi	British captures
Schwere Kampfwagen-Abteilung Nr 15	Roux, near Charleroi	British captures
Schwere Kampfwagen-Abteilung Nr 16	Roux, near Charleroi	British captures

Interesting group of German tank crewmen, 1918 – the death's-head on the front of the A7V tank suggests a very tentative identification of Abteilung 5. *The driver or mechanic on the left wears a grey-painted crash helmet, a* Bluse *of which the collar* Litzen *are just visible, and a grey suit of either leather or heavy cloth. The centre figure, wearing a British mail face-mask, certainly wears a suit of cloth rather than leather. Both have uniform buttons and cloth loops on the shoulders, indicating the occasional attachment of uniform epaulettes. The middle figure has a slung gas mask canister, and a Luger holster on his belt. The* Unteroffizier *(right) wears, apparently,* Kraftfahrtruppen *distinctions on collar, shoulder, and cap. His jacket is very non-standard, being neither a* Bluse *nor a 1910 service tunic.*

lers, one medical orderly and six supernumeraries. The crew of an A7V has been quoted variously as 18 or 23 men – apparently spare machine-gunners were sometimes carried in the tanks, and the gun crew varied between two and three. (Doubtless some members of this milling crowd could also have 'doubled up' at need!) Ten or 12 machine-gunners, two signallers, and either two or four mechanics were carried in addition to the commander, driver and gun crew.

Crews were drawn from various branches according to their trades: gunners from the artillery, signallers from the communications branch, machine-gunners from the infantry machine-gun units or 'Machine-Gun Sharpshooter Detachments', and drivers, mechanics and commanders from the *Kraftfahrtruppen*. They had no special uniform or insignia, and kept the distinctions of their original organisations.

The standard field uniform was the field cap and/or steel trench helmet; the 1915 *Bluse* jacket; straight, baggy trousers, and puttees, all in field grey. The field cap was the pork pie type for enlisted ranks and the peaked type for officers; senior

Another member of the same unit, wearing what certainly appears to be a grey leather tank suit, the domed helmet, British mail mask, gas mask canister and holster. The collar Litzen *of the Transport Troops is clearly visible, and again, buttons and loops on the shoulders allow attachment of uniform shoulder straps.*

NCOs also wore peaked caps and, in the last months of the war, even junior ranks seem sometimes to have received them. The band was coloured, and coloured piping followed both edges of the band and the crown seam. For all crew members the colours would have been identical, except for the machine-gun crews. *Kraftfahrtruppen*, signallers and artillery all wore black bands and red piping. Machine-gunners would generally have worn red bands and piping. All ranks wore two cockades on the cap front; the black/white/red *Reichs* cockade on the crown, and the state cockade on the band. For most personnel this would have

been the black/white/black of Prussia, but *Abteilung Nr 13* would have worn light blue/white/light blue. The peaked version of the cap appeared with or without a black chinstrap, the variation being without apparent significance.

The *Bluse* was a fly-fronted, single-breasted field grey jacket of generous cut. It had deep but entirely plain turned back cuffs, a plain fall collar, two skirt pockets with back-slanting buttoned flaps, and shoulder straps. *Kraftfahrtruppen* and signallers would normally wear double *Litzen* on the collar – the traditional lace bars of the Prussian Army – in white for enlisted and silver for commissioned ranks. Machine-gunners and artillery would not. The shoulder straps of the commanders, if commissioned, would be of the usual silver cord with grey underlay and a gold cypher 'K'. Enlisted ranks of the *Kraftfahrtruppen* wore a red embroidered 'K' on a plain, unpiped field grey strap. Red unit numbers from previous postings might be seen below this 'K'. Signallers would wear identical straps but with 'T' replacing 'K'. The artillerymen would wear red straps with a yellow 'bomb' above yellow unit numbers, if from a Field Regiment; and yellow straps with red numbers below red crossed cannons, if from a Foot Regiment. Machine-gunners would normally wear straps of field grey piped either red or white; numbers would be red, and if the piping was white a common number would be '13'. If from a 'Machine-Gun Sharpshooter Detachment', gunners might wear a grey oval patch on the upper left arm with a red stylised machine-gun on it. All buttons were nickel.

As mentioned above, leather patches were worn on knee and elbow. The steel helmet would be either grey, or painted in camouflage segments of subdued shades such as brick red, dark green, purple, ochre, etc, often divided by black lines into angular shapes. Personal equipment was limited to holsters for either the Luger automatic or the M'79 revolver; fighting daggers; and gas mask canisters.

The overalls worn for dirty work around the vehicles seem to have been simple black two-piece denim suits, as worn by aircraft mechanics. The rather more dramatic one-piece suits worn by the crew in the photos accompanying this chapter were apparently restricted to the drivers, and sometimes the mechanics. (Doubtless other crew members managed to 'wangle' them if they admired them!) They were grey, and seem to have appeared both in heavy cloth and in leather; the latter surely a wasteful use of a scarce strategic commodity at this late stage. They were worn with a heavy belt with a frame buckle and metal eyelets, and with a low, padded, dome-shaped crash helmet painted field grey. Photos show that loops and uniform buttons were attached to the shoulders, so the shoulder straps from the service dress were certainly worn on the overall sometimes.

Like other German troops of this period, the tank crews doubtless included some men who sported weird transitional jackets displaying characteristics both of the old 1910 field tunic and of the *Bluse*. Some wore *Blusen* piped round the collar, front closure, and/or cuffs in the colours of their branch. Others had pockets where none should have been. Some even had exposed buttons up the front. If such branch-colour pipings did survive among these crews, the likely colours would be red on the trousers of all branches; red at the front and black at collar and cuff for all technical branches; and red at all points for machine-gunners.

The ranking of NCOs followed this sequence: *Gefreiter* – Small button each side of collar, level with straps; *Unteroffizier* – Lace round front and bottom of collar, sometimes limited to short L-shapes in dull silver-grey; *Feldwebel* – Collar lace, plus large button each side of collar; *Offizierstellvertreter* (officer aspirant) – As *Feldwebel* but with lace round the edges of the shoulder straps.

Officers wore straps in silver corded finish. Company officers' straps had four double strips of cord down the length of the straps, with no pips, one gold pip and two gold pips respectively for *Leutnant*, *Oberleutnant* and *Hauptmann*. Field officers wore a strap with entwined cords showing rather more of the underlay down the edges, and no pips, one pip and two pips respectively for *Major*, *Oberstleutnant* and *Oberst*. These pips were square sunbursts with a raised circular centre, set diamond-wise on the strap.

United States

The only other country to put tanks into combat in the First World War was the United States. The 304th Tank Brigade had two battalions of Renaults, the 344th and 345th, which went into action for the first time on September 12 1918 at St Mihiel. A third battalion, the 301st, was equipped with British Mk V vehicles and always operated with the British Tank Corps – its first action seems to have been at Second Cambrai on September 27 1918. The 331st Battalion was activated only days before the Armistice. The 304th Brigade, being equipped and

Mixed American and French tank corps personnel work on Renault tanks on railway flatcars. The US soldiers wear light summer olive service dress and overseas caps, or one-piece overalls and overseas caps (US Signal Corps).

1918: American Renault crews in France, wearing khaki one-piece overalls and overseas caps (US Signal Corps).

trained by the French, seems to have had a large number of attached French tank personnel; during training, if not actually in battle, it seems that mixed French/American crews were to be seen.

United States tank personnel seem from photographs to have worn no special uniform items or insignia at all, apart from one-piece working overalls in what appear to be shades of brown or khaki. The steel helmet was issued, but the normal headgear in the vehicle was the rather shapeless khaki* 'overseas cap' or sidecap, with its 'envelope' shape usually distorted by being tugged down square to the ears! The top of the doubled turn-up sloped down and back to meet the lower edge of the cap on the right side at the front. The cap was not piped for enlisted men, but was piped around the turn-up top edge in branch colours for officers. At this date the piping of the wearer's original branch would have been worn – bright blue for infantry, yellow for cavalry or red for artillery, in most cases. At the left front of the cap enlisted men sometimes but not invariably wore a bronze disc branch badge. Officers wore the ranking in this position: none for 2nd Lieutenants, one and two silver vertical bars for Lieutenants and Captains, a gilt maple leaf for Majors, a silver leaf for Lieutenant Colonels, and a silver eagle for Colonels.

Normal service uniform was worn with or without overalls on top. It appeared in two weights – a

*US Army 'khaki', at this point, resembled the British uniform colour.

khaki serge for cold weather, and a khaki cotton material for summer. Both were of identical cut. The tunic was single-breasted with five bronze front buttons, pointed shoulder straps and a stand collar with square corners. There were two breast and two skirt pockets, all of patch type with buttoned pointed flaps and no pleats. Khaki breeches or pantaloons completed the uniform, with brown laced ankle boots. Enlisted ranks wore either khaki puttees or neutral coloured knee-length laced canvas leggings. Officers wore, to taste, either puttees, knee-length buckled brown leather gaiters, or brown riding boots.

Enlisted men wore a bronze disc badge on each side of the collar front. Officers wore a bronze 'U.S.' cypher on the front of each side of the collar, and a cut-out branch badge (eg. crossed sabres for the cavalry) on the sides in line with the shoulder straps. Officers' ranking, as described above, appeared at the end of the shoulder straps; these were plain for enlisted men. Officers were also distinguished by a broad stripe of brown braid around the top of the round false cuff.

The chevrons of NCOs appeared on both upper sleeves, in 'Olive Drab' – in practice, a light khaki shade. They took the form of slightly 'scooped' chevrons, point upwards, and for senior NCOs the lower ends of the lower chevron were joined either by straight 'ties' or concave 'rockers'. Examples are one, two and three chevrons (Lance-Corporal, Corporal, Sergeant); three chevrons above an open diamond (First Sergeant); three chevrons above two 'rockers' (Battalion Sergeant-Major); three chevrons above one straight 'tie' (Supply Sergeant).

Officers normally wore Sam Browne belts of British type. Occasionally the webbing belt for the russet leather Colt automatic holster or the cutaway revolver holster was worn in addition to the Sam Browne, and sometimes it was substituted. Webbing double magazine pouches for the automatic pistol were worn on the left front of the belt. Enlisted men seem to have worn a brown belt with a plain single-prong brass frame buckle when not wearing the 1910 web rifle pouch belt – which would be a useless encumbrance in a tank unit. British gas mask satchels were often worn slung on the chest.

Late in 1918 the wearing of colourful shoulder patches at the top of the left arm to identify formations and organisations became widespread in the AEF, but it does not appear that these divisional, etc, insignia were worn in action. Photos exist of an AEF Tank Corps patch of triangular shape, made up of the colours of the three main contributing branches, and illustrated on Colour Plate 1; it was certainly worn in France, but whether before or only after the Armistice seems unclear.

THE INTERWAR YEARS

Great Britain

The Tank Corps did not have to struggle to maintain its identity after 1918, surprisingly enough, although it was a period when antedeluvian senior officers were emerging from their filing cabinets to 'cut down to size' the young whippersnappers who had had the effrontery to win the war, and the motto in too many corridors of power was, 'Now we can get back to some *real* soldiering!' Paradoxically it was the huge success of horsed cavalry in Allenby's last great Palestine campaign which saved the Corps. Since it gave invaluable ammunition to those wedded to the continuity of the horsed cavalry, and since tanks had demonstrated beyond question their value on the Western Front, the Corps would neither be taken over by the emergence of an armoured cavalry, nor disbanded, and was allowed to soldier on – though greatly reduced. The interwar years saw much vigorous 'police action' in armoured cars and light tanks in the less hospitable Imperial possessions, and, in the 1930s, the bitter war between those visionaries who saw and preached the full potential of the mobile all-arms force, and the defenders of traditional tribal boundaries within the Army.

The uniform remained that of World War 1 in most respects. The field cap got its wire stiffener back in short order, but was itself replaced in 1924, after prolonged argument, by the famous black beret which was to remain the proud mark of the 'tanky' from then on. General Elles and Colonel Fuller had

Above *Royal Tank Corps cap badge, October 18 1923 to January 30 1953; there was no change of badge when the Corps became the Regiment in April 1939 (Mike Chappell).*

Right *A veteran field officer of the Tank Corps posing with his men in about 1919. In the original print it can be seen that all still wear two-coloured shoulder strap tallies; the white tank arm badge; and the white letters 'T.C.' at the top of each sleeve. The Corporal, seated left centre, has five insignia on his right arm and shoulder: the coloured tally on the end of the shoulder strap, the 'T.C.' cypher immediately below the shoulder seam, the tank badge, the crossed hammer and pincers in white identifying an artificer, and his rank chevrons. All wear standard khaki service dress (R. G. Harris).*

first got the idea when dining together in May 1918, and personally borrowed berets from the French *70ᵉ Chasseurs Alpins*, billeted nearby. The beret hid oil stains, and was vastly more practical than the khaki peaked cap. King George V finally approved its use in March 1924.

The white tank arm badge of a qualified tank soldier was taken into use by all officers and men of the Corps in 1919, and has likewise survived ever since. The coloured shoulder strap tallies disappeared in about the same year. The Corps went through two changes of name in the interwar period: it became the Royal Tank Corps in 1923, and subsequently the Royal Tank Regiment in 1939. A new cap badge marked the Royal honour in 1923, which has remained in use (with a minor change of detail in 1953) up to the present day: a crowned wreath with the left profile side view of a stylised Mark IV tank across the centre above the scroll 'FEAR NAUGHT'. For a time in the immediate post-war period a sewn shoulder title in the form of the white capitals 'T.C.' was worn at the top of both arms of the khaki tunic.

In overseas service the crews of light armoured vehicles wore the tropical dress of the Army as a whole: khaki drill shorts, 'greyback' shirts and solar topis. In the late 1930s khaki drill bush shirts and khaki drill slacks, seem to have been issued in Indian and Middle Eastern armoured units. The steel helmet was still to be seen in occasional use by the crews of open-topped vehicles such as tracked carriers and tankettes of various types. The famous black overalls nowadays worn by RTR units were officially approved as a vehicle uniform in 1935, but photos suggest that this was only a regularisation of a habit which had been catching on at unit level for some years. Rank chevrons seem to have been worn on both sleeves of the overalls in those days.

The mechanisation of the cavalry – against fierce opposition – began in earnest in 1928-29 with the conversion to armoured cars of 11th Hussars and 12th Lancers. Various other units experimented with partly mechanised establishments in the years that followed, but in 1935 the most die-hard horse-men had to recognise that the evil day could be put off no longer. The 3rd Hussars were the first to go, and others quickly followed – although for a long time they had to make do with trucks and light scout vehicles to 'represent' tanks which were not yet available. Finally, in 1937, re-armament began in earnest. The disbanded 7th and 8th Battalions, RTC, were resurrected in that and the following year. Territorial tank battalions were formed from infantry units, and numbered from '40th Battalion' upwards. In April 1939 the Royal Armoured Corps

was born, embracing the old RTC, now renamed Royal Tank Regiment; the mechanised cavalry regiments, both Regular and Territorial; and – within a year – six entirely new mechanised cavalry regiments.

The newly armoured cavalry regiments seem to have clung to their old regimental uniforms. By the time of the formation of the RAC this meant, in practice, little more than the retention of insignia and certain 'tribal' eccentricities, for by now the whole Army was wearing (or awaiting the issue of) the 1937 khaki battledress and the ugly khaki Field Service cap, or sidecap. The use of the black beret was extended to the whole RAC in 1940, but photographs show that in practice the khaki FS cap was worn by cavalry tank regiments, in significant numbers, into 1942. In the pre-Second World War period it was not unusual to see cavalry officers in the turrets of tanks wearing their full service dress (Sam Browne belts, with the four-pocket khaki tunic, and coloured regimental sidecaps).

The battledress is covered in detail in Part 3.

Royal Air Force
Several RAF armoured car companies served in the Middle East in the 1920s and 1930s. When

July 1935 – the first official recognition of the black RTR tank overalls, coinciding with parades to mark King George V's Jubilee. This crew displays the two box-pleated breast pockets with straight flaps, low standing collar, and single left thigh pocket without pleats, which characterised this first issue of black overalls (R. J. Marrion).

raised in 1921, they wore standard grey-blue RAF home service dress, which soon faded in the desert sun. From early 1922 a summer uniform of collarless 'greyback' shirt with sandy KD shorts and large sun helmet was authorised. The helmet soon acquired a flash on the side of the paggri – thick dark blue, thin light blue, thick dark red, in vertical stripes. Long grey or khaki socks, and either canvas shoes or ammunition boots, completed the uniform. The spine pad was worn, and often a sun curtain from the back of the topi. In the field all ranks often wore the red and white checked Arab headcloth or *shemagh* with a black cord *agal*. Other variations from regulations were to be seen when safely in the desert: the peaked grey-blue cap in place of the topi, or long trousers in place of shorts. The occasional black beret was to be seen, too.

As the 1930s wore on the tropical dress became better cut; officers wore tropical tunics modelled on the home service dress, in KD, and other ranks wore KD bush jackets. The topi was generally replaced by the RAF grey-blue Field Service cap (sidecap) by about 1936. When 'up the desert' and far from the eye of the Station Warrant Officer, some incredible costumes were to be observed: white boiler suits, khaki sweaters, flying helmets, cap comforters, and old sets of No 1 dress were all used.

France

The uniform and protective clothing of the French tank crewman underwent a gradual process of modification between the World Wars; this became a frenzy of activity from 1935 onwards, resulting in the French tank arm entering the Second World War with an assorted collection of old and new items in simultaneous use.

Until the mid-1930s the horizon blue uniform was worn as it had been in 1917-18, with the same green branch insignia. (The artillery had lost responsibility for tank units in May 1920.) In some units, but not by any means all, a fall collar with a deep, loose shape was introduced in the early 1930s; this had collar patches of the type worn by all units on the greatcoat's similar collar – a squat diamond shape formed by the point of the collar, bearing the green unit number and 'cut off' by two curved green pipings. The *pantalon culotte* were sometimes but not always piped green. A blue stock was visible in the neck of the tunic.

Peacetime ranking reverted to large, 'scooped' chevrons worn point up above both cuffs, the 'legs' butting down against the top of the round false cuff. These were in green and silver, in the same rank sequence as during the First World War. Metal badges were worn on the right breast, usually in the form of the type of tank used by that unit, but

varying widely in detail; silver was the usual colour. In walking-out and parade dress units which had been awarded decorations in the First World War wore the ornate corded lanyard or *fourragère* in the ribbon colours of that decoration round the left shoulder, with the end hanging at the front tipped with a silver ferrule (eg, the green and red mixed lanyard of the *Croix de Guerre* worn by the 501st Regiment).

The small midnight blue or black beret was made official in August 1919, and was the normal headgear from then on. This *'poulie'* was supposed to be worn pulled to the left, but was usually crammed straight down across the forehead; veterans also tended to substitute a small civilian beret for the issue one, which at 285 mm diameter was considered unstylish for some reason. The crossed cannons and helm badge, in silver, was worn in metal, centrally at the front, by enlisted ranks, and in wire embroidery on the left side by officers. Officially the beret was supposed to be worn anywhere *except* in the tank itself, but this order was generally ignored.

Officers' képis were midnight blue (in practice, black) all over, with silver knots on top, silver ranking lace round the upper edge, silver false chinstraps and silver unit numbers. Career NCOs and troopers who re-enlisted for an extra term beyond their legal national service also wore the midnight blue képi in place of the beret, officially. Ranks below *Caporal-Chef* wore yellow unit numbers; a yellow ring of piping round the edge of the top surface, another round the top edge of the vertical surface, and four short lengths of yellow piping joining these two rings at front, back and sides; and black leather chinstraps with silver buttons. From this rank upwards, number and chinstrap were silver; the latter was purely ornamental, and an extra black one would be buttoned on for use when needed.

Officers wore a four-pocket tunic with a stand-and-fall collar. This had box-pleated breast pockets with three-point buttoned flaps, and unpleated bellows skirt pockets with straight buttoned flaps. The short wartime ranking bars above the edge of the false cuff were retained; buttons were silver. On the collar points were silver unit numbers enclosed at the top by double green pipings. Officers began to acquire khaki uniforms well before their men, and from the very early 1930s would often appear in a khaki tunic and pale beige ('mastic') breeches. Collar patches had a khaki ground, with silver numbers and ash grey pipings.

When serving in the vehicles the tank troops continued to wear the double-breasted black leather coat, with its black cloth collar now adorned with patches. These were black, with the unit number in ash (light) grey, and the double pipings in the same shade. Officers wore silver numbers and ash-grey piping. Normally the straight, rather loose trousers of the one- or two-piece working overalls of dark blue denim were worn over the horizon blue pantaloons and puttees. Some black leather motorcyclist's trousers were issued, but these were not very common. On the front of the leather coat a small cloth tab could be fixed from the edge of the front closure across to a small button on the horizontal seam, and this bore the ranking. Officers had short bars of silver, NCOs bars of green and/or silver according to rank. Photos of Renault tank crews supporting French infantry in Morocco during the Rif War of the 1920s seem to show dark blue one-piece overalls and small black berets.

The special tank helmet appeared in 1919 and went through several modifications; in the 1930s at least three main types were in use together. The first model had the skull of the Adrian helmet, with the top comb (ridged crest) and the large embossed badge at the front. A small, sharply-angled neck guard was fixed to the back, and several thicknesses of black leather were riveted across the front to make a brow pad. It had a simple leather chinstrap. Numerous variations of detail appeared over the years, the main one being the abandonment of the added neck-guard in favour of a one-piece skull with integral neck-guard. The comb and single chinstrap seem to have lasted until 1935. The helmet was generally painted blue, but in some units, purely for the sake of 'swank', it was painted black, with the raised details of the badge, and the comb, in natural polished metal.

The personal equipment of the tank soldier remained limited: a holster on a leather belt, with a half-frame brass buckle with two prongs and heavy leather 'keeps'; one or more haversacks of neutral beige canvas; the two-spout French Army canteen, usually covered with horizon blue coat cloth; and a cylindrical blue or khaki gas mask container with a fluted surface. The dagger lasted for quite a few years after 1918.

The remarks above apply equally to the Regiments of Combat Tanks and to the cavalry tank units known, for some reason, as Cavalry Armoured Car Groups, even though their equipment included tanks. In the cavalry the insignia and button 'metal' was silver but the branch colour was violet instead of green; the branch badge was a Medusa mask on a sunburst. The képi was sky blue with crimson top and unit numbers.

In the mid-1930s a mass of new regulations

French tank helmet of one of the many slightly differing intermediate models used between the M1919 and the M1935. In this case the shape is that of the M1935, with one-piece skull and neck-guard, small comb, no frontal badge, and thick brow-pad; but the chinstrap is still the narrow type. Steel painted horizon blue; black leather.

appeared. A new helmet, a new leather coat, new insignia and a new service uniform all began to reach the regiments.

The service uniform was in khaki. The tunic had a fall collar, cut generously, beneath which a khaki shirt and khaki stock could be seen. Insignia were unchanged, except that the collar patches were khaki and of the shape previously seen only on the greatcoat and leather coat, with green piping and numbers. The *pantalon culotte* began to be replaced, just before the war and in limited numbers, by *pantalon golf*; these came down to mid-calf before being gathered into shorter puttees, just like 'plus-fours'. In the khaki uniform the trousers never seem to have been piped green. Insignia of rank reverted to the short wartime cuff bars, in dark brown and silver. From 1938 officers generally, but not universally, adopted a tunic with a new, open collar with stepped lapels worn over a khaki collar and tie. Their collar patches were then worn in a pentagonal shape, the base butted against the upper edge of the step in the lapel, with the silver numbers and double ash-grey pipings around the top two edges unchanged. Beige breeches and brown top-boots were still worn, with a Sam Browne belt. When serving in the tanks officers wore enlisted men's puttees and black ankle boots.

In 1935 the undisciplined variety of 'tank type' metal badges worn on the right breast were supressed in favour of a single badge worn by all mechanised troops. This was a stylised representation of a set of tank bogies and tracks in right profile, above which was a star trailing a blazing stylised 'tail', the lower flames of which passed behind the tank tracks. It was worn in dull silver, and sometimes appeared on a surrounding wreath.

The most visible changes in the immediate prewar years were the new M.1935 helmet and coat. The helmet now appeared without the top comb. The frontal badge became smaller, and was embossed into the helmet itself instead of being on an applied disc. The brow pad became much thicker, a genuine pad instead of a series of leather strips, and was dark brown in colour. So was the new leather chin-harness; this was a broad piece of leather tapering to a chinstrap at each side of the jaw, with a hole just over the ear. The chinstrap had a substantial buckle on the right side.

The 1935 coat was also of brown leather, and single-breasted, with one row of five large composition buttons down the front. It was softer and less unwieldy than the old black type, and had a leather collar. This bore khaki cloth collar patches with pipings and numbers in ash grey, although one or two units seem to have retained green on these patches. The rank tabs buttoned to the front were also khaki.

A type of heavy, light khaki-coloured proofed trousers were also issued to crews from 1935 onwards. These *pantalon cachou* were loose and straight, gathered just above the bottom of the legs by buckled cloth straps. Early models had two patch pockets high on the front of the thighs, which were missing from batches manufactured later.

New two-piece working denims in light khaki were also issued. These had straight, loose trousers; and a short, round-bottomed jacket buttoning on the right of the chest, with two rows of six small buttons, and two small patch pockets low on the sides.

Germany

The birth of the Panzer branch of the revived German Army in 1934-35, and its rapid transformation from an experimental and largely clandestine department into an important fighting branch with divisional formations, saw the introduction of a uniform both original and striking. Unlike the other nations of the West, whose tank crews tended to wear protective overalls when working or fighting their vehicles, but whose service dress remained basically similar to that of the other fighting branches apart from applied insignia, Germany chose to outfit her tank troops in a wholly distinctive service uniform. It was dramatic and dashing, thus underlining in the public mind the élite nature of this new type of unit; its insignia echoed traditional Prussian images; and it was soundly practical in conception. It was to remain in service, largely unaltered, until 1945.

This *Sonderbekleidung der Deutschen Panzertruppen* consisted of a protective headgear, a short double-breasted jacket and long straight trousers, all in black cloth, to hide the inevitable oil-stains. The headgear was in two parts: an inner, protective cap of felt padding and oilcloth, covered by a large, loose black beret. The jacket reached just below the waist. It had a deep falling collar, and very broad lapels which were normally worn folded back and open, exposing a mouse grey shirt and a black tie. The slanted front closure had a fly front; the only buttons visible on the jacket were two, of black horn, high on the right breast, by which the left lapel could be fastened closed across the chest in cold weather. There were two grey metal buttons on the shoulders for the attachment of shoulder straps, but the deep collar normally hid these. The trousers, of straight, loose outline, were worn over the normal knee-length black marching boots. They were gathered above the ankle, giving a deep 'pull-down' effect; there were two slanting side pockets on the front of the hips, with buttoned flaps, a small fob pocket and a rear hip pocket.

The *Waffenfarbe*, or distinctive arm-of-service colour, of the Panzer troops was a bright rose pink. Piping in this colour edged the collar of the black jacket for all ranks, commissioned and enlisted. On the collar points were worn a pair of unique collar patches, which were also common to all commissioned and enlisted ranks: long parallelograms of black cloth, edged with pink piping, and bearing centrally a small white metal *Totenkopf* or death's-head. The shoulder straps worn on the jacket, which were sometimes sewn down to the shoulder all round to prevent snagging on projections in the vehicle, were of the usual German Army design (see illustrations) but, for enlisted ranks, were of black cloth. They were piped pink around the edges, and for NCOs from *Unteroffizier* upwards bore the usual silver-grey braid, 9 mm wide, around the edges inside the *Waffenfarbe* piping, and the normal system of rank pips in white metal. Officers wore the usual silver cord shoulder straps on pink underlay, with gold pips where appropriate. In peacetime the regimental number was also worn on the shoulder straps, top towards the neck; enlisted men had it embroidered on the

Above *Unidentified but fascinating group of German Freikorps armoured car crewmen, photographed shortly after the Armistice? The left-hand man wears a small silver death's-head badge between his cap cockades. The foreground figure wears the same insignia in white or silver on a black arm patch, and below it is the earliest example known to the author of a cuff title for armoured troops, lettered apparently in white capitals on black, KAMPFWAGEN. The right-hand man has a red on grey 'K' shoulder strap cypher, identifying him as a past or present member of the* Kraftfahrtruppen *or transport corps, who manned the German tanks in the First World War. Interestingly, the centre figure wears a silver badge beneath his Iron Cross which, from its clearly defined shape, is a First War flying badge of some type – it is* not *the retrospective tank assault badge of July 1921 issue* (Imperial War Museum).

Below *The German* Schutzmütze, *showing the two parts fitted together (left), and (right) the padded head protector without the outer 'beret'* (Courtesy Mike Ross).

black strap in pink, NCOs from *Unteroffizier* upwards wore white metal cyphers pinned to the straps, and officers wore gold metal cyphers. The rank chevrons of junior NCOs were of the usual design, but in silver-grey braid on a black backing, worn on the left upper arm.

Initially the jacket was unusual in that it did not bear the national eagle and swastika insignia, common to all branches of the Army, on the right breast; this was introduced at some point between 1935 and 1939. It was of the usual shape – straight wings with the ends 'clipped' upwards and outwards, the head facing right as viewed, and the mobile swastika surrounded by a wreath. It was in white or silver-grey thread on a black backing for enlisted and non-commissioned ranks, and in silver wire on black for officers.

The insignia on the black beret, or *Schutzmütze*, was the same for all ranks. A smaller version of the national eagle surmounted a large oakleaf wreath which surrounded the national cockade in black, white and red; eagle and wreath were in white thread on a black backing. Again, the national eagle was not worn on the beret at first, the wreath and cockade alone being sewn to the front of the headgear. At some point during the late 1930s it was added.

The uniform described was worn with the standard enlisted ranks' black leather belt, with a rectangular buckle-plate bearing a raised motif – an eagle and swastika, with folded wings, in a circular riband bearing the legend *Gott Mit Uns*. Officers wore a black 'Sam Browne' style belt in the pre-war years, with the cross-strap passing over the right shoulder. This was later discontinued, and the usual officer's brown field service belt with two-pronged frame buckle was worn without it. Early photos show that it was common for the uniform to be worn without a belt at all.

The normal decorations were worn on the black uniform where appropriate. One decoration should be mentioned in particular, as it is sometimes to be seen in photographs of the late 1930s and was peculiar to this branch. In 1936 General von Thoma, commanding the *Panzer Lehr* units in Spain during the Civil War, instituted a Tank Assault Badge for wear on the left breast by officers and men of his corps who qualified by reason of combat experience. It was in white metal, a pierced design in the form of a large oval wreath surrounding a large death's-head, over a small, stylised tank shape. It was officially confirmed by OKH in July 1939. There were certainly some veterans of the *Legion Condor* tank companies who would also have qualified for a wound badge of the 1936 pattern. This was also worn on the left breast; it was a black solid oval, in the form of a plaque surrounded by a raised wreath. On the plaque were crossed broadswords points up, with superimposed on them centrally the shape of a Spanish Army helmet charged with a mobile swastika.

A cuff title was issued to commemorate service in Spain, but the author has never seen a photograph or an order confirming whether or not it was worn on the black Panzer uniform; it was authorised in June 1939 for wear on the field-grey service blouse and the greatcoat, and would have been such a handsome addition to the black jacket that it seems likely that only a direct order would have prevented it being worn! Of red cloth 32 mm wide, with gold edges, it was worn on the right sleeve 15 cm up from the bottom of the cuff, and bore on the outer face the gold legend *1936 Spanien 1939* in Gothic script.

The rarest badge worn on the new uniform – if it ever was – would have been the 'retrospective' First World War tank crew badge, authorised on July 21 1921. A solid silver oval, it bore a motif of an A7V tank in action. It seems very unlikely that more than a tiny handful of officers of the new branch would have qualified for it.

United States

In America the traditional branches of service won the battle which had been lost in Britain; in 1920 the Tank Corps was disbanded, and vehicles and personnel were assigned to the infantry branch. A tank company was assigned to each infantry division, and the 1st Tank Group was formed with an HQ and five battalions. In September 1929 this latter organisation became the 1st and 2nd Tank Regiments. In October 1932 they became the 66th Infantry (Light Tanks) and 67th Infantry (Medium Tanks). In 1933 the 68th and 69th Infantry (Light Tanks) were constituted, on paper. The 68th took shape early in 1940, drawing on infantry divisional tank companies, but the 69th was disbanded without ever existing in practice.

The cavalry experimented with light armoured vehicles in the 1920s, although these were limited to the designation 'combat cars' to avoid breaking the Congressional prohibition on any arm except the infantry having 'tanks'. For the period 1928-31 an experimental all-arms mechanised force was formed under the command of Colonel Daniel Van Voorhis. In 1931 the US Army Chief of Staff, General Douglas MacArthur, decreed that in future all arms could experiment – separately – with armoured and mechanised equipment. This was a green light for the cavalry, who in 1933 – spurred by some tart comments on the future of the horse in war from MacArthur – mechanised the 1st Cavalry at Fort Knox, Kentucky. Vehicles were divided between

armoured cars and 'combat cars', which were in fact the same 'light tanks' used by the infantry. Other cavalry regiments followed the 1st into the new role, along with artillery and services, and in 1938 Brigadier General Van Voorhis took command of all these Fort Knox units under the collective identification 7th Cavalry Brigade (Mechanised). Later that year he was succeeded by Colonel Adna Chaffee, America's 'Father of the Armored Force'.

The obvious emergence of important combat armour formations in Europe could not be ignored, and after the usual wrangling the infantry and cavalry began a slow process of co-operation. Armour of both branches was assembled into *ad hoc* armoured divisions for manoeuvres in 1940. That year saw Germany's shattering successes in Holland and France; and in July 1940 the Armoured Force was created under Chaffee's command. (There was still no Congressional authorisation for a separate armoured branch of the service, so it was officially raised 'for test purposes'. The end of the Second World War would see the situation unchanged, on paper; the cavalry claimed the armoured forces as their own in the period 1947-50, and it was not until the latter year that a new, separate, totally legitimate Armor branch was actually recognised!).

Five days after the birth of the Armored Force, the first two Armored Divisions came into being: the 1st, at Fort Knox, drew its main units from the old 7th Cavalry Brigade, and the 2nd, at Fort Benning in Georgia, drew on the infantry tank units – the 66th, 67th and 68th Regiments, which had been designated collectively the Provisional Tank Brigade. By the time Japan attacked Pearl Harbor, five Armored Divisions and numerous independent tank battalions had been activated.

The infantrymen who maintained the continuity of America's tank forces alone from 1920 to 1933 wore standard US Army service dress of the time with the insignia of their parent formations. In 1926 the old high-collared tunic gave way to one with an open, stepped collar worn over a white shirt and black tie. The trousers were now better cut, being definitely flared breeches instead of baggy pantaloons, and were worn with knee-high brown leather gaiters instead of puttees. On the collar of the new tunic the enlisted ranks wore disc-shaped brass badges on the upper lapels – these were charged with the national cypher on the right, and the branch badge of crossed rifles on the left. Coloured enamel regimental crests were sometimes worn on the lower lapels.

A new peaked cap, almost identical to that of the officers, was worn for formal duties and walking out; this had a glossy brown leather peak and strap,

August 1941 – a crewman of the 68th Armored Regiment, 2nd Armored Division, photographed during the Louisiana Manoeuvres. The cavalry tankers had now given up their khaki breeches and high boots in favour of the one-piece herringbone twill overalls and 'doughnut' crash-helmet. A few of these brown leather helmets were being used at about this time in North Africa by British crews, being supplied along with the Stuart tank to, among others, the 8th King's Royal Irish Hussars – who even wore them for a brief period! (US National Archives).

a stiff olive drab crown and band, and a brass disc insignia with the national arms. The Montana-peaked campaign hat with branch-colour cords was the usual field headgear; photos show this being worn when working with tanks, which sounds

hilarious – one can only assume the hat was removed on entering the vehicle. In summer a shirtsleeve uniform was worn, in a light sandy drill material. The shirt was worn with a black tie tucked between second and third buttons; the breeches were cut the same as the 'olive drab' ones.

Officers wore a very similar service dress. Their peaked caps had a cut-out national arms insignia, and their campaign hats mixed gold and black cords. Tunics were more finely cut, with box-pleated breast pockets. The upper lapels bore cut-out 'U.S.' cyphers on both sides, and the lower lapels cut-out branch badges. Rank was indicated by unchanged insignia at the end of the shoulder straps, and the enamel regimental devices were also worn on the shoulders. Sam Brownes, sabres, finely cut riding breeches and boots completed the uniform. Cuff lace was retained by officers. The use of olive tunics with 'pink' (fawn) breeches was normal.

In 1933 the Air Corps and armored units were authorised to wear a sidecap – 'overseas cap'. This was rather more stylishly cut than the First World War model, but retained the turn-up with a slanted flap on the right front. Infantry (and shortly thereafter, cavalry) branch colour piping was worn along the edge of the turn-up by enlisted men, and gold/black piping by officers. The disc branch badge was pinned to the left front of the turn-up by enlisted men, and officers wore their ranking in this position.

By the late 1930s, with the armored forces expanding, differences were becoming marked between infantry and cavalry. The former now wore a one-piece overall when serving with the vehicle. This was also 'olive drab' but was a light grey-green in colour. It had a simple fall collar, patch breast pockets, slash side pockets and hip pockets; buttoned tabs were sewn outside each ankle, back from the side seams, and there was an integral cloth belt with a simple frame buckle. The cavalry, meanwhile, still wore service dress in the vehicle, with a knee-length brown leather boot laced from top to instep. The overseas caps of officers now bore a branch-coloured circular backing to the rank insignia. A leather composition crash helmet appeared, in several developing models during the late 1930s. The early type, worn from about 1938, had a dome-shaped greenish olive drab skull pierced with ventilation holes, a narrow padded brown leather strip across the brow, and a short semi-circular guard at the back of the skull; the side-pieces were generously cut, like those of an airman's helmet, and had holes for earphones. By 1941 a modified version was in

The technical skill, and glorious phoneyness of the sub-
ject, make this one of the most memorable posed shots
of the early 1940s – a period when official photographers
were all too prone to fake effects for the public's con-
sumption. 'Abandoning their tank under fire' during the
Tennessee Manoeuvres are a white officer and coloured
troopers of the 758th Tank Battalion. The officer has the
battalion patch on his left breast – mainly as an instant
identification of his commissioned rank, since all ranks
now wore identical overalls and headgear. He has a gas
mask satchel slung round his body, and a .45 automatic
on a pistol belt; the other crewmen have dismounted the
machine-guns from the M3 light tank. All now wear
the definitive version of the tank helmet, in OD-painted
leather (US National Archives).

use, with a thick ring of padding all round the head at brow level; this helmet seems usually to have been left in natural brown leather colour.

Personal equipment was limited to a webbing pistol belt, with holster in brown leather, web double clip pouch, small first aid pouch, and water canteen where appropriate. Personal kit was stowed in a musette bag of webbing, which could be hung over the shoulder or worn on the back by attachment to belt braces – in fact it was usually stowed on or in the tank. Commanders wore binocular and map cases in brown leather. Boots

for the infantry tankers (and the cavalry, by about 1941) were laced ankle type; officers often wore a modified field boot with spiral strap fastenings.

The formation of the Armored Force in 1940 produced rapid changes. The grey-green coverall became standard for both infantry and cavalry – indeed, the distinction between the two disappeared from the uniform apart from the overseas cap piping. A new branch badge with a First World War tank motif appeared in that year. Divisional and independent battalion insignia appeared, and were worn initially on the left breast of overalls and field jackets by officers. All were of the same design – the blue, yellow and red triangle of 1918, now charged with a black number over a black stylised tank track in the centre.

The US Army's 1941 field jacket, a hip-length garment in light fawn proofed cloth, was sometimes seen in use by tank crews in that year. It had a stand-and-fall collar, normally worn open and stepped; a buttoned fly covering a zip front; two slash pockets in the ribs, with slanted openings; buttoned tabs at wrist and hip, an integral half-belt at the back, and plain shoulder straps. Ranking was worn on it in the usual way – on the shoulders by officers, on both upper sleeves by NCOs.

Ranking seems seldom to have been worn on the overalls at this period – this was presumably the reason for officers identifying themselves by wearing the unit patch on the chest.

During 1941 the first examples of a special windcheater-style jacket began to reach the tank crews of the new Armored Divisions. This was a most popular garment, both practical and stylish. Of light fawn or pale greenish khaki proofed cloth, it had a knitted wool stand collar, cuffs and waist; a zip front; a sturdy lining of olive drab blanket material; and two pockets in the chest. These were initially interior pockets with slanted slash openings on the ribs, but later batches sometimes had patch exterior pockets without flaps, set on either slanted or vertically.

Photos of the late 1930s show some personnel wearing light 'airmen's helmets' of sandy coloured cloth, instead of the leather crash helmet. These appeared in a number of different versions; with and without holes for earphones, or actual housings; with buckled or snap-fastened chinstraps, etc. A deep neck flap could be tucked into the collar.

Finally, it should be noted briefly, and with some regret, that the US Army turned down General George S. Patton's suggestions for a new tank crew outfit of his personal design. It featured a 'football-type' crash helmet, reputedly to be painted gold, and a green leather suit with a zipped plastron front .

Soviet Union

The following notes cover the uniforms worn by Soviet armoured troops in the period 1935-41, during their involvement in the large-scale frontier incidents with Japan in Manchuria, and the invasion of Finland. It should be borne in mind that this huge army, wracked by political purges and administrative inefficiency, and with its procurement and supply organisation spread over enormous areas, did not present at any stage of the 1930s and 1940s as uniform a picture as those of more modern and cohesive nations, and there were certainly local variations from regulation dress and equipment.

In 1935 the armoured forces received a new uniform, in steel grey instead of the khaki of other arms, but otherwise identical apart from insignia. The basic service dress comprised a pullover shirt-tunic – *rubaha* – with a stand and fall collar, a fly front reaching to the breastbone, two patch pockets with pointed, buttoned flaps, and two-button cuffbands; semi-breeches, loose in the thigh but tight in the knee and calf; knee-length soft black leather boots, or puttees and laced ankle boots. The shirt had no shoulder straps, and the only insignia were rectangular patches worn on

each collar point. For officers, the bottom and front of the collar and the top edge of the cuff-band were piped in arm of service colour: for armoured troops this was red. The headgear for enlisted ranks, which from photographic evidence seems also to have been worn in the field by many junior officers, was the *pilotka*, a simple sidecap with a deep turn-up reaching almost to the top edge. For officers this turn-up was piped along the top edge in red, and another line of piping appeared above it, following the edges of the top gusset. All ranks wore a red star badge on the front of the turn-up; for armoured troops this was supposed to be pinned through a slightly larger star of black cloth. Although the *pilotka* was authorised in 1935, there were still numbers of the old *shlem* headgear in use in the late 1930s – the pointed, peaked cloth helmet with turned-up ear-flaps, and a red cloth star on the front. Officers usually wore a peaked cap, known as a *furashka*; of the characteristic Russian outline, with a small, flattish crown, this had a steel grey crown piped red at the crown seam, a black band piped red top and bottom, a stiff black leather peak and chinstrap, and an enamelled red star badge on the front of the band, outlined gold.

It must be emphasised that the evidence for the actual use of the steel grey version of the shirt-tunic and breeches is scanty; it is safe to say, at the very least, that large numbers of tank troops continued to wear the khaki uniform. The grey *furashka* described above seems often to have been worn with a khaki shirt-tunic and breeches.

From 1935 to 1940, the collar patches of arm of service and rank worn on the shirt-tunic by armoured troops were black, in the shape of long canted rectangles, piped round the long and outer edges in red for non-commissioned ranks and in gold for officers. A yellow metal tank motif was pinned at the outer end, facing inwards, and for ranks above private symbols of rank, in the form of red enamelled shapes with yellow metal backing showing round the edges, were pinned along the length of the patch, centrally.

The sequence was as follows; the author uses here the traditional rank titles, although in keeping with Communist sensitivity the Red Army of this period in fact used euphemisms such as 'section commander', 'junior platoon commander', and so forth: Corporal to Sergeant-Major – one, two, three and four triangles, point up; Junior Lieutenant to Senior Lieutenant – one, two and three squares; Captain, Major, Colonel – one, two and three short upright bars.

In addition, officers wore a sequence of red cloth chevrons on the outer forearms of each sleeve, in the following manner: Junior Lieutenant – one

28

medium chevron; Lieutenant – two medium chevrons; Senior Lieutenant – three medium chevrons; Captain – one thick chevron; Major – two thick chevrons; Colonel – one thick chevron edged with thin gold chevrons top and bottom.

The greatcoat or *kaftan* was grey; enlisted ranks had a double-breasted version with concealed buttons, a deep fall collar and deep turned-back cuffs cut on a bias so that the highest point met the rear sleeve seam. Officers' coats had round cuffs, piped in red round the top of the turn-back, and two rows of four visible brass buttons. Special collar patches of rounded lozenge shape were worn on the greatcoat. These were black, piped round the upper two edges in red for enlisted men and gold for officers. A brass tank motif was pinned high in the centre, with the same rank symbols as described above ranged in a row across the middle of the patch below it. The officers' chevrons appeared on the *kaftan* sleeves.

In 1940 the system of rank and insignia was changed as follows. In theory it seems that Privates were still to wear plain black collar patches without symbols of rank, but in practice, photographs suggest that ranks below Corporal frequently wore no patches at all.

The rank and arm-of-service collar patches of NCOs of the mechanised branch, as worn on the shirt-tunic, remained basically black. A broad red stripe ran down the centre, about a third the width of the whole patch; and red piping ran around the long and outer edges. The inner edge, lined up with the edge of the collar itself, remained unpiped. In the top outer corner was pinned a brass pyramid-shaped stud. Immediately 'inside' this, pinned centrally on the width of the patch, was a brass tank motif. Corporals wore no additional insignia; higher ranks wore red-on-yellow enamelled metal symbols arranged along the central red bar of the patch. A triangle was the mark of a Junior Sergeant; two triangles, a Sergeant; three, a Senior Sergeant; and four, with gold piping round the inside of the red patch edging, a Sergeant-Major.

Officers' patches were less elaborate. They were still in the basic arm colour (in the case of tank troops, black) edged with gold piping along all but the inner edge. The brass tank motif was pinned at the outer end. Rank symbols were one, two and three squares for Junior Lieutenant, Lieutenant and Senior Lieutenant; and one, two, three and four upright bars for Captain, Major, Lieutenant-Colonel and Colonel. In addition, officers wore a new sequence of red and gold chevrons on the forearms of both sleeves. The sequence was as follows, from the top: Junior Lieutenant – thick red, thin

gold, thin red; Lieutenant – medium gold, thick red, thin gold, thin red; Senior Lieutenant – thin gold, medium red, thin gold, medium red, thin gold, thin red; Captain – medium gold, thick red, thin gold, thin red; Major – medium gold, thick red, thick gold, thin red; Lieutenant-Colonel – As Major; Colonel – medium gold, medium red, medium gold, medium red, thick gold, thin red.

The *kaftan* collar patches also changed in 1940. Enlisted ranks now had a stripe of piping colour (ie, red) across the middle of the patch, and the metal ranking was pinned to this stripe. Officers' patches were unchanged.

In the interwar period the normal cold-weather headgear was the grey *shlem* or *budionovka* cloth helmet. When worn by tank troops it was supposed to have a large cloth star in black sewn to the front, in the centre of which the red-on-gold metal star badge was pinned. How widely this was observed in practice is unknown. A new winter cap began to replace the *shlem* during the 1940 Finnish campaign; of grey cloth, with fur front and neck/ear flaps which could be worn up or down, it often had the red metal star badge pinned to the underside – the furry side – of the front flap, which was usually worn up. Officers' caps had real fur or astrakhan, enlisted men's caps, imitation.

When actually serving the vehicles, Russian tank men of the late 1930s wore a one-piece overall in either black or dark blue; by the entry of the Soviet Union into the war in July 1941 some khaki overalls were also being issued. These simple boiler-suit garments had a zip front, the zip concealed by a flap; a fall collar, on which the collar patches were sometimes but not invariably fixed; a buttoned patch pocket with a pointed flap on the left breast and another on the front of the right thigh; cuffs fastened with small buckled tabs; and an integral cloth belt with a metal frame buckle. There were no shoulder straps. Very deeply cuffed brown leather gauntlets with strapped wrists were issued with the suit, the cuffs having a cutaway section on the back of the forearm. The suit was worn either over or tucked into the black knee-boots, in the former case giving a visibly tight, stretched effect on the calf.

The familiar padded Russian tank helmet was at this time produced in brown leather; there was a pocket housing on each side for earphones, although only senior command vehicles were fitted with radio at this time and most inter-tank signalling was by flag. Brown leather belts with simple frame buckles were worn at the waist, with either leather or webbing holsters for either the old 1895 Nagant revolver or the 1930 Tokarev automatic. Lanyards were sometimes attached to the rear of the belt. Officers wore a Sam Browne belt, the crossbelt passing over the right shoulder. When the collar patches were not attached to the tank suit, the suit was normally worn well open at the neck to display the patches on the collar of the shirt-tunic beneath.

Italy

Although negotiations for the licence production of the Renault FT by Fiat were concluded and an Italian Government order for 1,400 tanks was placed in spring 1918, the Armistice intervened before the Italian tank arm could progress beyond the establishment of evaluation teams and instructors' schools. In December 1918 an Autonomous Assault Tank Battery of two sections, each of four tanks, was formed at Turin; each section had one heavy Fiat 2000 tank and three Fiat-built Renaults. Most of the large wartime order was cancelled, however; and despite the limited use of one section against Arab rebels in Tripoli in 1919, it was to be October 1927 before a full tank regiment was formed. This comprised five battalions, each of four companies; a depot and an armoured car group. In September 1931 the regimental headquarters moved from Rome to Bologna. Almost exactly four years later the regiment was disbanded and four new units were formed: the 1st Tank Regiment at Vercelli: I, II and III Battalions (L3 light tanks), IV Battalion (Fiat 3000 heavies); the 2nd Tank Regiment at Verona; took title 32nd Regiment in 1938: IV, V, XII Battalions (light), III Battalion (heavy); the 3rd Tank Regiment at Bologna: VI and VII Battalions (light), I Battalion (heavy), plus mechanised company and instruction school; and the 4th Tank Regiment at Rome: VIII, IX, X and XI Battalions (light), V Battalion (heavy), and a company on Sardinia.

In 1937 the 31st Tank Regiment was raised; and in that year two Armoured Brigades were formed by combining a tank regiment with a *bersaglieri* regiment and services: the 1st, *Centauro*, at Siena and the 2nd, *Ariete*, at Milan.

Some 157 light L3 tanks were in Africa at the outbreak of the Ethiopian War – 112 in Eritrea and 45 in Somaliland. In all some 500 tanks saw action in this campaign, including significant numbers of vehicles fitted with flamethrowers. Tanks were used in small units rather than massed, for obvious reasons of terrain and type of opposition. Their unsurprising success against the Negus's primitive army contributed to a dangerous overconfidence in their quality.

The Italian *Corpo Truppe Volontarie* in the Spanish Civil War had two tank battalions of light L3s grouped in a *Raggruppamento Carri*. Experience against Soviet types showed that the L3 was

now seriously obsolete, but Italy was much slower than Germany to apply the lessons learned in Spain to new procurement policies. Studies were begun for a medium tank, but the specifications were far too modest.

On February 1 1939 the *Ariete* Armoured Division was formed, followed on April 20 by the *Centauro* Armoured Division; these formations took the numbers 132nd and 131st respectively. The 33rd Tank Regiment was formed and posted to the *Littorio* infantry division, which was transformed to an armoured division with the number 133rd. These divisions had each a tank regiment; a two-battalion *bersaglieri* regiment; a motorised artillery regiment with two batteries of 75 mm guns and one detachment of 20 mm anti-aircraft weapons; and an armoured engineer company.

Tanks were also assigned to *Celere* Divisions, each of which had two horsed cavalry regiments; a *bersaglieri* regiment; a light tank group manned by cavalry personnel; a motorised artillery regiment, and services.

The occupation of Albania in 1939 saw tanks employed by infantry, cavalry and *bersaglieri* units, but no fighting.

During the last months of the First World War personnel assigned to the fledgling tank schools kept their old branch insignia; armoured car units were manned by cavalry personnel. In the 1920s and early 1930s the tanks were considered to be part of the infantry, and personnel wore the collar insignia of infantrymen unassigned to a named

Line-up of gun- and machine-gun-armed Fiat light tanks, Italy, late 1930s. The officer, second from left, wears the light grey uniform of his rank; collar flames, Captain's sleeve ranking, and breeches stripes are clear on the original print. All other personnel wear overalls in varying shades of blue, and all wear the leather tank helmet (Imperial War Museum).

brigade – a double red 'flame' at the front corners of the standing black collar, with a silver star superimposed. The headgear was the general issue grey-green képi with black peak and chinstrap, and a silver (after 1933, gold) frontal badge showing a flaming grenade superimposed on a crossed gun and machine-gun, over a stylised arc of tank track. Equipment followed cavalry practice; an accompanying photo shows the parade uniform of a tank soldier at this period.

In 1934 the képi gave way to a flat-topped peaked cap, or a *bustina* forage cap. The collar of the enlisted man's grey-green service uniform was opened and stepped, and worn with a grey-green collar and tie. The single-breasted tunic had four patch pockets, all box-pleated with buttoned three-point flaps. There were plain pointed shoulder straps and an integral cloth belt fastening at the front with two horizontally spaced buttons. The cuffs had a pointed false turnback seam. The enlisted ranks wore semi-breeches with black, strapped, knee-length leather gaiters over laced ankle boots. Officers wore fuller-cut breeches with double black stripes flanking piping in branch colour, and black jackboots. Enlisted ranks' peaked caps were grey-green with black peak and chinstrap and the branch badge on the front of the band. Officers wore larger, stiffer caps with an embroidered branch badge of bullion wire on the front and ranking round the band in the form of lace stripes – eg, two 10 mm gold lace stripes for First Lieutenant, one 10 mm above one 17 mm for a Major. The cap, like the whole uniform, was of lighter grey for officers. They tended to wear straight pocket flaps, and the lower lapel was much longer than on the enlisted man's tunic.

The whole upper half of the collar, down to the step of the lapels, was black – velvet for officers and cheaper cloth for enlisted men. The collar insignia of all ranks were double red 'flames' at the bottom of the upper lapel, with the silver stars common to the whole army. Tank personnel of cavalry units, ie, in the *Celere* divisions, had a bright blue upper collar with double white flames.

The *bustina* sidecap was in mouse-grey for officers, grey-green for enlisted ranks. It had a frontal peak of cloth, normally worn folded vertically up at the front of the crown, on which was worn the branch badge in gold – gilt wire for officers and NCOs, brass for ranks from Corporal-Major down. There was a neck-and-ear flap in the form of a turn-up with a cloth 'chinstrap' buttoned over the top of the crown. Officers wore ranking on the side of the crown at front left, between 'peak' and 'chinstrap'. In 1934-35 these were in the form of short sections of rank stripes following the se-

quence worn round the band of the peaked cap, set at a tilt, rear high. Thus a Second Lieutenant had one 10 mm strip, a 'First Captain' (promoted after 20 years as an officer if still in that grade) had three 10 mm strips above a star, and a Lieutenant-Colonel had two 10 mm strips above one 17 mm strip. In 1935 these rankings were changed to five-point stars: one, two and three for Second Lieutenant, Lieutenant and Captain; two or three, each above a 10 mm strip, for 'First Lieutenant' and 'First Captain'; and one, two and three enclosed in a gold lace 'box' for Major, Lieutenant-Colonel and Colonel.

On the grey uniform officers wore their ranking on the cuff, in the form of lengths of gold lace with a 'curl' in the top length, in the manner of traditional naval officers' ranking. The sequence was as for

Private of the Italian Tank Regiment posed with a Fiat 3000 at the Fort Tiburtino barracks, Rome, circa 1930. The grey-green uniform includes the stiff képi of the day; the pocketless tunic; the cavalry carbine, bandolier, and gaiters. The collar is black, with two scarlet flames and a silver star each side (Furio Lorenzetti).

the cap ranking: one thin, two thin and three thin for Second Lieutenant to Captain; one thin above one thick, two thin above one thick, and three thin above one thick for field officers; and Lieutenant's or Captain's ranking above a five-point gold star for 'First' Lieutenants and Captains. Stiff grey shoulder boards with an elongated front outer point were piped in branch colour (red, at this period, for tank units, and white for cavalry tank troops) all round the edges, and bore a repetition of the branch badge as worn on the cap, in gold. (It should be remarked here that Colonels commanding units wore all branch and rank badges on a brick red backing instead of the usual grey-green.)

The ranking of NCOs was worn in large chevrons right along the top edge of the false Polish cuff. Sergeant-Majors and Sergeants wore respectively two and one thin chevrons above one thick, in gold. Corporal-Majors and Corporals wore the same sequence in black. Warrant Officer ranks – *marescialli* – wore a mixed black and gold braid cap band stripe, and one, two and three stripes of such braid along the shoulder boards, according to grade, from the outer end to the button in a 'crow's foot'.

From 1934 divisional arm badges were often to be seen. These were in the shape of simple 'heater' shields, edged with gold, bearing an upright Roman sword in the centre, a number below the pommel; lettering up each side of the shield; and oakleaves across the top. For tank units the background seems, from Del Giudice's *Uniformie Militaria Italiane*, to have been black, while that of *Divisioni Celeri* was red.

In 1939, before Italy's entry into the war, various uniform changes took place. The divisional arm shields were forbidden in 1940, but some were still occasionally to be seen. The NCOs' rank chevrons became much shorter; they were moved to the upper arms, and reversed, so that, eg, a Sergeant now wore one thin over one thick chevron, point down. Shortly afterwards gold chevrons were ordered to be worn in yellow thread. Branch cap badges of enlisted men were generally worn in black thread instead of brass from 1939/40 onwards. Coloured upper collars now became grey-green, with 'flames' sewn at the end: some were sewn directly to the grey cloth, others over coloured rectangular patches which showed between and behind the 'flames'. Tank regiments now wore double (ie, two-pointed) scarlet 'flames' on a bright blue patch, with the usual silver star. The piping of shoulder boards on the officers' European uniform became bright blue.

In Africa a sandy drill uniform was worn, rather redder in tone than the British or American equivalent. It was similar in cut to the grey-green European uniform, but had buttoned, plain cuffs and straight-cut pocket flaps. With this uniform officers wore their ranking on the shoulders rather than the cuffs, on black, stiff cloth shoulder boards of asymmetric shape (see illustration in Part 3). There was a tropical *bustina* in the same drill material.

In the Spanish Civil War regular Italian Army uniforms were worn, both in European and tropical versions, but usually without any official insignia apart from ranking. Most personnel obeyed the order to remove collar flames and stars; some persisted in wearing them. There were many unofficial insignia observed during this campaign. Partly Spanish and partly Italian uniform items were often seen; and the sidecap (*isabellino*) of the Spanish Foreign Legion, in grey-green with red piping and tassel, was popular. The Italian involvement was initially disguised by posting contingents to the Foreign Legion, and *Tercio* insignia seem to have survived in some cases throughout the war. Spanish ranking was also worn by many officers. The optional tropical tunic style popular with Italian officers in Africa, the *sahariana*, with its single fall collar and caped chest pockets, was often worn in Spain (see also Part 3).

When serving with the vehicles in all theatres the normal dress was a dark blue one-piece overall, a simple working 'boiler suit' worn without insignia. In the mid-1930s a three-quarter length black leather coat was issued, and this traditional item remains in use in the 1970s. It was double-breasted, with two rows of three buttons, an integral belt with a frame buckle (often replaced

Text continued on page 38

Captions to plates on pages 33 and 34.

1 *Lance-Corporal, 'H' Battalion, Tank Corps, November 1917. A soldier of the leading wave of tanks in the Cambrai attack of November 20, holding a round for the 6 pdr main armament of a Mk IV Male tank. Normal vehicle uniform of the time: service tunic over one-piece brown dungarees, with leather equipment set of 1916. Tank badge on right upper arm identifies trained soldier; red/blue flashes on helmet and shoulder straps identify 'H' Battalion (later 8 RTR). Rank chevron on both upper arms, and service chevrons, one for each year's overseas service, on the right forearm only.*

2 *Cannonier, Artillerie Speciale, 1917. French crewman of a St Chamond or Schneider tank, carrying oil can. He wears full vehicle uniform apart from the Adrian helmet. Note leather driver's coat with cloth collar: civilian beret: red artillery piping down trouser seam: fighting knife. The flat gas mask canister, painted blue-grey, would be slung on the right side.*

Plate captions continued

3 *Ordnance Sergeant, US 304th Tank Brigade, 1918.* Standard US Army service tunic, trousers, puttees and overseas cap, the latter bearing a bronze collar insignia, as was often the case – the US cypher on a disc, which was worn each side of the stand collar by enlisted men. Chevrons of rank and speciality on both upper arms in light 'olive drab'. The Tank Corps patch was worn at about the time of the Armistice, but probably not in action, on the left shoulder only.

4 *Lieutenant, Royal Naval Armoured Car Division, Russia 1918.* The uniform is an Army khaki service dress, with naval insignia. The cap has a black ribbed band and the gold wire RN officer's cap badge. The tunic has bronze Army rank pips on the shoulder straps – three, as a naval Lieutenant was equivalent to an Army Captain; and gold naval ranking on the cuffs. Bronze 'collar dogs' in the shape of Rolls-Royce armoured cars are worn. The Sam Browne was frequently worn with both shoulder braces in this unit, vertical at the front and crossed at the back. This officer has the DSC ribbon above the left pocket, and two vertical gold wound stripes on the left forearm.

5 *Feldwebel, German field artillery, seconded tank branch, 1918.* The peaked field cap has the black band and red piping of most technical branches of the Imperial German Army, with Reichs-cockade on the crown and Prussian cockade on the band. The tunic is the Bluse of 1915 vintage, with the large collar buttons and abbreviated silver-grey Tresse typical of this rank at this date. The field artillery shoulder straps, in red with yellow regimental number and 'bursting shell', are retained. The ribbon of the Iron Cross is worn in the fly front, and the elbows are leather-reinforced; the belt worn with the tank driver's suit is shown here, with a Luger holster; the cloth strap round the body supports the gas mask canister.

6 *Gefreiter, Schwere Kampfwagen-Abteilung Nr 13, 1918.* We have reconstructed this uniform from separate references. The basic tank crewman's outfit includes field cap, Bluse and trousers with leather reinforcement, puttees and ankle boots; belt supporting holster, dagger; and slung gas mask canister. The cap colours are those of the Transport troops which provided large numbers of the crews of A7Vs, with the Bavarian blue and white state cockade on the band referring to the Bavarian Army background of the personnel of this particular battalion. The plain grey shoulder straps have the red 'K' of the Transport troops; the rank is indicated by the button on each side of the collar; the Litzen on the collar are standard insignia in the Transport branch. We have gone out a little way along a limb in adding, for visual appeal, the blue/white checkered lace completely round the collar. References show this State peculiarity being worn by Privates – not just NCOs – of both infantry and cavalry units of the Bavarian Army in 1918, so it seems a fair assumption that it might have been seen in the Bavarian tank battalion.

7 *Chasseur, French 511e Régiment de Chars de Combat, circa 1933.* Apart from the evolution of the helmet, which now has a thin leather pad in place of the front peak of the Adrian type, little has changed since 1918. The leather coat now bears collar patch insignia in ash grey; note that the stand collar of the tunic still has green numbers and soutaches. Green trouser piping was observed in

some units into the 1930s. The Ruby automatic now replaces the revolver.

8 *Major, 'Legion Condor', Spain 1938.* Jose Maria Bueno illustrates this outfit in his Uniformes Militares de la Guerra Civil Española: it is extremely striking, but strictly non-regulation, and if accurate may be a personally ordered 'one-off' outfit. The cap is a dark blue version of the Spanish gorro piped in German Panzer pink, bearing the single eight-point star of this rank in yellow on a pink backing. The mono is obviously of Spanish manufacture, but again, the rank is worn on a 'biscuit' not of Spanish Nationalist black, but of German Panzer pink. Shirt, belt, holster and marching boots are German – the latter are interesting, on an officer.

9 *Brigada, Spanish Republican tank unit, Madrid 1936.* An interpretation by the author of a photo showing a Republican Renault FT 17 unit in the streets of the University City during fierce fighting in November 1936. The cap is civilian, and the colour is conjectural. The khaki cazadora jacket has typical ranking on the breast patch – note large size of star, most noticeable in the original photo; the rank is equivalent to Sergeant-Major. The trousers, slightly flared at the thigh, appear in the photo to be leather; several other men in the same group wear both leather trousers and crutch-length leather coats, with either laced or one-piece knee-boots, and dark berets – probably black or very dark blue.

10 *Alferez, Compañias de carros, Spanish Foreign Legion, 1938-39.* This Second Lieutenant or Ensign of the Tercio's tank companies, which were equipped with German PzKpfw I vehicles and possibly Italian L3s as well, is taken, again, from Bueno. The black beret is typical of Nationalist tankers, and bears the single gold six-point star of this rank, which is repeated on a black 'biscuit' on the left breast. The cazadora and flared officer's breeches are in the Legion's distinctive grey-green cloth; the shirt is slightly paler. Bueno shows the white metal tank troops branch badge, shaped like a Renault, on the right breast. Both braces for the black belt are worn; the holster is for the issue Astra automatic. Note interesting laced and buckled 'motorcycle' style boots.

11 *Unteroffizier, 'Legion Condor', Spain 1938-39.* Taken from a photo which fails to show the legs, this may illustrate a one-piece overall or a lightweight summer tunic; it is definitely in pale drill, rather than the khaki woollen material of the Legion Condor service dress. The gold bars on pink backing on the breast are rank insignia. A dark leather belt with a rectangular buckle-plate is worn in the photo on which this is based. The skull above the swastika on the beret (both in white metal) is of the jawless kind seen on German Panzer collar patches, but significantly larger.

12 *Captain, US 7th Cavalry Brigade (Mechanised), Fort Knox 1938.* Summer 'khaki' uniform as worn by all ranks of this first 'cavalry tank' unit, including flared breeches and high, laced boots. The officer's 'overseas cap' is piped in mixed gold and black, and bears rank bars on a branch-colour patch on the left front. Bars are worn on the shirt shoulder straps. The web belt bears the .45 automatic in its russet leather holster, a double clip pouch, and a first aid pouch on the left rear of the hip. The riding crop is a cavalry officer's affectation. This unlikely uniform was worn in the tank, with the addition of an early model leather tank helmet.

1

2

3

4

5

6

Captions to plates on pages 35 and 36.

13 *Mladshii Leitenant, Soviet Army, 1940. Grey peaked cap piped red; black band, peak, and strap; enamelled red and gold badge. The dark blue overalls have one pocket on the left breast and one on the right thigh, and are tucked into knee-length black boots. Junior Lieutenant's rank patch is black, piped gold, in 1940 style, with gold tank badge and one red/gold square. Red-piped collar of shirt-tunic just visible in neck of overall. Brown leather belt, revolver holster and map-case on cross-straps, helmet, and gauntlets; signalling flags.*

14 *Obergefreiter, German 2nd Panzer-Regiment, 1939-40. The regulation black vehicle uniform as it might be worn in peacetime or behind the front lines. White insignia on beret and breast; silver-grey chevrons of rank on left arm only. Note pink regimental number on shoulder straps, and forward-buttoning pocket flaps on front of both hips.*

15 *Lieutenant, Polish 10th Mechanised Brigade, 1939. Beret with national and rank insignia, the latter repeated on cloth shoulder straps of long, officers' model leather coat. Khaki service dress tunic, with black and orange collar pennants and zig-zag silver lace; flared khaki breeches with black jackboots. Brown 'Sam Browne', with holster for VIS automatic; brown binocular case and gauntlets.*

16 *Caporal, French 24e Bataillon de Chars de Combat, 1939-40. M1935 tank helmet in khaki steel and brown leather; goggles have off-white rubber pads and amber, steel-rimmed lenses. The brown leather coat has khaki cloth collar patches with ash grey soutaches and battalion number; a khaki rank tab bears two green bars. The pale khaki pantalon cachou are gathered at the ankle. The brown holster for the Ruby automatic is broad, with 'bellows' sides. He carries a commercial Michelin road-map – all that was usually available in 1940.*

17 *Sergeant, Japanese tank troops, China, winter 1938. Domed winter helmet with fur-lined face and neck piece. Deep fur collar (note longer point and fastening tab on his left side) on jacket of two-piece padded overalls in pale khaki. Single rank patch of Gunso on left breast – red patch, yellow bar, two white stars. Note slanted top line of thigh pocket – mirrored by another on his right thigh, obscured here. Felt and leather winter gauntlets and boots; the former, with separate thumb and forefinger but otherwise mitten hand, have tapes at wrist, and leather lining inside palm and fingers. Revolver holster on cross-belt has deep clam-shell cover.*

18 *Major, Grenadier Guards, 1944. Regimental badge, embroidered in gold thread for an officer, on RAC black beret. Battledress, privately tailored, of the dark khaki favoured by the Guards; collar tailored open and faced with khaki. Crown of rank on red infantry backing. Shoulder title in regimental colours, above Guards Armoured Division patch on both sleeves. Medal ribbons for wartime campaigns were not much worn in the front line, but this selection would be typical of a regular officer: the Military Cross, a General Service ribbon for prewar overseas service, and the Africa Star.*

19 *2nd Lieutenant, Inns of Court Regiment, 1944. In this unit officers wore the green beret, and WOs the black*

beret, both with this embroidered badge – a red devil on a padded oval of black cloth. Other ranks wore the black beret with a larger version of the regimental badge seen here on the collar points in bronze. The sleeve badges illustrated were worn by all ranks on both sleeves, although some or all were sometimes omitted in the front line. The RAC shoulder title was worn on normal duty BD; on walking out dress 'best BD' it was often replaced by a white on dark green title: INNS OF COURT REGIMENT; and a white lanyard was added to the left shoulder. The 11th Armoured Division patch was worn from mid-July 1944; between D-Day and that date the white spearhead on red diamond of I Corps was worn by this armoured car unit. The blue and green diamond below the RAC strip was a regimental insignia (Courtesy Patrick Leeson).*

20 *Officer, 15th/19th King's Royal Hussars. The regimentally coloured 'forage cap' sometimes seen in the front line as an alternative to the beret and SD cap. Red piped with gold was common to Hussar regiments. This unit served in 11th Armoured Division in NW Europe, 1944-45, with Cromwell tanks.*

21 *Sergeant, 4th County of London Yeomanry, June 1944. Wartime 'utility' BD with insignia worn between this Sherman unit's return from Italy in winter 1943/44, and the amalgamation with 3rd CLY in July 1944, as a result of casualties in Normandy. Black RAC beret with regimental cap badge. Regimental shoulder strap tallies in dark green, yellow, and 'old gold' or mushroom colour. Light khaki lanyard on right shoulder. Non-regulation SHARP-SHOOTERS shoulder title in yellow on green. 7th Armoured Division patch above RAC strip and rank chevrons. All sleeve insignia worn on both arms. (From the BD blouse of Sergeant G. H. Lockwood, RAC Tank Museum, Bovington.)*

22 *Lieutenant-Colonel, 1st Armoured Regiment, 1st Polish Armoured Division, 1944. Free Polish insignia is described in detail in the main text. The black RAC beret bears the national badge above the silver ranking. The left shoulder bears the black shoulder board of the 10th Mechanised Brigade; Polish ranking appears on this and the right shoulder strap. Regimental pennants in black, crimson and orange on both collar points. Regimental orange lanyard on left shoulder. National shoulder titles on both sleeves; divisional patch on both sleeves until late 1944, when this unit adopted arms of St Niklaas Waas on right sleeve.*

23 *Officer, 8th King's Royal Irish Hussars. The unique 'tent hat' worn by officers of this unit; photos show it in use in the front line both in the desert and in NW Europe, 1944-45. The gold braid fell vertically from the edge of the turn-up to the headband at the rear centre, in two strips one each side of the seam.*

24 *Officer, Royal Scots Greys. An example of the khaki service dress cap worn by some officers of armoured cavalry, here with the regimental badge on a black patch.*

25 *Sikh Jemadar, 'C' Squadron, 7th Light Cavalry, Indian Army, 1944-45. Black regimental initials, NCO's red and gold shoulder stripe, and 'pip' of rank all worn on khaki drill slip-over on shoulder straps of jungle green tropical battledress blouse. Photos of this squadron in action with its Stuart tanks in Burma show that white turbans were worn.*

by officers with their Sam Browne) and buttoned cuff-tabs. At the same time a heavy, domed black leather crash helmet was issued, with a soft leather neck-flap (see photographs). In summer the overalls were often worn without the leather coat. Officers wore their ranking on the left breast of the leather coat, in the form of metal stars pinned directly to the leather.

Personal equipment worn over the leather coat was limited to a Sam Browne and holster for officers; and a grey leather cavalry style pouched bandolier, with the pistol holster slung from it on the right hip, for enlisted men.

Japan

In the late 1930s and 1940-41 the Japanese armoured forces were committed to the war against China. Three main uniforms are relevant to this period: the normal service uniform, the summer tank suit and helmet, and the winter tank suit and helmet.

The Japanese soldier's temperate zone field uniform was entirely of a brownish or mustard shade of khaki, and consisted of field cap, tunic, semi-breeches, puttees and boots. The cap was shaped rather like a peaked sidecap, with a central top gusset, a rounded cloth peak, and a brown chinstrap. National insignia was a yellow five-point star in cloth, stitched to the front low down. The tunic of the 1930 uniform was single-breasted with five buttons; two concealed breast pockets had external, buttoned flaps with a single point. There was a low standing collar, on which were worn small swallow-tailed patches in branch-of-service colour with yellow metal regimental numbers applied. (The author has been unable to discover a separate branch colour for Japan's small armoured organisation; given the complete subordination of the arm to the infantry, and its employment in detached units in infantry support rather than in concentration, it is a reasonable assumption that infantry red collar patches were worn.) At the outbreak of war in 1941 there were four tank regiments.

On the point of the shoulder of the 1930 uniform, ranking was worn on transverse rectangular strips, similar in size and placing to US officers' traditional 'boxes'. These were red, with a yellow central star for the lowest rank of Private, and two and three stars for higher grades. A Corporal had a red patch with a central yellow stripe and a white star; two and three stars, and a patch with two yellow stripes, identified higher grades of NCO and Warrant Officer. Officers' tunics were similar but had two concealed skirt pockets, with external rectangular flaps without buttons. Officers wore the same collar patches, and rank straps in the same style as enlisted men. These were of gold braid, with two red stripes and one, two and three white stars for subalterns, and three stripes with

This Japanese crew re-ammunition what appears to be a Type 89B, with a Hiragana character painted on the turret which has been identified as a Chutai marking within the 13th Sensha Rentai – a tank regiment which served in China. Apart from the summer-pattern tank helmets worn by three of them, the crew wear normal 1930-pattern uniform without special features. The nearest man wears some kind of bandaging or light-coloured face mask (Imperial War Museum).

Plate captions continued

26   *Sergeant, Special Service Battalion, 6th South African Armoured Division, 1944-45. The divisional patch was worn on BD at all times during the formation's service in Italy. National shoulder tallies in orange. Silver regimental cap badge on black beret, above qualified instructor's ribbon in orange, white, royal blue.*

27   *Private, 116th Regiment RAC (Gordon Highlanders), 1944-45. In Burma this regiment retained the khaki Balmoral bonnet with regimental cap badge. The US leather tank helmet was sometimes worn, alongside the rimless RAC steel helmet.*

Close-up of the Japanese summer tank helmet, left side; it is in brown cloth with brown leather straps (courtesy Mike Ross).

one, two and three white stars for field officers. Other ranks wore baggy khaki semi-breeches gathered into khaki puttees, and brown laced ankle boots; officers wore flared khaki breeches and black knee boots, or buckled leather knee-length gaiters and ankle boots. Officers wore swords of the traditional *samurai* design suspended from an internal belt under the tunic with one strap. The scabbard was brown with brass fittings, the grip was wound with brown cord, and the fist strap and knot were of flat gold braid backed with blue for company and red for field officers.

In 1938 a new uniform was authorised, of the same colour and basic design but with a stand-and-fall collar. The ranking moved from the shoulders to the collar, but was unchanged in design, the shoulder boxes simply becoming collar patches.

The summer tank overall was of one-piece design, in a greenish khaki cloth. It had a simple fall collar, on which the rank patches were normally worn. It had a fly front from throat to crotch, buttoned tabs at the wrists, and a single pocket on the left side of the chest. This appeared both with and without a pointed, buttoned flap, and was patch-type. The legs of the suit were sometimes worn loose to the ankle, and sometimes confined from knee to ankle with khaki puttees and tapes. The helmet was of padded cloth, with a brown cloth cover. It had a padded rim or headband, and Y-straps passed each side of the ear and united beneath it. There was an arched cut-out each side over the upper ear, partly covered by a laced fabric section, to house earphones. The usual yellow star was sewn to the front above the padded band.

The winter outfit was a two-piece fawn or light khaki suit. The jacket was waist length and round

bottomed, with a deep fall collar of fur or fleece, usually fawn or tan. It was single-breasted, with four brown plastic or horn buttons down the front, and single buttons at the wrist. On the left breast was a patch pocket with a buttoned pointed flap. The ranking was usually worn as a single patch above this chest pocket. The jacket was worn over a pair of bib-fronted overall trousers, with a chest piece and shoulder straps. This was of similar colour to the jacket, and had a vent from armpit to hip each side closed by four plastic buttons. The baggy legs tied with tapes at the ankle, either round the ankle or under the boot. There were pockets on the front of each thigh, with pointed, buttoned flaps; the top line of these pockets sloped out and down. There was a similar pocket on the right breast, the top line sloping down and inwards. The boots could be of three kinds: either normal laced brown ankle boots, or knee-length brown leather boots with fur lining, or knee-length grey-brown felt

The commander of a Type 89B, near Shanghai, China, 1937. He wears the green one-piece summer overall tucked into his jackboots; the summer helmet; and a number of pieces of kit slung on cross-straps, of which a map case and a canteen are visible (Steven Zaloga).

boots with a fleece lining showing round the top, and black rubber welds down the front centre and round the edge of the sole.

The winter helmet had a rigid skull which resembled the dome-shaped summer helmet, but in brown leather. There was a complete neck and ear piece, like that of a pilot's flying helmet, in leather with fur lining, and earphone housings. It bore the usual yellow star in cloth or light leather. The personal equipment of tank crews was limited to waist belts; pistol holsters, in brown leather or greenish proofed canvas, were slung round the body to the right hip on a crossbelt which passed under the waist belt.

It is common to find photographs showing tank crews riding in standard field dress rather than special helmets and overalls.

Spanish Civil War

Tanks were employed by both sides in the Civil War, by Spaniards and by foreign 'volunteer' expeditionary forces. There seems to have been little uniformity of dress or insignia, and information is somewhat scanty. The following notes are culled from photo research and from the book by J. M. Bueno, *Uniformes Militares de la Guerra Civil Española*.

Spanish Nationalist tank crews seem to have worn the ubiquitous native *mono* or one-piece overall in dark blue, light khaki or dark brown. It varied in details such as pockets and buttons; a typical example is illustrated in this chapter. The normal headgear was a small black beret, pulled down at either side or backwards, to individual taste. A white cloth or white metal skull-and-cross-bones badge was often worn, unofficially, on the beret, and sometimes on the right breast of the overalls as well. Officers were supposed to wear ranking on the beret. Company officers wore one, two and three small six-point yellow metal stars in a row, and field officers one, two and three larger eight-point stars. These were normally repeated on a strip of black cloth sewn to the left breast of the overall above the pocket, if any. Another breast badge was the pre-war tank corps insignia, a white metal silhouette of a Renault FT 17 tank in left profile, pinned to the right breast. Shirts of all shades of khaki, grey, green and blue were observed. Sam Browne belts, and the holster for the Astra service automatic, were normal for officers.

The German *Legion Condor* tank instructors, who saw action as unit and sub-unit commanders early in the war but handed over their Panzers to Spanish crews as soon as they were trained, seem from photographs to have worn the Legion's khaki

service tunic, cut something like a German Army field grey tunic. It was thigh-length, with four box-pleated pockets with pointed buttoned flaps, and an open collar with stepped lapels. Light khaki shirts, with or without black ties, German-style

Typical appearance of a Spanish Nationalist tank officer, after Bueno. See text for details of mono *and insignia (G. A. Embleton).*

belts, and black marching boots or jackboots were worn with either straight trousers or, for officers, flared breeches. The small black Spanish beret was worn.

In theory ranking was worn vertically on the beret and horizontally on the left breast above the pocket. This comprised, for enlisted men and NCOs, gold braid bars edged with pink Panzer *Waffenfarbe* backing: one bar for a *Legionär*, two for an *Unteroffizier*. The insignia for all grades of *Unteroffizier mit Portepée* was a single six-point yellow metal star edged with pink backing. *Leutnant* and *Oberleutnant* wore two and three such stars; *Hauptmann* and *Major* wore one and two eight-point stars, and *Oberstleutnant* and *Oberst* wore three. Photographs suggest that in fact the ranking was sometimes omitted from the beret, and two white metal badges were substituted: a Panzer death's-head above a swastika. A colourful variation on this uniform is illustrated on Colour Plate 2.

Republican tank units, like the rest of their army, wore a motley collection of clothing. In the vehicle the *mono*, in shades of khaki, blue, brown and grey seems to have been common. Leather coats and windcheater jackets were much in evidence, and so were various types of *cazadora* – a short, round-bottomed jacket cut much like a British battledress blouse, with patch chest pockets and a falling collar. Details varied widely, but a brownish khaki shade was normal. Khaki breeches or trousers, calf- or ankle-length laced brown boots, and khaki or black berets all appear in photos. Leather semi-breeches are shown in at least one photograph of a group of Republican tank men. The pre-war breast badge shaped like a Renault tank was to be seen among Republicans, and a shirt in the Imperial War Museum, London, bears a version of it on the right breast, worked in fawn cloth with black and gold thread details.

Ranking was sometimes worn on the beret, nearly always on the left breast pocket. For NCOs a red star was worn above a small upwards-pointing red chevron (*cabo*), a single vertical red bar (*sargento*) or two bars (*brigada*). For officers a red star outlined in gold was worn above one, two and three thin horizontal gold bars by company officers, and above one, two and three thick bars by field officers. These chest rankings were normally worked on a patch of khaki cloth sewn to the pocket of the *mono*, shirt, *cazadora* or leather jacket, and to the beret. It is possible that Russian tank instructors were present on the battlefield wearing their own black or dark blue overalls and brown leather padded helmets; it is also possible that the Russian helmet was provided in some numbers for Republican crews.

Poland

The few tank units which saw action in the 1920 Russo-Polish war of independence wore French uniforms, as they had been formed within the French army. In the aftermath of the war the tank units were divided between the different arms of service, only being reunited as the *Brón Pancerna* in 1930. At the time of Germany's invasion in September 1939 the Polish tank troops were wearing a basic vehicle uniform of beret and steel helmet; overalls; and black leather coat.

The beret was small, black, and worn pulled down square. A silver national cap badge was worn centrally – the crowned eagle above a cartouche (the latter is actually an 'Amazon' shield). Below this appeared the ranking, also in silver. Lance Corporals, Corporals and Lance Sergeants wore one to three silver horizontal bars. Sergeants and Staff Sergeants wore one and two shallow chevrons, point down. Warrant Officers wore a red bar and a single silver star; a star alone identified Second Lieutenants. Lieutenants and Captains wore two and three silver stars, in a line; and field officers wore one, two and three stars above two horizontal bars.

The helmet, painted khaki of a green shade, was the old French 1919 model armoured crew helmet. This was basically an Adrian skull with a riveted, sharply down-swept neck guard (nearer the vertical than the horizontal), a comb or ridge running front to back across the top, a single chinstrap and a thin pad of leather laminations across the brow. There was no embossed frontal badge. In 1938 the two battalions of 7TPdw light tanks began to receive a new helmet for commanders only, designed to receive headphones; this was larger and deeper than the old type, and of simpler shape, without the separate neck guard and brow pad.

The overalls were one-piece greenish khaki 'boiler suits' worn without insignia, apparently. They had simple fall collars usually buttoned closed; about seven drab buttons visible between throat and waist, down a central closure; buttoned cuff-bands; two patch breast pockets with straight flaps buttoned at the corners; and conventional slash side pocket openings. They were worn with black ankle boots, and very short ankle-puttees in khaki. The usual Polish soldier's belt was worn over them, a brown leather item with a single-claw frame buckle and leather keep. The black leather coat does not seem to have been universal wear, and when the overalls were worn alone, a holster and gas mask satchel were worn over them. The holster for the VIS automatic was brown leather, noticeably square and untapered in appearance, with a long central strap for the rounded

Cadets of the Polish Central Officers' Training School parade with their 7TPdw light tanks. The colour party, foreground, wear the black beret with the national eagle above silver rank stars, and the black leather coats with cloth collars are clearly visible. On those in the background one can just make out the large, square holster for the VIS pistol, and the French helmet (Janusz Magnuski).

flap, a magazine pocket on the front surface and another strap and stud on the rear surface; a brown braided cord lanyard was worn to the neck. The light khaki web gas mask satchel resembled the British type in its shaped, square appearance. It hung around the neck on a web strap, bottom surface just below the breast pocket flaps when properly adjusted. It had a pointed flap which came down in a V-shape on the outside (exposed) face, fastening at the point with a drab metal button, about half way down the total depth of the satchel. Brown leather gauntlets with deep cuffs were issued to all ranks.

The leather coat appeared in two slightly differing models, for NCOs and officers. The former came to mid-thigh and had two vertical rows of six buttons (visible) on its double-breasted front. The deep fall collar and the shoulder straps were of black cloth, contrasting with the black leather body and sleeves. The longer officers' coat had no visible buttons. A heavy horizontal seam crossed

the chest, sweeping down in points on each breast; it is illustrated on Colour Plate 3. Officers and NCOs wore their ranking on the black shoulder straps. The distinctions are described above; bars were transverse and stars in line up the straps, the bars of field officers being worn at the outer end. Officers wore a brown leather Sam Browne belt with double-claw buckle and diagonal cross-strap over the right shoulder. The automatic holster was worn on the right hip butt backwards by all ranks; officers and NCO commanders also wore binocular cases, map cases, etc. Typical legwear for both was flared greenish khaki breeches and knee-length black boots, those of NCOs being rather heavier and less tightly cut than those of officers.

The fall collar of the black leather coat was quite loosely cut, and the stand-and-fall collar of the khaki tunic normally showed in the neck. Readers may care to note a few details of collar insignia. The edges of the collar, both front and bottom, were braided for officers and NCOs in the traditional Polish zig-zag silver lace; that of officers was noticeably broader than that of NCOs and Warrant Officers. On each collar point were worn 'pennants' – elongated triangles of cloth recalling lance pennants, about 16 mm deep by 55 mm long. For armoured units these were halved horizontally, black above orange.

THE SECOND WORLD WAR

Great Britain

Tank and armoured car crews, Europe

The normal dress of AFV crews from the outbreak of the war was the khaki 1937 battledress for all ranks. This comprised a round-bottomed waist-length blouse and straight-cut trousers of khaki serge which buttoned together (inadequately – all who have ever worn it will recall the sensation of fresh air around the kidneys when one bent over vigorously!). The blouse was single-breasted, with a stand-and-fall collar which hooked closed at the throat, and front buttons concealed by a fly. An integral belt at the waist fastened from left to right with a patent metal buckle on the right hip. Two patch breast pockets had pointed flaps, with concealed buttons, and box pleats. There were khaki shoulder straps permanently attached, fastened close to the neck with a khaki composition button.

The trousers had four spaced belt-loops, buttoned at the top end, around the sides and back, which accommodated the webbing belt when in shirt-sleeve order. There were conventional slash side-pockets; a single right hip pocket with pointed flap and concealed button; a large pocket in front of the left thigh, with pointed flap and concealed button; and a small unflapped pocket with a box pleat, high on the front of the right hip, for the field dressing. Small tabs were attached to the bottom inside edge of the leg, and three spaced buttons round the bottom of the leg allowed the cloth to be gathered tight.

An 'economy' model appeared from 1940, and the two types were seen in simultaneous use throughout the war, although the prewar pattern naturally became scarcer as each year passed. The 1940 type had no fly at the front, and the five khaki composition buttons were exposed. Pocket buttons were also exposed, and there were no pleats on the pockets, except for a single one on the field dressing pocket. The leg tabs also disappeared. (It should be noted that fashion-conscious officers sometimes had their BD privately tailored, retaining the fly front and pleats.) All buttons, at the front, on the pockets and the shoulders, were identical.

Other ranks wore this uniform over a collarless khaki shirt, but officers wore a khaki shirt and tie. Officers' blouse collars were therefore always worn open, with the collar hooks and top button sometimes removed altogether. The collar was pressed open, the top part of the front closure thus forming two small triangular lapels. Some officers wore the blouse unaltered, in which case the partial lining of sandy khaki drill cloth showed on these 'lapels' and inside the collar band; many had

Brewing up during an exercise in the UK, this RTR Matilda crew displays the two-piece khaki drab denim version of battledress (right) and the greatcoat (centre and left) – these two troopers also wear rubber Wellington boots. Note full webbing including shoulder braces, and map case fixed to the front of the gas mask satchel (left) (Imperial War Museum).

khaki serge tailored over these areas to make a uniform-coloured facing. In about the last year of the war some enlisted men were also issued collars and ties, and wore the BD blouse open, but this was not universal.

Ranking was worn on the shoulder straps by officers and on the sleeves by enlisted men. Lance-Corporals, Corporals and Sergeants wore one, two and three large white herringbone on drab brown chevrons, point down, on both upper sleeves. Staff Sergeants and Colour Sergeants wore a crown above the chevrons in white thread on brown. Warrant Officers wore the Royal Arms (WO 1st Class) and a crown (WO 2nd Class) on each forearm. Second Lieutenants, Lieutenants and Captains wore one, two and three 'pips' respectively on the shoulder straps. These were square 'stars' bearing a Maltese cross shape with a circle in the centre, and were set diamond-fashion on the strap. They were embroidered in light buff thread, the cross and circle detail being picked out in brown thread. Their backing, which showed in a thin line all round, was yellow for cavalry regiments; black for the RTR; and red for infantry battalions which had been converted into numbered Royal Armoured Corps regiments, and for the converted Foot Guards regiments of the Guards Armoured Division and 6th Guards Tank Brigade. Majors wore a single crown embroidered in the same manner; Lieutenant-Colonels a crown 'inside' a single pip,

The crew of the RSM, 2nd Irish Guards, during an inspection of the battalion's Covenanters somewhere in the UK, 1942. The RSM (left) looks suitably embarassed by the outlandish outfit he is called upon to wear, one of the bright ideas for tank uniform which luckily did not survive into the front lines! The helmets are of thin, pressed and riveted black fibre composition, like a miner's helmet of the day; note that the unit's tactical code, '53', is painted on the front of each. A sleeveless jerkin, apparently machined together from many small pieces of scrap leather, is worn over the BD. Full insignia are worn on the sleeves: the RSM has his large and beautiful warrant badge on the upper arm, and all wear the white on dark green Irish Guards shoulder title, trade badges, long service and good conduct chevrons, etc. Note the microphone handset tucked into the front of the jerkin (Imperial War Museum).

and Colonels a crown inside two pips. Ranking was worn in full and at all times on battledress, except in very exceptional circumstances.

On both upper sleeves of the blouse, about five inches below the shoulder seam, all RAC personnel were supposed to wear a strip of felt two inches long by a quarter inch wide, halved red and yellow, yellow to the front on both arms. Photos show this to have been worn in the front line as a general rule, but equally that it was quite often discarded.

Formation insignia – of Corps, Division or Brigade – were worn on both upper arms about two inches below the shoulder seam. Again, they were almost invariably worn when not in the front line, and very often when in the presence of the

The various experiments with crash helmets and other special clothing items did not lead to any general issue. This RTR Valentine crew of 8th Armoured Division, 1942, wears battledress with standard insignia and webbing. The black on khaki 'RTR' tally is worn on both shoulder straps. The divisional sign, in black and green, appears above the red/yellow RAC arm strip, and the RTR tank arm badge. Open holsters are worn on the long leg strap, with the cartridge pouch on the right-hand side of the belt. Gas mask satchels are worn on the chest – not an item normally seen in the front line (Imperial War Museum).

A British Lieutenant and one of his crew re-ammunition their Sherman with 75 mm HE rounds. The enlisted man seems to wear a khaki one-piece denim overall, the officer a two-piece denim battledress with bronze rank pips on the shoulder strap. From the scrubbed webbing this was taken in Sicily or Italy (Imperial War Museum).

enemy. They were supposed to be removed for security purposes, but often were not. Some examples will be found in the accompanying photos and on Colour Plate 4; a few other commonly seen examples may be described:

5th Corps Black square with white Viking longship, red cross on sail.

8th Corps White solid silhouette knight with plume and lance on charger facing left, on red rectangle.

12th Corps Three trees, in black or black and green, on a white horizontal oval, on a black rectangle.

13th Corps Red solid silhouette of gazelle leaping up to left, on upright white oval, on upright red rectangle.

2nd Armoured Division White silhouette of lavishly plumed knight's helm, facing left, on red square.

6th Armoured Division Stylised white knight's gauntlet, set diagonally across black square with wrist low right, fist top left.

79th Armoured Division Black bull's mask, full face,

with horns and white details, on yellow triangle point down, sometimes with white outer edge.

Brigade patches were not commonly worn, since armoured brigades were either attached to an armoured division, or moved rapidly from higher formation to higher formation at need as Army and Corps troops. A few may be cited, however:

4th Armoured Brigade Black jerboa, facing right, on white square.

8th Armoured Brigade Yellow disc with red/brown edge, red/brown fox mask.

22nd Armoured Brigade Red stag's head facing right on white square.

23rd Armoured Brigade Black 'liver bird' on white background, square or circular.

These patches all appeared with slight or chronic variations of detail from time to time.

The independent Army Tank Brigades almost invariably had patches of various colours made up of the same shape – a 'diabolo', or two solid triangles meeting point-to-point, one above the other.

The other main type of insignia seen on the BD blouse during the war was the regimental title at the shoulder. This is a subject fraught with peril for the researcher, and the nearest one can achieve to a firm rule is that all rules were constantly ignored, and many completely unauthorised practices were observed at unit level. Briefly – and with many thanks to Paul Cross for his advice – the situation was as follows:

Before the war, metal regimental shoulder titles were worn on the end of the BD blouse shoulder strap, usually in the form of initial capitals in yellow metal in a bar or an arc – eg, 'XIIRL' for 12th Royal Lancers. In 1940 these were abolished; but the order did not 'take', and individual examples of their use on BD can be found in wartime photos They were officially replaced by a khaki cloth slip-over tab bearing black lettering and worn at the end of the shoulder strap – eg, 'R.T.R.' for Royal Tank Regiment, '14/20H' for 14th/20th King's Hussars, etc. In the summer of 1943, in the UK, there began to appear in the Army as a whole coloured felt shoulder titles in an arc shape, sewn to the top of the sleeve immediately below the shoulder seam, and replacing the khaki slip-ons. For all armoured units these were supposed to take the form of a yellow arc bearing 'ROYAL ARMOURED CORPS' in red. These were certainly seen quite often in the front lines, although they should have been removed. They were most often worn, it seems, by some of the armoured Yeomanry regiments, RAC training regiments and infantry battalions converted into numbered RAC regiments. They were rarely worn by RTR personnel. Many cavalry regiments, both Regular and Yeomanry, seem to have adopted unofficial, regimentally-coloured titles of this type. Again, these were sometimes seen in the front lines, and often on a soldier's 'best BD' for walking out, leave, etc. Examples are '17/21 LANCERS' in white on black; 'SHARPSHOOTERS' in yellow on dark green, for County of London Yeomanry; and 'INNS OF COURT REGIMENT' in white on dark green, for that armoured car unit.

The coloured slip-overs worn on the shoulder straps by the numbered RTR regiments were revived in 1940 (see table) but were unevenly worn. They were certainly in evidence in the desert, but do not seem to have been very widely worn in the European front lines. Some Yeomanry tank regiments adopted their own coloured slip-overs, and an example is illustrated in Colour Plate 4. Regimentally coloured lanyards worn round the shoulder and disappearing into the top pocket were also to be seen occasionally, but no comprehensive listing of these is known to the author.

Royal Tank Regiment shoulder tallies, 1940-45
The first 11 numbered RTR regiments used the same

colours as the same numbered Tank Corps battalions in 1918 – see Part 1. An exception was the red lanyard which replaced the red slip-over of 1 RTR, to avoid confusion with the orange-red tally worn by all South African servicemen. The yellow tally of 2 RTR acquired a crosswise central stripe of green, red and brown; and 11 RTR used white and black, in place of the white and red of the First World War. Additional regiments formed for the Second World War used the following colours; in some cases written and pictorial records at RTR HQ differ.

40 RTR – blue/vertical red/blue
41 RTR – yellow/green
42 RTR – yellow/blue
43 RTR – green/maroon (? or purple)
44 RTR – yellow/maroon (? or purple)
45 RTR – green/thin yellow/black
46 RTR – green, red Welsh dragon superimposed
47 RTR – white/green/white (? or grey/pink/grey)
48 RTR – yellow/black
49 RTR – green/maroon (? or purple/grey)
50 RTR – black/vertical green/black (? dark blue in place of black)
51 RTR – green/black (? or grey/black)

To recap, then, the whole mind-boggling subject of BD blouse sleeve insignia worn by AFV crews in the front lines in Europe:

In France, pre-Dunkirk, the small armoured force wore no arm insignia at all apart from ranking, and the RTR's white tank badge. In the UK, 1940 to 1945, black-on-khaki unit titles were worn on the shoulder strap, gradually replaced 1943-45 by coloured felt titles at the top of the sleeve – either the RAC title in red on yellow, or unofficial regimental titles. The khaki slip-ons; the RAC or regimental coloured titles; and isolated examples of old brass shoulder strap titles were all to be seen in the front line in north-west Europe and Italy, 1943-45, but were officially forbidden. The red/yellow sleeve strip was commonly worn both at home and in action, but not universally. The formation sign – either a Corps, Divisional or, less often, a Brigade sign – was worn in the UK almost universally, and very often in action. Regimental 'tribalism' in the form of coloured slip-overs on the shoulder straps, lanyards, etc, were observed in action and at home but followed no authorised pattern.

Headgear
The Royal Armoured Corps as a whole was granted the right to wear the black beret in 1940. The Royal Tank Regiment always wore this beret, with its own silver cap badge, regardless of rank. The armoured Regular cavalry units wore their own regimental cap badges on the black beret, some-

times pinned through patches of coloured cloth according to tribal tradition: the 15/19th King's Royal Hussars and the 10th Royal Hussars had red patches, the Royal Scots Greys black patches, the 4th/7th Royal Dragoon Guards and 5th Royal Inniskilling Dragoon Guards a maroon and a green patch respectively. These patches normally followed the shape of the badge, showing round the edge in a narrow strip. In fact, as mentioned in Part 2, many armoured cavalry regiments did not receive the beret until well into 1942, and until they received it enlisted ranks wore the khaki 'sidecap', the 'cap, Field Service'. Cavalry officers, both before and after the issue of the black beret, could and often did wear the khaki service dress peaked cap, with brown chinstrap; it will bear repeating that this cap was never worn by RTR officers.

The black beret was also worn by Yeomanry tank and armoured car regiments, with their own cap badges. These were as various in design as those of the Regulars, and no listing can possibly be made here. A couple of attractive examples might be quoted, however: the Lothians and Border Horse, who wore a brass corn-sheaf on a bright blue patch; and the Warwickshire Yeomanry, who wore the silver 'bear and ragged staff' – a standing bear, facing left as viewed clawing an irregular tree trunk its own height.

Those infantry battalions which were converted later in the war to tank regiments seem generally to have retained their county infantry cap badges

British tank regiments – representative cap badges: (top left) 1st King's Dragoon Guards – silver; (top right) 9th Lancers – silver; (bottom left) 10th Hussars – gold crown, gold lower scroll, remainder silver; (bottom right) 17th/21st Lancers – silver (Mike Chappell).

on the black beret, and not to have worn the mailed fist cap badge of the Royal Armoured Corps. Examples are the silver *fleur-de-lys* of the Manchester Regiment (111th Regiment, RAC); the silver bugle-horn surrounding a Tudor rose of the King's Own Yorkshire Light Infantry (149th Regiment, RAC); and a silver lion's torso emerging from a crown waving a banner, above a silver scroll, all above a brass scroll, and worn through a red patch – the Duke of Wellington's Regiment (West Riding), which provided the 114th, 115th, 145th, and 146th Regiments, RAC. The Gordon Highlanders of 116th Regiment, RAC, in Burma retained their khaki tamoshanter and wreathed stag's mask badge.

The Royal Armoured Corps cap badge seems to have been a pretty unpopular item. In the form of an upright mailed fist, under a crown, with a circular frame formed by arrowed 'pincer movements' on each side, this silver badge only seems to have been worn by RAC training units and depots. It was predictable that British soldiers, whatever their culture-shock at being torn from their natural element and thrust into tanks, would cling grimly to the cap badges which alone linked them with their 'real' identity.

It need hardly be added that the Foot Guards regiments converted to the armoured role retained their regimental cap badges: the grenade of the Grenadiers; the stars of the Order of the Garter, Thistle and St Patrick, worn by the Coldstream, Scots and Irish Guards; and the leek of the Welsh Guards.

Apart from the black beret and the khaki peaked SD cap, officers of armoured cavalry not infrequently wore the regimentally coloured sidecaps – No 1 Dress caps – traditional to their units. Photos show that these were popular in the Middle East, and still sometimes worn in north-west Europe – although rather less often, in an altogether uglier and more crowded theatre of war. Examples are the 3rd, 4th and 7th Hussars, all of whom wore red sidecaps with gold piping around the edges of the top gusset, down the front and back of the crown, and around the edge of the turn-up. These regiments served together in Italy from November 1944, incidentally – the 3rd and 7th in Shermans and the 4th in Kangaroos. The 13th/18th Hussars, who fought in Europe from August 1944 in Shermans, wore caps with a dark blue turn-up and front 'peak' and white top gusset and crown, piped gold. So did the 17th/21st Lancers, who crewed Shermans in 6th Armoured Division in Italy in 1944. Examples of other regiments, including the most colourful of all, may be found on Colour Plate 4.

It should perhaps be recorded that the true

Supposedly the CO (right) of the 10th Mounted Rifles, the armoured recce regiment of 1st Polish Armoured Division, 1944. Note headset and handset; rimless RAC pattern steel helmets, with stencilled Polish national eagle badge just visible on front; and the 1943 tank suit (right) (Imperial War Museum).

'tanky' always wore his beret pulled down square on both sides, with the badge as near to central as he could get away with – 'It's these 'ere earphones, Sarge, honest . . .'

Protective clothing

When working in and around the vehicles, British tank crews often protected their uniforms with one-piece 'boiler suits' or dungarees, which came in many shades of brown, khaki or sand-coloured cloth. They normally had a small fall collar, interior breast pockets with external pointed flaps, and internal left thigh pockets with pointed flaps. Buttons were of khaki or brown composition or horn, and they often had integral cloth belts with metal buckles. Details varied widely. Some pre-war black RTR overalls are to be seen in photos of the 1940 French campaign.

Two-piece 'denims' were also to be seen, often as fighting dress. These were suits of coarse cloth cut generally like the battledress, but with exposed composition buttons and simple unpleated pockets. They were of a thin, shoddy cloth, usually of a drab earth-brown shade – that is, a colour mid-way between brown and grey, without much green in it. On both working dungarees and two-piece denims it was normal for sleeve ranking to be worn on the right arm only, often either temporarily fixed with snap-fasteners or worn on brassards of khaki cloth.

The khaki greatcoat was the normal cold-weather addition to the tank crewman's uniform from 1939 to the winter of 1944. This was of heavy khaki serge, double-breasted, calf length, with a deep stand-and-fall collar and four pairs of large bronze buttons on the front. It had an integral half-belt at the back with three bronze buttons equally spaced; two large interior skirt pockets with backwards-slanting flaps; and plain shoulder straps. Ranking was normally the only insignia worn on the coat, although formation signs are sometimes seen in photos. The practice of officers wearing greatcoats piped in 'branch colours' around the shoulder straps was not widespread in the front line but was sometimes observed; a photo accompanying this chapter illustrates a very flamboyant example.

The sleeveless brown leather thigh-length jerkin or 'trench waistcoat' beloved of British soldiers of both World Wars was also much in evidence in armoured units as in all other branches of the service. It had four large buttons of brown horn or composition material, and a round, collarless neck; it was partly lined with khaki blanket material, and appeared in a range of brown shades, usually fairly light with an orange tinge.

In the winter of 1944 crews in north-west Europe received for the first time the 1943 tank suit – usually christened 'zoot suit' or 'pixie suit' by the troops, who took to it enthusiastically. It was of a light sandy khaki shade, lined with a warm khaki woollen material, and had two long zips from neck to ankle at the front, for easy access. Cunning manipulation of these zips turned it into a sleeping bag. It had numerous pockets on the chest, thighs and lower legs; a zip-on hood; and specially strengthened shoulder straps, by which casualties could be pulled from a tank turret.

With all these uniforms the standard dish-shaped steel helmet, painted khaki, was issued as battle-field head protection. It was worn by exposed commanders when the danger from small-arms fire was great, but was obviously impractical for those inside the vehicle and was normally hung on the outside of the turret. From 1943 a more practical rimless helmet, identical to that of the paratroops but with a simple web chinstrap, was issued to the RAC, and this was much more widely worn in action.

Regulation footwear for enlisted ranks, throughout the war and in all theatres, was the black, laced, hobnailed ankle-boot with reinforced toe-cap. In armoured units the hobnails and heel and toe plates were normally removed. Officers sometimes wore these, sometimes brown laced boots or shoes.

Self-propelled artillery

The crews of self-propelled guns of the Royal Artillery and Royal Horse Artillery wore basically similar uniforms to their counterparts in towed artillery units: battledress, with the khaki field service cap until 1943 and the khaki 'cap GS' thereafter. This latter, easily mistaken for a beret in photos, was in fact made up from several pieces of cloth like a Highland tamoshanter, rather than from a single shaped piece like a true beret. It had a cloth headband instead of a leather rim, and was made of coarse khaki serge. Officers wore either the khaki peaked SD cap or a khaki beret. Cap badges were, for the RA and RHA on the officers' SD cap, the artillery's cannon badge in bronze; for RA enlisted ranks, on the FS and GS caps, the cannon badge; for RA and RHA officers on the khaki beret, the gold bursting shell-and-scroll badge and the silver RHA badge respectively – the latter being a crowned garter around a monogram above a scroll; and for RHA enlisted ranks on the GS cap, the RHA badge in nickel. The dish-shaped steel helmet was worn in the open-topped SP guns until 1943, and increasingly after that date the rimless RAC pattern. The US leather tank crash-helmet was also to be seen in some M-10 units.

When insignia were applied to the BD, they would take the form of one or all or some combination of the following. The shoulder title from mid-1943 was

Three anonymous squaddies shortly after VE Day; the centre man wears the light khaki 1943 tank suit.

'ROYAL ARTILLERY' in red on blue. The arm-of-service strip was halved red and blue. Formation signs for Corps and Divisions, and sometimes Armies, would be worn in the usual position. Artillery Sergeants had the cannon badge repeated in the 'dip' at the top of their chevrons, or superimposed on the top chevron. Officers' rank pips were on red backing.

Greatcoats were worn, as was the leather jerkin, in cold weather; the latter was preferred as being less cumbersome in the vehicle. In the depths of winter extra items such as rubber Wellington boots, seaboot socks, balaclavas, snow gloves and white camouflage clothing were sometimes issued.

Reconnaissance Corps

This organisation, whose regiments were attached to infantry divisions and took their numbers from the parent formation, was founded in 1941 and taken into the Royal Armoured Corps in December 1943. Personnel wore conventional BD uniform, with parent formation patches, and from 1943 a yellow-on-green shoulder title with the Corps name. They also wore a khaki beret (a true beret, predating the 'cap GS') with their Corps badge in yellow metal: an upright spear, flanked by two lightning bolts so placed against each side of the shaft as to make a sort of cartoon 'fir tree' shape, above the scroll.

The Middle East

Armoured crews in Africa and the Middle Eastern countries wore normal tropical drill uniform in hot weather, and battledress as described above in cold weather. The tropical uniform comprised the European headgear; a pullover shirt; and shorts or long trousers. The shirt had an open neck, box-pleated breast pockets with three-point buttoned flaps, and shoulder straps. The front closure ended at the level of the pocket bottoms; all buttons were fawn plastic composition. The shorts were generously cut – to modern eyes, ludicrously so! They had wide legs, reaching to the kneecap. Some batches, manufactured in India, were even longer, and could be turned down to tuck into the socks; usually they were worn folded up from the knee and fastened with buttons on the thigh through buttonholes in the bottom hem. The waist-band was broad, with loops to accommodate the webbing belt, and two cloth strap-and-buckle fastenings at the front. There were conventional slash side pockets, and a small flapless, buttoned, box-pleated field dressing pocket high on the front of the right thigh. Slacks had side pockets but not the big left thigh pocket of the BD trousers. All these items were in a light sandy material known as khaki drill – KD. Shorts and/or slacks were worn according to individual unit orders; some commanders ordered slacks to be worn at all times to protect the men against the sores inseparable from any scratch or insect-bite in that climate.

The khaki serge greatcoat was much worn at night, and officers would often provide themselves with such unofficial additions as hooded naval watch-coats in camel-coloured blanket material, or native *poshteens* of more or less inadequately cured goatskin which could usually be smelt a good way off. All ranks often wore khaki wool V-neck sweaters.

Officers wore either the same uniforms as their men, or sometimes a KD version of the service tunic. This was a bush-shirt or safari jacket style, thigh-length with four large pockets – usually box-pleated breast pockets with three-point flaps and plain skirt pockets with straight flaps. There was an integral cloth belt with a narrow metal frame buckle at the front and cloth 'keeps'. Buttons were of brown plastic, of leather, or of brass regimental patterns. This jacket was usually worn open-necked, without a shirt underneath. Neck-scarves were common. (A veteran reports that a considerable *cachet* was enjoyed by some officers who continued to wear the khaki service dress tunic in all its full-skirted glory, in place of BD. This identified the wearer as having been serving in India or Egypt since before the war, thus missing the issue of BD, and confirmed the officer in question as an 'old tropical hand.')

Ranking on the tropical uniform was conventional. Enlisted ranks often wore chevrons only on the right arm, snap-fastened or on a brassard. Officers' shoulder ranking was sometimes sewn

February 1945: two crewmen of 3rd Carabiniers on a ferry with their M3 Lee tank. They wear standard jungle green shirtsleeve order, and, typically of this regiment, dark green webbing complete with shoulder braces. The Lance-Corporal has a chevron sewn to his right sleeve; in this unit NCOs sometimes wore small white chevrons, points outward, on khaki shoulder strap slip-overs. Note regimental cap badge on black berets (Imperial War Museum).

in place, sometimes worn on KD cloth slip-overs. Since rolled sleeves were normal for all ranks when in shirtsleeve order, Warrant Officers usually wore their forearm ranking on leather wrist-straps, usually on the right wrist only. One published photo shows a Royal Scots Greys Sergeant-Major wearing a broad leather patch on a wrist-strap, bearing a metal regimental cap badge above metal ranking; this practice may have been common. Cavalry Corporals and Sergeants often wore a regimental device – sometimes the cap badge, sometimes a derivation of it – on or above the chevrons on the sleeve: eg, the Prince of Wales's feathers worn by the 11th Hussars. (This regiment, which provided the armoured car regiment of 7th Armoured Division, also had a special headgear: a milk-chocolate coloured beret with a broad red band, worn without a badge.)

Arm of service strips and formation badges were not much seen in action on tropical uniform. When out of line the formation patches were sometimes added, either snap-fastened to the conventional position, or worn on KD slip-overs on the shoulder straps. As mentioned above, the coloured slip-overs of the various RTR regiments seem to have been worn quite widely in the desert, but the tank arm badge was not worn on the KD shirt.

The normal legwear when in shorts was long khaki wool socks, and either web anklets or short brown-drab puttees at the ankle, fastened off with a light khaki tape; the usual ankle boot was worn. Officers in this theatre often wore non-standard items such as pale fawn corduroy slacks,

Battledress (left) and light khaki one-piece working overalls worn by M3 Lee crewmen in North Africa, 1942 (Imperial War Museum).

washed until they were almost off-white, and the popular suede chukka boots, or 'brothel creepers' with thick crêpe soles.

The Far East

At the outbreak of the war with Japan, Britain had no armour in the theatre. 7th Armoured Brigade was pulled out of the desert and sent to Burma in time to cover the retreat, arriving in February 1942. They wore tropical uniforms in sand-coloured KD, exactly as described above. By the time of the Arakan fighting in early 1943 jungle-green clothing was being issued. It appears that initially a cellular, jungle-green version of the battledress blouse was issued, corresponding in most respects to the khaki serge type, with a fly front and pleated pockets. This proved impractical and unpopular, and by the end of 1943 a jungle-green 'bush shirt' had replaced it. This seems to have been worn either tucked into the slacks, or hanging outside them to expose the skirt pockets; it is hard to tell from photographs, but there seems to have been only the one garment, not a separate two-pocket shirt and a four-pocket bush jacket. The situation is confused by the fact that, when the unpopular tropical BD blouse came in, it was replaced by individuals and units with locally acquired and dyed shirts of various types. Shirtsleeves were normally worn rolled, and photos which show a rather bulky sleeve buttoned to the wrist invite closer inspection – it is sometimes possible to make out, on the front of the right hip, the buckle of the integral cloth belt which identifies this as the tropical BD blouse. The jungle-green trousers normally had the large left thigh pocket, unlike the KD model worn in Africa.

Whether in BD blouse or rolled shirtsleeve order, however, tank crews wore very little in the way of insignia in the front line. Normally it was limited to ranking. Often the chevrons of NCOs were worn on the right sleeve only, sometimes temporarily attached, sometimes permanently sewn on, sometimes on a brassard. Officers' ranking was usually worn on light khaki shoulder strap slip-overs. The black RAC beret was normally worn, although some units seem to have made use of the US leather tank crash-helmet. The rimless RAC steel helmet was much in evidence in the 1944-45 reconquest of Burma, due to the ferocity of Japanese snipers. As mentioned above, the Gordon Highlanders of 116th Regiment, RAC, retained their khaki Balmoral with regimental cap badge. The broad-brimmed Australian-type khaki felt bush hat was the usual headgear of SP artillery crews and was also carried by some tank units for use outside the tank.

Webbing equipment

This was kept to a minimum. It was unnecessary, since personal kit was stowed in and around the vehicle; and it could be dangerous – crews had a horror of being trapped in a 'brewed up' vehicle by some snagged belt or pouch. It was usually limited to belt, holster, cartridge pouch, and in some regiments but not very many, webbing anklet gaiters. This was all standard 1937 web equipment, identical to that of the Army as a whole, with the exception of one piece of kit – the long Royal Armoured Corps leg strap for the holster.

Holsters were of both the standard issue closed type, and the open-topped type. The latter had a narrow web strap across the top to retain the revolver; a trip of six cartridge loops slanting down and forwards on the outer face; and a narrow vertical pocket on the front edge to hold a cleaning rod, whose looped wire end stuck out the top. It was sometimes worn on the belt, sometimes on the RAC leg strap. This was a broad web strap which fitted over the belt, to the bottom of which the holster was attached so that the muzzle came just above the knee. A narrow transverse strap secured it round the leg. It was felt to be more comfortable for soldiers who spent their working lives largely in the sitting position, and this was true; it was also rather stylish, and had something of a 'Western gunslinger' air. In sober fact, of course, it was also far more prone to get snagged on protrusions in the tank than the waist-mounted holster.

Both holsters were worn indiscriminately, on either side of the belt – on the right, butt backwards, or on the left, butt forwards. The small cartridge pouch of soft webbing, with a deep pointed flap with a bronze snap, was mounted on a slightly larger rectangle of webbing which hooked over the face of the 1937 belt. It could be worn either on the opposite side of the holster, to balance it, or on the same side with the holster hooked to the bottom of the pouch itself. Webbing shoulder braces were sometimes worn in regiments which took uniform neatness seriously, such as the 3rd Carabiniers in Burma; these rose vertically in front of the shoulders from the belt, and crossed in mid-back to engage with the opposite buckles on the rear of the belt. They had the usual wide sections for the 12 inches in the middle which passed over the top of the shoulder.

Webbing colour varied in Europe from grey-green with a hint of yellow when newly blancoed, to dark mustard when unblancoed. In Asia it was usually coloured dark green, and in the Middle East it was bleached almost white.

Text continued on page 58

Captions to plates on pages 53 and 54.

28 *Unterfeldwebel, Deutsches Afrika Korps, 1942. Tropical sidecap and tunic in olive, fading towards khaki; trousers could be either long straight slacks, flared semi-breeches, or shorts, in any shade of olive or khaki drill. Panzer pink piping on cap front, round shoulder straps; eagles on cap and breast in blue-grey on tan brown, as are Litzen on upper lapels. Copper-brown rank Tresse round shoulder straps inside pink piping, and round collar and upper lapels; white metal skulls on lower lapels; first pattern cuff title on right forearm. Webbing belt with olive-painted buckle; standard headset and throat-mikes; Luger holster.*

29 *Panzerschütze, 116th Panzer-Division, France 1944. Black Einheitsfeldmütze with one-piece badge on crown front; black and white divisional badge of greyhound pinned above left ear. Reed-green working denim suit with breast eagle and collar patches added. Note pocket detail – small slanted pocket with forward-buttoning flap on left hip, above large pocket (here with bundle of cotton waste); these were not repeated on right leg.*

30 *SS-Hauptsturmführer in one-piece camouflage suit, 1943-44. The one-piece camouflage overall for tank and assault gun crews was peculiar to Waffen-SS units. He wears the small 'old style officer's field cap', with SS insignia and pink Panzer piping. Note goggle and binocular details. Regulation rank patch for use on camouflaged clothing, on left arm only. Vertical, buttoned side pockets in each leg seam.*

31 *Feldwebel, Sturmgeschütz Brigade XII, France 1944. This unit was raised from paratroopers, and wore Luftwaffe headgear and insignia with the field grey assault gun uniform. We take this figure straight from an interesting photo of two NCOs of StuG Brigade XII, Oberfeldwebel Berndl and Feldwebel Stangassinger. Luftwaffe NCO's Schirmmütze piped in the yellow Waffenfarbe of the paratroopers, with dark blue-grey crown and black ribbed band, black strap and peak. Blue-grey and yellow Luftwaffe shoulder straps and collar patches, with usual silver-grey Tresse and pip on former, but no Tresse on latter, which bear only the three silver-grey metal 'wings' of rank. Luftwaffe breast eagle, and on the left breast the Iron Cross 1st Class, the silver Luftwaffe Ground Combat badge, and the Fallschirmjäger's qualification badge in silver and gold. Luftwaffe belt, Walther holster. Note light shade of grey uniform.*

32 *SS-Panzerschütze, 1st SS Panzer Korps 'LSSAH', France 1944. We take this figure from the well-known photos of crewmen of the Tiger tank regiment schwere SS Panzer-Abteilung 101. Black sidecap of SS cut with silver-grey SS eagle and skull insignia. Field grey shirt and black tie. Two-piece camouflage uniform in faded light and dark greens, browns, ochres, and brick pinks, cut to same lines as Panzer vehicle uniform. The only insignia are the black shoulder strap piped pink, taken from the black vehicle uniform, with the pink-on-black slip-on tally bearing the 'LAH' monogram of this premier SS formation; and the Panzer Assault badge in dull silver on the breast.*

33 *Hauptmann, Sturmgeschütz Brigade 277, Russia 1944. Taken from a photo of Hauptmann Bernhard Flachs, who rose to command StuG Brigade 277. The use of the black Panzer uniform, with skulls removed from the collar patches, by assault gun personnel is discussed in the*

text. *Several photos from different units late in the war also show the combination of grey Einheitsfeldmützen and black uniforms; note green backing to silver eagle and national cockade turned and sewn in a T-shape, and silver officer's crown piping. Decorations are the sunburst of the War Order of the German Cross, and on the left breast the General Assault Badge, the Iron Cross 1st Class, a wound badge in black, and the ribbon of the Iron Cross 2nd Class. At his throat hangs the Knight's Cross.*

34 *Colonello commanding Italian tank regiment, Libya 1942. The bustina cap, sahariana jacket and flared breeches are of the slightly pink shade of sandy drill characteristic of Italian tropical uniform. The three stars of rank, in gold, appear in an open gold 'box' on the left side of the cap, set at a slant; the tank branch badge is on the turned-up peak, and both are in gold on the special red backing of a unit commander. Tank branch collar patches in red and bright blue. Black shoulder boards with gold branch and rank insignia, gold inner edging, bright blue outer piping. Below medal ribbons on left breast, the gold badge of a tank unit commander – a horizontal wreath and scroll surrounding a dragon and tank motif. Brown leather 'Sam Browne', small Beretta holster, and jackboots.*

35 *Major, US 8th Tank Destroyer Group, Remagen, March 1945. (Taken from the published notes and sketches of H. C. Larter, Jr, of the Company of Military Historians, to whom we make due acknowledgement.) Steel M1 helmet with four separate insignia: decal of Tank Destroyer patch above brazed-on Major's leaf badge, on front; decal of 8th TD Group pennant on sides; and painted white bar, identifying an officer, centrally at rear. Cavalry yellow scarf; 'tanker's jacket' in light OD with rank leaf pinned to leather patch on shoulders, and TD Forces patch on left sleeve; brownish olive wool trousers of the service uniform; light greenish OD webbing belt and shoulder braces. The M1 carbine was carried as well as the pistol, and magazine pouches and bayonet are fixed to the belt.*

36 *Corporal, US 2nd Armored Division, Europe 1944-45. Standard tanker's crash helmet in green-painted leather; see photos in text. Tanker's windcheater jacket, with divisional patch on left sleeve only, and rank chevrons in light OD on midnight blue on both sleeves. Bib-fronted winter overtrousers in pale OD.*

37 *Starshii Leitenant, Guards tank unit, Soviet Army, 1944. This Senior Lieutenant wears the pilotka cap with red officer's piping at crown and turn-up, and enamel badge. The 1943 shirt-tunic, with stand collar, has officer's patch pockets, and is worn with flared breeches and black leather boots reaching the top of the calf. Field pattern shoulder boards of khaki are piped and striped red, with silver tank badge and rank stars. Above the right pocket are the enamel Guards badge, awarded as a unit citation, and the gold stripe signifying a serious wound. The medal for the defence of Leningrad hangs on a white and green ribbon on the left breast. 'Sam Browne' belt; winter sheepskin coat.*

38 *Major, Soviet tank troops, 1941-42. Winter model tank helmet in black fabric with fleece lining. Pre-1943 shirt-tunic with red-piped fall collar, and collar patches of rank and branch, repeated on wartime production khaki overalls: black patches piped gold, with silver tank badge, red and gold enamel bars.*

39 *Serzhant, Soviet tank troops, 1943-45. Grey cloth and*

46

47

48

49

50

51

Captions to plates on pages 55 and 56.

fleece ushanka *cap with metal badge. Grey* kaftan *coat of enlisted men's pattern, with concealed buttons, and post-1943 collar patches of khaki piped red. Khaki field shoulder boards piped red, with red rank stripes and - for enlisted ranks - brass tank badge.*

40 *Capitaine,* 1er *Chasseurs à cheval, French Indo-China 1954. Taken mainly from a photo of Captain Hervouet, the outstandingly courageous commander of the Chaffee tank squadron at Dien Bien Phu. Note prominent band and seams of sand-coloured beret, and small silver cannon-and-helm badge above left ear. The photo shows the beret pulled down on the right, the opposite side to normal French practice. The silver on black ranking bars are worn round the shoulder straps of the jungle-green fatigue shirt. We have added the regimental badge on a leather pocket fob, clearly visible in photos of other personnel of the* 1er *RCC in Indo-China.*

41 *Lieutenant, 1st Battalion, US 77th Armor, Viet Nam 1969. (Taken from Company of Military Historians Plate 415 by W. H. Bradford.) Olive green jungle fatigue suit – note canted chest pockets; green glass fibre CVC helmet with black rubber rim, and plastic and wire radio boom on left side only; green canvas and leather jungle boots. Black rank bar and armoured branch patch on right and left collar points respectively. Red diamond patch of parent formation, 5th Infantry Division (Mechanised), on left sleeve; this was one of few formations to opt to keep full-colour patch rather than use 'subdued' green and black style. Black name and* US ARMY *tabs worn above right and left breast pockets. Locally-made blue and white 1st/77th Armor patch on left pocket – a tiger sejant, with a battleaxe, red tongue and claws, and white scroll on a blue shield. Note wristwatch hung from pocket, apparently common practice.*

42 *Major, Egyptian armoured troops, 1973. This very plain uniform, distinguished only by the eagle of rank on the shoulder straps and bearing no distinctive branch insignia at all, is described in the text. Photos of an Egyptian Army parade in Cairo in 1978 show olive green shirtsleeve order worn by T-54 crews, with black Russian tank helmets and black paratrooper-style boots.*

43 *Četař, Czechoslovak tank troops, 1960. The three red rank bars identifying this grade of Sergeant, together with the colour and design of the helmet, overall and boots, give this soldier an almost totally Russian appearance. The earth-brown overall has four buttoned pockets and slash side pockets. Note the long straps and large jack-plug of the winter pattern fleece-lined brown leather helmet, which has built-in laryngophones. Only the brass buckle plate, bearing a raised Czech lion motif, and the German-looking holster, relieve the Soviet appearance of this outfit. (From a colour photo.)*

44 *Areef, Jordanian 1st Tank Regiment, circa 1970. This Corporal is taken largely from a colour photo of Jordanian M-48s parading after the rebuilding of the Jordanian Armoured Corps following its losses in 1967. The wearing of yellow shoulder patches could be made out, but not the regimental badge – we have added the crossed lances, wreath and crown of the 1st Regiment. Ranking is worn on a brassard on the right only. British 1937 webbing, scrubbed almost white. See text for further background.*

45 *Segen, Israeli Armoured Corps, 1973.* **This** *1st*

Lieutenant wears the olive tank suit which seems to have been universal in the Yom Kippur War, with British web belt, dusty black high-lacing 'paratrooper' boots, and black beret. Bronze corps badge pinned through red cloth. Khaki shoulder strap slip-over with two green rank bars. He carries a machine-gun ammo box. Note slanted zips of chest pockets; vertical zip at inner edge of left thigh pocket. The right thigh pocket has a horizontal zip across the top.

46 *Desátnik, Czechoslovakian tank troops, 1977. Soviet-pattern helmet and overalls in black fabric. Two white metal buttons of this rank – roughly, Corporal – on black patch above the single right breast pocket. Note APDS round, and light buff straps of helmet chin-flaps and throat microphone yoke.*

47 *Maggiore, Italian 15th Recce Group 'Cavalleggeri di Lodi', 1974. Black beret with gold cavalry badge and gold ranking; the latter, a single star in a 'box', is repeated on both shoulder straps as an open metal slide, the star moulded with the rim in one piece. White national stars on collar points. Red/black halved regimental scarf. Pale khaki webbing belt and holster, the former British 1937 pattern, the latter the small pattern for the Beretta automatic. US-style double buckle boots. The Italian camouflaged combat uniform was replaced by one in brownish olive shortly after this date.*

48 *Feldwebel, Panzerjäger troops, Bundeswehr, 1976. Brown beret of AFV units other than battle tanks, with printed cloth national insignia of a cockade above grey sabres. Standard tank overall, with ranking patch below national flash on both sleeves.*

49 *2nd Lieutenant, Queen's Royal Irish Hussars, 1974. Standard tank denims, with ranking slip-over on shoulder straps. Dark blue beret, with regimental cap badge in gold and silver wire for officers, and emerald green silk ribbon headband. Green regimental scarf. Standard headset and microphone, the cables uniting in 'chest plate' slung round neck on khaki strap. Khaki ankle puttees. Dark green webbing belt.*

50 *Korporaal* 1e *klasse, Dutch tank regiment 'Huzaren Prins Alexander', 1975. Black beret with silver cavalry cap badge on regimentally coloured cloth patch. Dark green tank overall, with yellow braid ranking on brown shoulder strap slip-overs. Cavalry-coloured scarf. The hair length is unusually moderate by Dutch army standards . . .*

51 *Serzhant, Motor Rifle APC unit, Soviet Army, 1978. This painting is taken from a photo supposedly showing an exercise in the field. The addition of walking-out dress shoulder boards and left arm patch is unexplained in these circumstances; though normal enough for a full dress parade with the vehicles, it seems unlikely for an exercise, and may be simply a feature of a posed propaganda shot. This NCO is the commander of a unit of BMP-76PB armoured personnel carriers within a Soviet armoured division. Such crews are drawn from the Motor Rifle branch, but wear tank clothing when in the vehicle. He wears the latest two-piece black tank suit of the Soviet Army; note the turret number of his vehicle painted on the brow pad of the helmet. Rank is indicated by three gold bars across the shoulder board, which has the Army's 'CA' cypher at the end. The red and gold of the Motor Rifles also appear in the branch of service patch on the left sleeve. In tank units the shoulder boards and patch would be black with gold features.*

The Commonwealth

Australia

The Australian Armoured Corps had a rather anti-climatic career in the Second World War. From tiny beginnings it was built up to a considerable strength and dispersed around Australia to guard against the expected Japanese invasion. As the threat receded these armoured units were generally disbanded and the personnel assigned to other types of unit, since there was no real need for large numbers of tanks in the Pacific island campaign.

The three Australian divisions first raised for overseas service, the 6th, 7th and 9th, each included a Divisional Reconnaissance (later, Cavalry) Regiment. The cavalry regiments of the 6th and 9th Divisions fought in the North African campaign with diverse equipment including Stuarts and Crusaders, and captured French Renault R35s and Italian M13/40s, apart from Universal Carriers and odd Vickers light tanks. They wore regulation tropical KD with the black RAC beret, and British style ranking; in most orders of dress they were only

South African armoured personnel sightseeing in Egypt, 1941-42. Note large bonnet-type black beret with broad cloth headband. The others wear the South African 'polo' sun helmet and khaki drill one-piece overalls.

identifiable by their cap badge, which was the national design – a crown on a broad semi-circular sunburst over a scroll, in bronze. On the khaki BD blouse the cavalry regiments wore shoulder patches of divisional shape (a horizontal rectangle for the 6th; a disc for the 9th in 1941, changed to a squat T-shape in 1942) in equal vertical stripes of brown, red and green, always within a narrow grey border round the edge of the patch.

The Aussies went home after Second Alamein and from 1943 onwards fought in the islands, and New Guinea in particular. Operating in virtually independent squadrons under the overall command of 4th Australian Armoured Brigade, the Matildas of 1st Australian Tank Battalion and 2/4th Armoured Regiment fought in the close support role on New Guinea and Bougainville. The 2/9th Armoured Regiment and the 2/1st Armoured Brigade Reconnaissance Squadron also fought in Borneo, with gun- and flamethrower-armed Matildas. From photos it seems clear that crews in this theatre generally wore standard jungle green shirts and slacks, with a khaki cloth beret. Some photos suggest that this was sometimes worn without a badge.

Canada

Canada raised in all 32 armoured car and tank regiments during the war, the traditional territorial regiments being given numbers from one to 32.

Canadian tank regiments – representative cap badges: (top left) Fort Garry Horse – gold maple leaf, remainder silver; (top right) British Columbia Dragoons – gold; (bottom left) Governor General's Foot Guards – silver; (bottom right) Three Rivers Regiment – gold crown and foliage, central device silver (Mike Chappell).

These units played a major part in the campaigns in Italy and north-west Europe. The major formations were two armoured brigades operating independently, the 1st and 2nd Canadian Army Tank Brigades, renamed Armoured Brigades from summer 1943; and the 4th and 5th Canadian Armoured Divisions. The first unit to see action was the 13th Armoured Regiment, the Calgary Regiment, from 1st Canadian Army Tank Brigade, which suffered heavy casualties at Dieppe in August 1942. The brigade went on to fight in Sicily in July 1943, in Italy from September 1943 to February 1945, and in north-west Europe from February to March 1945. The 2nd Armoured Brigade landed in Normandy on D-Day and fought in this theatre until VE Day. The 4th Armoured Division landed in Normandy in July 1944 and fought through the European campaign until the end of the war; and the 5th Armoured Division fought in Italy in 1943-44, transferring to the Netherlands in February-March 1945.

The tank regiments of these formations were as follows:

1st Armoured Brigade: 11th Armoured Regiment – Ontario Regiment; 12th Armoured Regiment – Three Rivers Regiment; 13th Armoured Regiment – Calgary Regiment.

2nd Armoured Brigade: 6th Armoured Regiment – 1st Hussars; 10th Armoured Regiment – Fort Garry Horse; 27th Armoured Regiment – Sherbrooke Fusiliers.

4th Armoured Brigade, 4th Armoured Division: 21st Armoured Regiment – Governor General's Foot Guards; 22nd Armoured Regiment – Canadian Grenadier Guards; 28th Armoured Regiment – British Columbia Regiment.

5th Armoured Brigade, 5th Armoured Division: 2nd Armoured Regiment – Lord Strathcona's Horse; 5th Armoured Regiment. – 8th Princess Louise's (New Brunswick) Hussars; 9th Armoured Regiment – British Columbia Dragoons.

Canadian uniform was almost identical to British. The material used for battledress was of a better quality, and of an 'almond' green shade – notably greener than British khaki, and much sought after by British personnel. The black RAC beret was worn with regimental badges, a selection of which are illustrated here. The rank badges were identical to British insignia. The rimless RAC steel helmet was worn, and in the last winter of the war, the 1943 British 'zoot suit'. Coloured formation signs were worn on the upper sleeves of battledress. That of the 1st Army Tank Brigade was originally (1942) a black rectangle bearing a yellow maple leaf charged with a black ram. In 1943 this changed to a black diamond, with the horizontal dimension longer than the vertical, with a broad red horizontal central stripe. The sign of the 2nd Brigade was the same shape, with a blue central stripe. The 4th Armoured Division wore a plain green rectangle, and the 5th, a red rectangle.

The author has seen a poor quality colour photo of 1944 vintage which purports to show a Canadian-crewed Cromwell tank in north-west Europe; the visible crew members all appear to wear red berets. Further research has been fruitless: if any reader can shed light on this the author would be delighted to hear from him.

India

The history of the mechanisation (first in name and then, some long time afterwards, in fact) of the Indian cavalry is a long and complicated one, and has no real place here. Certain Indian regiments did serve in Iraq, Persia, East Africa and Egypt as 'armoured car' units, but their equipment consisted very largely of trucks and Universal Carriers. The following remarks are limited to those tanks and armoured car units which actually saw action in the reconquest of Burma.

Various armoured divisions came and went on paper, but in physical fact the brigade was the highest armoured command level to have any reality in the jungle fighting of 1944-45. The Stuarts of 7th Light Cavalry fought with 254 Indian Tank

Left *Men of the Royal Deccan Horse being inspected by General Auchinleck at Imphal, 1944, wear light tropical shirts and slacks, probably in faded 'jungle green', with black on khaki 'R.D.H.' shoulder strap slip-overs. Webbing is dark green, as are the turbans worn by the three Sikhs. Third from left wears an intriguing shoulder patch which is tantalisingly hard to make out. It appears to be a bull's or buffalo's head, full face, superimposed on a section of track in dark on lighter colours, the track receding in perspective. This insignia is unknown to the author, but it immediately recalls the 'tracks' of 254 Indian Tank Brigade, and the buffalo skull insignia of HQ 44th Indian Armoured Division* (General C. Pert).

Brigade at Imphal, alongside the Grants and Lees of the 3rd Carabiniers and 'C' Squadron, 150th Regiment, RAC. On the Kohima front the 11th PAVO Cavalry had Daimler armoured cars, and 45th Cavalry had Stuarts. After the repulse of the Japanese Arakan offensive, General Slim launched his own drive across the Chindwin in December 1944. IV Corps had 255 Indian Tank Brigade in support, comprising 5th Probyn's Horse, 9th Royal Deccan Horse, 7th and 16th Light Cavalry, and a British contribution in the formidable form of 116th Regiment, RAC (Gordon Highlanders). The support for XV Corps in the Arakan was provided by 50 Indian Tank Brigade with 19th KGO Lancers and 45th Cavalry, alongside 146th Regiment, RAC (Duke of Wellington's). The armoured brigade of XXXIII Corps was 254 Indian Tank, with the armoured cars of 11th PAVO Cavalry acting as eyes and ears for the tanks of 3rd Carabiniers, and 149th (KOYLI) and 150th (Yorks and Lancs) Regiments, RAC.

Indian armoured regiments were uniformed almost identically to those British units with which they were brigaded. The jungle green battledress blouse and slacks seem to have been regulation, and the blouse lasted a lot longer among Indian crews than among their British comrades; it is well in evidence in photos of the 1945 fighting. Rolled shirtsleeve order is also to be seen, usually on officers, or troops out of the front line; and one-piece khaki drab working dungarees were also pressed into service as fighting dress. Ranking was worn on both sleeves of the BD blouse by enlisted men, but normally on the right sleeve only of the shirt. Officers wore slip-overs in various khaki shades on the shoulder straps, bearing British ranking. Viceroy's Commissioned Officers – ie, Indian officers – wore British ranking, with an additional insignia at the outer end of the slip-

Left *A Stuart crew of 'B' Squadron, 7th Indian Light Cavalry in Burma, 1944-45. All wear the regimental badge on black berets. The right-hand man wears jungle green shirt and slacks; two others, the jungle green tropical BD blouse and slacks, rarely seen among British troops but often among Indians. The left foreground figure wears one-piece khaki denim overalls* (H. Travis).

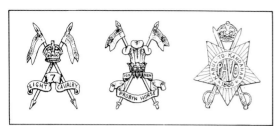

Representative Indian Army cap badges: (left to right) 7th Light Cavalry – silver; Probyn's Horse – silver; Prince Albert Victor's Own Cavalry – gold (Mike Chappell).

overs: one red stripe edged gold for *jemadars*, and two stripes for *risaldars*. Black-on-khaki shoulder titles in the British manner – eg, 'R.D.H.' for Royal Deccan Horse – were worn at the extreme end of the shoulder straps, but were often discarded in the front line. Regimentally coloured alternative patterns were known.

Headgear varied according to squadron. Indian cavalry regiments were recruited by squadrons from the 'martial races', and Sikh squadrons wore the *puggri* (turban) instead of the black berets worn by other sub-units. Captain Harry Travis, to whom the author is indebted for access to contemporary photos, recalls that in 7th Indian Light Cavalry 'A' Squadron was composed of Jats, 'B' of Punjabi Mussalmans, 'C' of Sikhs, and 'HQ' was mixed. The Sikh *puggri* was white in some regiments, dark green in others, and was worn without a badge. 'Beret' squadrons wore regimental badges in brass, silver, or a mixture of the two; officers wore embroidered bullion badges.

Webbing equipment was of the usual British 1937 pattern; shoulder braces and anklets seem to have been worn more often than among British units.

New Zealand

The New Zealand Divisional Cavalry Regiment, NZAC, operated with Universal Carriers and Marmon-Herrington armoured cars in the 1941 Greek campaign. In the Western Desert they acquired Stuart tanks in place of the Marmon-Herringtons; and in Italy in 1943 they operated Staghounds. After the controversial failure of British armour, in the desert battles of mid-1942, to protect the infantry of 2nd NZ Division effectively – largely due to lack of communication, let it be added – the New Zealand government withdrew one of the division's infantry brigades (the 4th, comprising 18th, 19th and 20th Battalions) for retraining as an armoured brigade. 4th NZ Armoured Brigade, with these three numbered battalions, was back with the division in time for the Italian invasion, equipped with Shermans.

Uniforms were virtually identical to the British

RAC crews in the same theatres – khaki battledress and tropical KD, with black berets. At the very beginning of the war the Divisional Cavalry regiment wore a slouch hat (of conventional shape, *not* the famous 'lemon-squeezer') with a *puggri* in khaki/green/khaki – the colours of the old NZ Mounted Rifles regiment. The beret appeared in January 1940, officially for wear strictly when working on the vehicles or in action, but it was soon to become everyday headgear. The cap badge was a crowned wreath containing 'NZ', all over a scroll, in brass or bronze. The other insignia were all of British pattern. A black slip-over with white lettering 'NEW' over 'ZEALAND' was worn on shirt and BD shoulder straps, but not usually on the greatcoat. Working dungarees in various brown and khaki shades were worn for dirty jobs.

A single squadron of Valentines supported 3rd NZ Division in the Solomons in 1943.

South Africa

Although the South African Tank Corps was formed in 1940, the Union's contribution to Allied armour was mainly in the form of armoured car companies until 1943. The 1st, 2nd and 3rd Armoured Car Companies of 1st Battalion, SA Tank Corps, all served in East Africa in January-May 1941, and moved to Egypt in May. (There was also a light tank company, with obsolete equipment, but this seems to have played little part in the fighting.) The 1st, 2nd and 3rd Armoured Car Companies were formed into the 3rd Reconnaissance Battalion, which operated with 1st South African Division until late 1942. The 7th Reconnaissance Battalion, one of several extra units formed from the South African territorial organisation during 1941, served with 2nd SA Division, and was lost with its parent formation at Tobruk in June 1942. The 4th and 6th Armoured Car Regiments, amalgamated into the 4th/6th Regiment shortly before Alamein, served with British 1st Armoured Division.

In late 1942 the South African contingent returned home on leave, and a major reorganisation took place. The Tank Corps was disbanded, and the armoured car units were broken up and absorbed by new units then forming. The 6th South African Armoured Division was raised during 1943, and went to the Italian Front in April 1944, where it served under US 5th Army and fought with distinction until VE-Day. The armoured element, equipped with Shermans and Fireflies, was 11th SA Armoured Brigade comprising three regiments: Prince Alfred's Guard, the Pretoria Regiment, and the Special Service Battalion Regiment (*sic*). The reconnaissance regiment was the Natal Mounted Rifles.

South African troops wore basically British

Working up with the Grant during the winter of 1942/43, this South African Captain seems to wear the denim version of battledress over a long khaki sweater. Note full webbing harness, and orange tally under outer pip on shoulder strap slip-overs. He is seen here with a Captain of the 14th/20th Hussars whose greatcoat, of dashing cut, bears cavalry yellow piping not just around the shoulder straps but also around the collar front and bottom edges, and the tops of the deep cuff turn-backs.

uniform with minor variations. In the desert the khaki drill shirt, shorts and slacks were worn, with khaki battledress, sweater and greatcoat for cold weather; in Italy, the battledress was normal for winter and khaki drill shirt and slacks for summer. Shorts were noticeably briefer than the voluminous British style. Webbing was of British pattern, scrubbed almost white; an unusual item sometimes seen in the desert, although generally discarded by 1944, was a longer type of web anklet with three buckled straps.

Headgear of armoured crews comprised either the black beret, the steel helmet, the South African 'polo' pith helmet, or the khaki SD cap for officers. The beret seems from photos to have varied in size, some troops wearing the normal British style and others – sometimes within the same crew – wearing

a much larger type like an Irish bonnet. Regimental cap badges were worn by the tank regiments in 1943-45; some are illustrated here. The SA Tank Corps badge was the normal insignia of the armoured car units in the desert, although the 4th wore a large silver Roman 'IV'; generally, cap badges were larger than was the British fashion. The pith helmet sometimes sported a cap badge on the front, at the top of the *puggri*, and in the field a sun-curtain was often improvised and worn tucked under the back of the helmet. The formation sign of 6th SA Armoured Division was a yellow triangle, point up, outlined bright green; this was usually worn on the upper sleeves of the BD blouse, even in the front line, and also appeared on a light khaki slip-on tab on the shoulder straps in some cases. Ranking was as for the British Army. All SA personnel wore an orange stripe sewn at the outer end of the shoulder straps of the battledress blouse, and very frequently on the shirt also. The laced ankle boots were of brown leather.

France

The French tank force went into the May 1940 campaign fatally dispersed; split between infantry support duties in the *Divisions Cuirassées*, and 'cavalry' duties in the *Divisions Légères de Cavalerie* and *Divisions Légères Mécaniques*, they were unable to bring their overall superiority in numbers, and partial superiority in equipment, to bear on the fast-moving Panzer Divisions.

Their combat uniforms remained very much as described in Part 2. The majority wore the 1935 khaki-painted tank helmet, but some older models with top comb and single chinstrap are believed to have been in service. The single-breasted brown leather coat was worn by the bulk of the crews; but again, the old black double-breasted type had

Representative South African cap badges: (left to right) Special Service Battalion – silver, after change to armoured role in 1942; Pretoria Regiment – gold; SA Tank Corps 1941-42 – silver (Mike Chappell).

not been phased out entirely during the rapid prewar mobilisation of the French forces. There is an impression that the older gear was more likely to be seen among the cavalry *Auto-Mitrailleuses* units than among the *Chars de Combat*, but the author is unsure how much weight can be put on this. Legwear when in the vehicles was still either the baggy, ankle-strapped *pantalon cachou*, or the straight, coarse denim working overall trousers – the latter generally in khaki but probably still in dark blue in isolated cases. The belt and holster were unchanged. The canteen would by 1940 have been covered in khaki cloth in virtually all cases. A gas mask haversack in pale greenish khaki webbing with a fawn leather fastening strap and a coarse greenish slinging strap would be worn at all times by all ranks – when regulations were observed . . .

During the winter of 1939-40 the three-battalion regiments of tanks had been split up into a pool of independent battalions, and the collar patches changed to show the battalion number. Battalions were re-assembled into Groups of Tank Battalions (*GBCs*), and battalion numbers seem to have borne no relationship to the old regimental association: eg, the *511eGBC* now consisted of the *3e*, *9e*, *37e* and *51e* Battalions, and crews wore these numbers on their collar patches in ash-grey on khaki. When hostilities began in earnest patches were normally removed from the leather coat, but not invariably. Ranking was still worn on buttoned tabs on the front of the coat, in green and silver bars on khaki tabs – although the old black tabs were very often observed still in use in 1940.

Some of the cavalry armoured car units were posted to Reconnaissance Groups, which were light, mobile, mixed-arm forces assembled at the outbreak of war from many units and attached to higher formations. Armoured car crews of Army Corps Recce Groups would (officially) have worn dark blue collar patches with triple white edge piping and white unit numbers: Divisional Recce Groups wore triple green piping and green numbers.

Free French armour
The 'orphaned' French units in Africa which continued the fight alongside the British 8th Army wore their prewar uniforms until they wore out, and then a mixture of British BD and KD, old French items from stores in Syria, and their pre-war headgear and some insignia; it was a chaotic period, and no useful generalisations can be made. After the incorporation of French troops in Algeria, Tunisia and Morocco into the Allied armies in 1943, the US Army took over the equipment and clothing

This Free French Stuart tank crew in Italy, 1944, wear the US leather tank helmet over the olive drab wool 'beanie', and M1941 Mackinaw jackets with olive wool shawl collars (ECPA).

of French forces, just as the British provided for the Poles, Dutch, Czechs and Belgians. Tank and armoured car units of the famous *2eDB* – the *'Division Leclerc'*, standard-bearers of French homecoming in the invasion of summer 1944 – seem to have worn basic American uniform with their own headgear and ranking. This normally meant, in practice, the light grey-green OD herringbone twill one-piece overalls. In contemporary photos of both the *2eDB* and the other Free French divisions in the south of France and Italy it is rare to find crewmen wearing the US tanker's windcheater jacket over these overalls; it was a sought-after item in the American forces, and probably could not be spared in numbers. The usual substitute in French service was the 1941 US Army field jacket, in light sandy drab. Photos accompanying this chapter show some alternatives, including mackinaws with shawl collars faced with blanket material, and leather jackets. The US leather tank crash helmet was normally worn, and the US steel helmet by crews of open-topped vehicles. French 1935 vehicle helmets were sometimes worn, particularly by officers.

Out of combat the headgear reflected French traditions. In the *2eDB* the Sherman crews of the *501eRCC* wore black British berets with their old silver French branch badge. Those of the *12e Cuirassiers* wore dark blue French sidecaps with a madder red centre gusset. Tank destroyer crews of the *Fusiliers-Marins* kept their sailors' bonnets, in navy blue with red pompons, white cord chinstraps, and white cap-tally lettering; their senior Petty Officers and Officers wore the navy blue

Free French M10 tank destroyer crewmen of the 9e Chasseurs d'Afrique wear US leather tank helmets and OD fatigue trousers with interesting waist-length leather jackets of uncertain origin: 1e Division Blindé, near St Tropez, August 1944 (Steven Zaloga).

Mixture of French and US items worn by two Free French officers in Italy, 1944. (Left) Colonel Bonjour, commander of the Groupement Blindé and the 3e Spahis Algeriens wears the French 1935 tank helmet with five rank bars painted on the brow pad, the US one-piece herringbone twill overall in light OD, US webbing and gaiters, and his French ranking and regimental badge on the front of his overall. (Right) Colonel Van Heoki of the 7e Chasseurs d'Afrique, 3rd Algerian Division, wears a steel helmet, a twill overall with exposed buttons, and high-lacing boots. His personal equipment is a mixture of US and German, and he too wears his ranking and his regimental badge on the front of his overall (Imperial War Museum).

peaked cap with prewar naval insignia. All ranks usually wore a dark blue square patch on the left upper arm, with crossed red foul anchors. The *12e Chasseurs d'Afrique* wore light blue sidecaps with a yellow gusset, and the *1er Regiment de Marche de Spahis Marocaine* wore all-red sidecaps. In the 1st French Army the light armoured regiment of the Foreign Legion wore their famous white-covered képis whenever practical: those of NCOs and officers were midnight blue with red tops and conventional lace in dark blue and silver respectively; a silver seven-flamed grenade was the front badge. Officers and Warrant Officers sometimes wore a dark green sidecap with a dark blue gusset. Ranking was worn on all these sidecaps *en chevron* on the front of the crown, usually in the form of silver stripes but in gold for Spahis.

Ranking practice as a whole was rather chaotic in Free French units. Officially it should have been worn on both upper arms by NCOs in the form of the short diagonals of dark brown and the corps 'metal' worn on the forearms in 1940; officers normally wore their stripes on black backing in the form of slip-overs at the base of the shoulder straps. In fact one sees many examples of NCOs wearing ranking in the form of small chevrons, point inwards, on shoulder strap slip-overs, and many officers wearing chest tabs and no shoulder ranking. (In both the Combat Tank regiments and

the Legion, green replaced brown in the junior NCOs' ranking.) An interesting photo of a *brigadier-chef* commanding a *2e DB* Stuart M5A1 tank during the liberation of Paris, and therefore presumably a soldier of the *12e Chasseurs d'Afrique*, shows the light grey-green herringbone twill overall with one silver and two brown diagonals high on the left arm, and just below it what appears to be an old prewar collar patch in dark blue with yellow double piping at the top edge and a yellow '12' – assuming the colour from the light shade and the probable unit identification. Typical ranking for a naval Petty Officer commanding an M-10 tank destroyer in the same operation would be a dark blue shoulder strap slip-over with three small red chevrons pointing to the neck, identifying a *Quartier Maitre 1e Classe*.

Germany
Army tank and armoured car crews
The crews of Germany's Panzer units entered the Second World War wearing the uniform described

in Part 2: the black double beret or *Schutzmütze*, the short black crossover jacket, and long black trousers gathered at the ankle over marching boots. During the Polish campaign of 1939 the only deviation from the uniform previously described was the progressive abandonment of the regimental number on the shoulder straps. This was impractical in a war situation, given the necessity to move men from unit to unit, and was also, clearly, bad security in a combat zone. Increasingly these numbers were omitted from the shoulder straps, and only worn in rear areas. The metal cyphers of NCOs and officers could obviously be pinned on or removed at will; enlisted men generally had the number embroidered on small cloth loops which were slipped over the shoulder strap when desired.

The first major change came with the abandonment of the black 'beret' during the winter of 1939/40. As not infrequently happens, an item of uniform which seems suitable on paper, and in service under peacetime conditions, proved impractical under battlefield conditions. It was rather unwieldy at the best of times, was particularly awkward when wearing a radio headset, and offered little practical protection. With the fitting of intercom radio in PzKpfw III and IV vehicles, and the consequent need for all crew members to wear headsets, it was decided to abandon the beret in favour of a black sidecap. It was to be many months before the black sidecap was available in sufficient numbers, and in the meantime the field grey sidecap of the standard Army service dress was often worn. The 1940 campaigns in France and the Low Countries saw the *Schutzmütze* and the grey sidecap both in use simultaneously, and one or two photographs suggest that in isolated cases the beret, the grey sidecap and the black sidecap were in simultaneous use in Poland in 1939. The black side caps in these pictures are worn by officers — it is quite feasible that officers' privately purchased uniform items would be in use far sooner than enlisted mens' issue items. Photographic evidence does show, however, that the *Schutzmütze* continued to be worn in the Balkans and Russia to as late as 1942.

The sidecap was of conventional Army cut, whether in grey or black. It had a deep turn-up all the way round, with a scooped lower section at the front. A small cloth eagle and swastika badge was worn on the front of the crown, and a national cockade on a diamond-shaped patch was sewn immediately below this on the front of the turn-up. The grey cap had a light grey on grey-green eagle and the cockade on a grey-green diamond. It is possible, but not confirmed by photographs known

to the author, that the normal inverted chevron of *Waffenfarbe* piping may have been worn on the front of the turn-up, in the pink appropriate to Panzer troops. The black sidecap had a white or light grey eagle badge (from 1941, increasingly, the latter), and the backing of both badges was black. The pink chevron was certainly worn on the black sidecap by all ranks. Officers' sidecaps, both grey and black, were of finer material, and had silver piping around the crown seam and around the edge of the 'scoop' at the front of the turn-up. Their eagle insignia were silver, and their national cockades were woven in the form of a raised boss.

At the same time as the *Schutzmütze* was discontinued, crews were ordered to draw steel helmets. These were painted in the usual dull grey, with the national decals on each side – a silver-grey eagle and swastika, with folded wings, on a black shield, worn on the left side, and a tricolour black-white-red shield on the right side. (Generally the steel helmets of armoured crews tended to retain the decals later than those of infantry, who

Described, but rarely photographed: an excellent study of the 'Armoured Pioneer' variation on the black Panzer uniform, with mixed black/white twist Waffenfarbe. *This* Oberfeldwebel, *photographed in Russia in 1941, wears helmet decals, a wound badge, and collar and tie; the MP40 adds a more warlike note* (Bundesarchiv).

Excellent study of an Oberfeldwebel *(Centre) and a* Leutnant *(right) of the Panzer Regiment* Grossdeutschland *– the shoulder strap monograms, and the NCO's cuff-title, are just visible. The NCO wears a jacket with the original pink collar piping, and a* Feldmütze *with a pink inverted chevron. His decorations include the General Assault badge, the Iron Cross 1st Class and the ribbon of the Winter 1941 Russian Front medal in his buttonhole. The officer has a cap without the pink chevron, and a jacket without collar piping. His decorations include the War Order of the German Cross, the sunburst just visible beneath his right breast eagle; the Iron Cross 1st Class; the General Assault badge; a wound badge; and a pre-1933 Sports Badge. All this strongly indicates that this man is a former ranker promoted after considerable front-line service (ECPA).*

removed or obscured them, for obvious reasons, soon after the Russian campaign opened.) Early in 1941 it was ordered that henceforward the long marching boots would not be issued to armoured crews, and that ankle-length laced boots would replace them, worn with short canvas webbing gaiters. Photos show that many troopers who already had marching boots clung on to them for at least two years after this order, and that both types were to be seen worn side by side throughout the Panzer arm until the last year of the war. The gaiters seem to have been largely ignored, and those crewmen who received ankle boots either bloused the trousers into them, or gathered them

over the boots; they were normally cut long enough to allow this.

As early as the Polish campaign, some officers had favoured wearing field grey peaked caps with the black Panzer uniform. These were increasingly seen as time passed, and were of two types. The less common was the standard service dress *Schirmmütze*; of the familiar high-fronted shape, this had a stiffened field grey crown, a dark green band, and a shiny black peak. Two silver cords were worn across the front, attached to the chinstrap buttons at each side. The crown seam and the top and bottom edges of the band were piped in pink. On the front of the crown was worn an eagle and swastika badge, usually pressed in silver-grey alloy but sometimes of woven silver wire on a dark green cloth backing. On the front of the band was a heavy, elaborate silver wire oak wreath device with the national cockade worn as a raised metal boss in the centre. More popular than the slightly unwieldy *Schirmmütze*, in the confines of an armoured vehicle, was the smaller, softer *Offizierfeldmütze älterer Art* – 'old style officer's field cap'. This was of similar shape to the *Schirmmütze* but was smaller in outline and unstiffened, with a peak either of field grey cloth or – commonly – of unstiffened black leather. It had a field grey crown, a dark green band, and the same pink piping as the service cap; however, it lacked the silver cords, and both insignia were in flat cloth finish, embroidered in silver thread on patches of dark green. Very occasionally one finds photos of officers wearing this cap with the addition of the silver cords. It was extremely common among tank officers right through the war, despite being officially withdrawn in April 1942.

To re-cap, then, on the appearance of Panzer troops in the initial stages of the Russian campaign in summer 1941: all ranks wore the black uniform over a grey shirt and black tie, with either marching boots or laced boots. Collars were piped pink; recently issued enlisted mens' jackets had light grey breast eagle insignia, but most would still have white, and officers, silver. Most officers would wear either the black sidecap with silver insignia and piping and pink chevron, or the 'old style officer's field cap'. Rankers would normally wear the black sidecap with white or light grey eagle badge and pink chevron, but in some cases would still have the field grey sidecap, and in isolated instances, the black 'beret'.

For winter wear at this stage of the war, tank crews were issued with the standard Army greatcoat – a field grey garment with a deep falling collar of dark green, double-breasted, with two rows of six silver-grey metal buttons on the chest. Shoulder straps and sleeve rank chevrons, if any, would be worn on this coat.

For working dress around the vehicle in dirty weather, for maintenance duties, and, in many instances, for an extra or alternative battle outfit, a variety of denim-type overalls were worn. Sometimes these were worn instead of the black uniform, sometimes in combination with it, and sometimes over it. The first issued seem to have been old sets of pre-war drill clothing, dyed reed green. These comprised single-breasted jackets with five buttons, slit skirt pockets, and small collars, with plain, straight trousers. One-piece overalls from Czech stocks also seem to have been issued to some units in 1941 – these were light neutral khaki or stone in colour, with a medium sized falling collar; there were two patch pockets with pointed flaps and plastic buttons on the chest, and slash side and patch hip pockets on the trouser part. Brown plastic buttons closed the front from neck to crotch. These loose-cut suits have been photographed worn by Panzer crews who had added breast eagles, shoulder straps, and even collar patches to them. It is certain that a wide miscellany of other overalls and 'boiler suits' were pressed into service, from obsolete or captured stocks of various origins, for use during dirty jobs.

A variation on the black uniform, ordered in May 1940 but probably fairly short-lived, was worn by

Superb portrait of a Panzer commander: Hauptmann *Walter Scherff, commanding officer of* 3. Kompanie, schwere Panzer Abteilung 503, *a PzKpfw VI Tiger battalion formed in 1942 from Panzer Regiments 5 and 6. Photographed in Russia early in 1944, Scherff wears the* Ritterkreuz *which he was awarded on February 23 that year, and the War Order of the German Cross. The battalion later served in Normandy* (ECPA).

men of *Panzer-Pioniere* companies – the integral armoured recovery and repair element in tank regiments. They were ordered to replace the pink piping around the collar, the collar patches, and on the sidecap with a mixed black/white piping.

The year 1942 saw the beginning of the abandonment of the pink piping round the collar of the black jacket, although it was retained on the collar patches. The pink chevron also began to disappear from the black sidecap. This discontinuation of collar piping, like all the other changes of dress ordered during the war, was extremely slow and inconsistent in the observance; old stocks would normally be used up before new items were issued, if available, and some stubborn individualists and units simply ignored such changes; various styles may therefore be seen in simultaneous use late in the war.

At this time a new type of cap began to be seen; the *Feldmütze* 1942 does not appear from photographic evidence to have been very widespread in issue, as it was superseded the following year. It was a version of the black sidecap with the scooped front of the turn-up divided and fixed with two small grey metal buttons, allowing the turn-up to be folded down around the face in cold weather. The national eagle and cockade badges were worn one above the other on the front of the crown section on this cap. It had rather broader dimensions than the sidecap proper, being in effect a 'peakless ski-cap'.

In 1942 a measure of uniformity began to appear in the matter of working and summer combat denim clothing. A new two-piece reed green denim suit, cut in the same style as the black uniform, began to appear in large numbers, and was increasingly seen in the front lines. It differed in small details from batch to batch, but a common version had a patch pocket on the left breast, either vertical or set at a slight inwards angle, with a pointed flap fastened by a plastic button. The loose trousers had a small pocket, again with a buttoned flap, on the front of the right hip, and a larger one low on the left thigh just above the knee. Shoulder straps, collar patches and breast eagles could all be seen applied to this suit in the latter half of the war.

During 1942 the formation of the 24th Panzer Division from the old 1st Cavalry Division was marked by an order that the armoured crews of that formation should wear golden-yellow cavalry *Waffenfarbe* in place of pink on collars, collar patches and caps. The collar piping was ordered discontinued at the same time as the pink piping of other units.

In the winter of 1942, the greatcoat, an unsatisfactory garment for men living and working in the cramped confines of armoured vehicles, was replaced with the German Army's padded, reversible winter combat suit. This heavy, generously cut uniform consisted of a long double-breasted jacket with attached hood, and straight trousers. It was completely reversible, and had a drawstring waist and two slanted, flapped pockets in the skirts. The front flap, offset to the right, was closed by metal buttons. Initial issues were white on one side and mouse grey on the other; the grey was later replaced by the two camouflage patterns adopted for all German Army camouflage clothing. The angular 'splinter' scheme in dark brown, dark green and light green, with a 'rain' overpattern of dark green, was later replaced by the softer-edged 'water' pattern of tan, dark green, dark brown and snuff brown with a light green 'rain' overpattern.

In the infantry, coloured cloth bands could be buttoned round the upper arms of the reversible jacket as temporary field signs. In the Panzer arm such details were seldom necessary. The only

Posing between a Bulgarian officer and private, this dashing young Oberstleutnant *of the Panzer Regiment* Grossdeutschland *wears the peaked 1943* Einheitsfeldmütze, *with two small silver front buttons, and silver officer's crown piping. Note cuff-title, decorations, jacket without collar piping and roll-neck sweater (ECPA).*

insignia normally seen on the reversible jacket among tank troops was the stylised rank patch introduced in August 1942 for wear with overall and camouflage-type uniforms. (This was officially worn on the reed green Panzer denims as well, but not consistently, since the popular practice of fixing the shoulder straps from the black uniform to the denims rendered it superfluous). This patch was worn on the upper left arm, and took the form of a black rectangle across almost the whole width of the arm, with ranking in the form of horizontal green bars and, for officers, horizontal pairs of green stylised oakleaves. One to five bars identified ranks from *Unteroffizier* to *Stabsfeldwebel*; one to three bars beneath one set of oakleaves, *Leutnant* to *Hauptmann*; and one to three bars beneath two sets of oakleaves, *Major* to *Oberst*.

In June 1943 the last major change in Panzer uniform was ordered. The cloth-peaked *Einheitsfeldmütze* was now to replace the sidecap throughout the German forces, and a special black version was issued to Panzer troops. It was of exactly the same shape as the field grey version worn by other arms – a 'ski-cap' with a stiffened cloth peak, and a deep turn-up 'scooped' and fastened with two small buttons at the front. It bore the national eagle above the national cockade on a triangular black backing on the front of the crown, the eagle being silver for officers and light grey for enlisted men. The officers' version was piped in silver round the crown seam, and in some cases, around the 'scoop' of the turn-up as well. The cap buttons were silver or silver-grey. Well into 1944 the side-cap was still to be seen, worn side by side with the *Einheitsfeldmütze* by officers and men of the same unit.

The German Army Panzer trooper thus ended the war wearing a uniform very similar to that in which he had begun it. The beret had been replaced by the stylish and practical 'ski-cap'; the cloth insignia were embroidered in light grey rather than white; and the collar had lost its pink piping. In practice, it must be emphasised that troops in the front line often wore a motley assortment of parts of several different uniforms, and presented the observer with an impression of anarchy. In 1944 a single crew might wear some black side-caps, some black 'ski-caps', and a peaked grey service cap for the commander; black tunics with or without collar piping, reed green denim jackets

Hungary, March 1944: a PzKpfw V Panther crew of Panzer Lehr Regiment 130 pose in their reversible winter combat uniforms of splinter/snow camouflage. Three wear felt and leather winter boots, most clearly seen on the right-hand man (ECPA).

with or without shoulder straps and collar patches; and black, reed green, grey or camouflage trousers. Officers sometimes acquired camouflage smocks, or had camouflage jackets made up to personal order.

The insignia most frequently seen on photographs of Panzer troops in the front line, and usually confined to the black jacket, were gallantry decorations and Assault Badges. The Iron Cross 2nd Class was not displayed, its ribbon only being worn, through the buttonhole at the top of the left lower lapel of the jacket. The ribbons of the War Service Cross, and the Russia Winter 1941-42 medal were also worn in this buttonhole. The pin-back Iron Cross 1st Class was worn on the left breast, low down. Tank Assault Badges, marking a varying number of separate engagements in which the wearer had participated, took the form of dull silver oval wreaths, pierced, and enclosing the stylised $\frac{3}{4}$-front view of a German tank. The details of the design varied as the war progressed. The first design, authorised in December 1940, had a small folded-wing eagle and swastika superimposed on the top edge of the wreath, and featured a stylised PzKpfw IV. From July 1943 the wreath had a small square cartouche superimposed at bottom centre bearing a number – 25, 50, 75 or 100 – signifying the total number of actions to date; the tank design changed to a more modern image, and was now shown crushing a log barricade. The final version changed the shape of the tank yet again,

giving it a longer gun and a mantlet with spaced armour; the wreath became squatter, the eagle larger, and additional oakleaves were placed in a spray at the bottom.

All ranks wore Wound Badges, where appropriate; like the Assault Badges, these appeared on the left breast. The design of the 1939 Wound Badge was a solid oval plaque edged with a wreath, bearing crossed broadswords point upwards, with a German helmet superimposed on the junction of the swords, charged with a swastika. It was awarded in black (one or two wounds), silver (three or four wounds) and gold (five or more wounds).

Holders of higher gallantry awards, usually officers, displayed them on the black uniform as follows. The sunburst star of the War Order of the German Cross, in silver or gold, with its central disc charged with a large black swastika, was worn on the right breast below the national eagle. The Knight's Cross was always worn at the throat, its ribbon passing under the shirt collar.

Cuff titles were not common among Army Panzer units, but two which are occasionally seen in photographs are the *Grossdeutschland* regimental cuff title, and the *Afrika* campaign title. The former, worn by all ranks of the tank regiment of the *Grossdeutchland* Division (later, Korps) was a 32 mm-wide black cloth cuff band worn on the right forearm, with silver edges and silver copperplate lettering. The *Afrika* cuff title was worn by veterans of the North African campaigns after returning to other fronts. It was sewn to the left forearm of the tunic; 33 mm wide, it was of a soft snuff brown with silver-grey edges, and contained the word '*Afrika*' in silver-grey between two silver-grey palm-heads.

Tropical uniforms

In North Africa, 1941-43, Panzer troops wore the same basic uniforms as all other German Army personnel. A well-known photograph of the first tank unit to arrive in the theatre parading in full black uniform should not be misinterpreted; the only part of the black uniform sometimes retained in the desert was the sidecap, seen in one or two photographs of crews otherwise dressed in tropical uniform.

The regulation uniform was an olive green four-pocket tunic with an open neck, worn over an olive shirt and tie; slightly flared olive breeches, or shorts, or long straight trousers bloused at the ankle; laced ankle boots, in either brown leather, or brown leather and olive canvas; or boots reaching to the knee, in leather and canvas, laced from instep to knee. The sunhelmet originally

A fine portrait of an officer wearing the Afrika Korps *regulation service uniform for officers. Oberst Gerhard Müller, wearing the Knight's Cross awarded to him on September 15 1942, displays the olive-coloured field cap with pink soutache and silver crown and turn-up piping; the olive tunic, with collar* Litzen *above Panzer skulls; field officers' shoulder straps with the two pips of this rank; and an array of decorations including a First World War Iron Cross 1st Class beneath the eagle clasp for a Second World War award of the same decoration (ECPA).*

issued was not popular and was seldom worn, for obvious reasons, by tank crews; it was of cork, covered with olive green cloth, and bore two large metal shield badges in the same design and colours as the decals normally worn on the steel helmet. The normal desert headgear was the well-known tropical field cap, a stylish peaked 'ski-cap' in olive cloth. An olive green, lightweight version of the sidecap was also issued and seems to have been quite widespread among vehicle crews.

Insignia on the tunic were of conventional design but in special colours. All ranks were supposed to wear a breast eagle in light blue-grey on a tan brown backing; officers occasionally replaced these with the silver-on-black eagles

A more typical view of DAK tank crewmen! This motley bunch display shirtsleeve order with shorts; the long canvas and leather laced desert boots; the tropical field cap; two examples of the black European field cap retained in the desert; and, slung on the turret (left), South African sun helmets pressed into service after capture, adorned with the pin-on national insignia from German sun helmets (ECPA).

from their black uniforms. Officers wore the pink-backed silver shoulder straps from their European uniforms, and other ranks wore olive shoulder straps on which the *Tresse* of senior NCOs was in copper brown, rather than silver. Normal pink *Waffenfarbe* piping edged these straps. Junior NCOs' left sleeve rank chevrons were also in copper brown on olive backing; and the upper lapels of the jacket were edged with brown *Tresse* for ranks from *Unteroffizier* up. All arms, Panzer included, wore the conventional *Litzen* of the German Army on the collar, in blue-grey on tan brown. Officers wore their European service dress collar *Litzen* – silver, with pink 'lights', on dark green backing. All ranks identified their arm of service by pinning the white metal death's-head from their black European collar patches directly

to the cloth of the lower jacket lapel. These death's-heads, and the pink piping on their shoulder straps, were all that distinguished Panzer troopers' tunics from other branches. The chevron of pink *Waffenfarbe* was sometimes, but not invariably, worn on the front of the tropical field cap and sidecap. The insignia on these caps were conventional – eagles and cockades – but the former was in blue-grey, and both were on tan brown backing patches. Officers had silver woven cap eagles on brown backing, silver crown piping, and the cockade in the form of a raised boss of embroidery.

Gallantry and wound decorations, and Assault Badges, were worn on the tropical jacket in the usual way. In fact, the jacket itself was very frequently discarded; in the desert the Panzer crewman's normal dress, except in the cold of night or deep winter, was a field cap, shorts, and canvas and leather 'sneakers'. Olive green shirts were worn, sometimes with uniform shoulder straps attached but without other insignia. The jacket sometimes displayed the two cuff titles issued in this theatre. The first, dating from July 1941, was worn on the right forearm; it was dark green with silver-grey inner and tan brown outer edges, and bore the word 'AFRIKAKORPS' in silver-grey. The second, issued from January 1943 to replace it, is described earlier.

The shade of 'olive green' displayed by all items of headgear and uniform varied very widely, from a true green, through every shade of khaki, to a bleached sandy yellow: field caps were often deliberately bleached.

Tropical clothing was also widely used in Sicily, Italy, the Balkans and southern Russia in the summer. Italy presents a confusing picture: Continental uniform was worn in winter, and olive tropical dress in summer, with frequent variations in the form of reed green denims, Luftwaffe tropical items in sandy yellow drill, and odd bits and pieces of Italian clothing. Reversible winter uniforms did not reach Italy until the winter of 1944-45.

Army self-propelled artillery

This is an area of uniform research fraught with confusion, due to inconsistently observed changes of regulations; an over-complexity of uniform difference between units of supposedly different functions: and a lack of precision in translations of German material. The author therefore presents his conclusions cautiously, with a warning against 'generalising from the particular', and a general rider that in actual front line practice there were certainly many exceptions to every trend.

Self-propelled artillery in the German Army fell into three main categories: SP anti-tank units, equipped with *Panzerjäger* vehicles of various marks, Marder, Nashorn, Jagdpanther, Hetzer, etc; assault artillery units, equipped with the Sturmgeschütz III and IV, Sturmhaubitze 42, etc; and SP heavy field artillery batteries, equipped with the Wespe, Hummel, etc. The distinction was blurred, and interpretation of photos made more difficult by the fact that the StuG III was increasingly pressed into use as an anti-tank weapon in the mid-war years.

The self-propelled *Panzerjäger* units seem to have worn the same black vehicle uniform and pink piping as the tank troops in the early part of the war, with the addition of a 'P' cypher on the shoulder straps in pink embroidery, white metal and gold metal according to rank. In February 1942 this was exchanged – when existing uniforms needed replacement – for the field grey version of the tank uniform. The black, pink-piped collar patches with metal death's-head were retained, as were the black, pink-piped shoulder straps with the 'P' cypher. There was no pink collar piping. Headgear comprised the field grey sidecap with normal national insignia, with or without the pink chevron;

Splendid portrait of a Sturmartillerie *senior NCO in front line uniform;* Oberwachtmeister *Richard Schramm of StuG Brigade 202, awarded the Knight's Cross on December 23 1942 for destroying a total of 44 Soviet armoured vehicles in his StuG III, which seems to bear the name 'Sea Devil' painted on the gun. Schramm wears the grey uniform of Panzer cut, with the later collar patches –* Litzen *on green or field grey patches piped red round the edge. The double bars of silver braid across the ends of the shoulder straps mark Schramm as an* Offizieran- wärter, *or aspirant for promotion to commissioned rank.*

Schirmmützen and old style officer's field caps, with pink *Waffenfarbe*; and, from mid-1943, the field grey *Einheitsfeldmütze*. Steel helmets were much worn, as these vehicles often exposed their crews to fire. In May 1944 a complex new set of regulations was issued; how widely they were obeyed is open to speculation. From this point until the end of the war, the following distinctions were officially drawn. SP anti-tank units serving under Army, Corps, or under infantry, rifle or mountain *division* command were to retain the uniform described above. SP anti-tank units under infantry, rifle or mountain *regiment* command were to wear the same field grey uniform of Panzer cut, but with conventional *Litzen* on green collar patches piped round the edge with white or green depending on the parent regiment's *Waffenfarbe*. It is to be assumed that shoulder straps of black, dark green and field grey would all have been seen in use together, piped pink, with the 'P' cypher. SP anti-tank units under command of Panzer and Panzer-Grenadier divisions, and units under Army or Corps command equipped with the Elefant heavy SP gun, were to revert to the black Panzer uniform, piped pink, with 'P' cypher on shoulder straps. Given the confusion, logistic difficulties, and shortages of the last year of the war, it seems highly unlikely that these fine distinctions were often observed in practice. The use of reed green denims and reversible winter clothing would further complicate the picture.

Assault artillery – *Sturmgeschütz* battalions – were ordered to wear, from May 1940, a field grey version of the black Panzer uniform, complete with the large beret. (It seems unlikely that it was issued in time to be worn in action by the four batteries of StuG IIIs which fought in France that May and June, although trials

A Major wearing the silver-piped officer's Feldmütze and the grey SP artillery jacket. He appears to have the shoulder strap cypher '33', and the Schwedteradler dragoon tradition badge on his cap further identifies him as serving with Aufklärungs Abteilung (Mot) 33, a reconnaissance unit of 15 Panzer Division. Of interest as well are the Knight's Cross at his throat, the Close Combat clasp on his left breast, and the Honour Roll clasp and Winter 1941 Russian Front medal ribbons in his buttonhole (ECPA).

batches may have reached the front. It was certainly in evidence in early 1941.) Initially the jacket was to have the upper lapels in dark green, with conventional *Litzen* collar patches, but in the event the jacket was issued completely in grey. Shoulder straps were of dark green with artillery red *Waffenfarbe* piping. Collar patches were of the same shape as the Panzer type, but in dark green, with silver-grey metal death's-heads and red piping round the edges. The great majority of these units seem to have worn the normal field grey sidecap, with or without red piping chevron, from the start of the Balkan and Russian campaigns until mid-1943. It had been thought that the grey version of the *Schutzmütze*, with the same eagle and wreath/cockade insignia as on the black version but in silver-grey on dark green, was never issued in quantity and never worn in action. However, a recently published photo definitely shows an NCO of the 192nd *Sturmgeschütz Abteilung* wearing the grey beret in the front lines in Russia in 1941. The other men in the photo wear sidecaps; how many berets were to be seen at the front must remain open to question. The field grey peaked *Einheitsfeldmütze* replaced the sidecap from mid-1943, but as in other branches, the two types of cap can be seen worn together in photos dating from late 1944 at least. Grey, later field grey, shirts and black ties were worn with this uniform, by all categories of gunners issued with the 'crossover' vehicle jacket.

Confusion arises with regulation changes affecting the collar patches. In 1942 the skulls were ordered removed from the patches – an order perhaps more honoured in the breach than the observance. In January 1943 the patch was ordered out of use altogether. From now on, assault artillerymen were to wear normal *Litzen* on the collar of the jacket, on grey or green backing patches edged with red piping. Officers would simply attach their normal silver braid *Litzen* from the service tunic, complete with green backing and red 'lights', to the vehicle jacket collar. From early 1943 until the end of the war, *Sturmartillerie* personnel in photographs display a mixture of the old skull patches and the new red-piped *Litzen*, apparently indiscriminately.

To indicate just how chaotic uniform practice could be in *Sturmgeschütz* units late in the war, the author – his head still reeling painfully from the discovery – need only mention a group photo which shows ten officers of *Sturmgeschütz Brigade 276* posing in the front line in November 1944, in East Prussia. Of the ten, two wear standard black Panzer uniforms with black, pink-piped collar patches bearing silver skulls, and black 1943

Einheitsfeldmützen. It is not possible to tell if a 'P' monogram is worn on the shoulder straps. Five wear grey *Sturmartillerie* uniforms of the same cut, with *Litzen* collar patches, and either grey *Schirmmützen* or *Einheitsfeldmützen*. Three wear black Panzer uniforms, *with Litzen collar patches!* Their headgear is mixed – two black *Einheitsfeldmützen*, and one grey *Schirmmütze*. The wearing of conventional *Litzen* on the collar of the black uniform is confirmed by another photo, of Hauptmann Bauszus of *Sturmgeschütz Brigade 239* at Sandomirz, Russia, in April 1944.

Yet another variation in this branch, as far as the author knows not mentioned in surviving regulations but confirmed by significant numbers of photographs of officers and men of at least three brigades in Russia, was the wearing of the black Panzer uniform with the skulls removed from the collar patches: an example is included in our colour-plates. Readers will readily appreciate that to attempt to fit all these variations into any artificially rigid code purporting to govern uniform and collar patch distribution in *Sturmgeschütz* units would be an act of folly.

The self-propelled field artillery batteries actually under the command of infantry and Panzer-Grenadier *regiments* in the infantry support rôle were now to wear the same uniform as assault artillery, but with the *Litzen* collar patches piped round the edge in white or green, depending on the parent regiment's *Waffenfarbe*.

The uniforms worn by men of field artillery batteries equipped with Wespe, Hummel and similar open-topped gun mountings are a puzzle. Lack of distinction between 'assault' and 'self-propelled' artillery in translated regulations bedevils this question. At the beginning of the Russian campaign, certainly, most photographs show such field artillery crews wearing the normal four-pocket service tunic of their comrades in other artillery units, with conventional *Litzen* on the dark green collar, and red-piped shoulder straps. As the war progressed, denim clothing was more in evidence – often the 1942 reed green denim version of the four-pocket service tunic, worn by all arms of service. In 1943 one sees in photographs occasional examples of the 'crossover' jacket worn by these crews; one, showing Wespen of the *Grossdeutschland* Division's armoured artillery regiment, has a crew dressed in 'crossover' jackets with *Litzen* – whether red-piped or not, one cannot tell – in July 1943. As 1943 wore on, and in 1944, photos increasingly show crews of Hummel and similar vehicles wearing the field grey uniform of Panzer cut with collar *Litzen*; but occasional examples of the old four-pocket service tunic are

still to be seen. By the end of the war the 'crossover' jacket was being issued to more and more categories of troops in motorised and armoured units, including some Panzer-Grenadier infantry. The four-pocket tunic was probably very little worn by SP field artillery by the beginning of 1945.

Waffen-SS tank, armoured car and SP artillery crews

At the beginning of the war – 1939-41 – the few SS armoured units of the *Leibstandarte SS 'Adolf Hitler'*, the *Reich* (later *Das Reich*) and the *Totenkopf* Divisions wore the Army's black Panzer uniform, initially with the black beret. The collar was not piped in pink. The shoulder straps were those from the field grey SS service uniform, black, with silver *Tresse* for NCOs and pink *Waffenfarbe* piping. Officers' straps had a double underlay – silver cord body, on *Waffenfarbe*, on black; and for officers the collar of the black jacket was piped silver. Normal Waffen-SS collar patches were sewn to the jacket, in the form of black lozenges, piped silver round the edge for officers. Isolated examples are known of Waffen-SS Panzer personnel wearing their collar patches with pink-piped edges. One photograph shows *Leibstandarte* armoured car personnel in the black uniform, including the padded beret, of 1939-40, with pink-piped collar patches but unpiped collars. A rare and much later example may be seen among the accompanying photographs in this chapter. Personnel of the *Leibstandarte*, *Das Reich*, and the later-formed *Wiking*, *Hohenstaufen*, *Frundsberg* and *Hitlerjugend* Division armoured regiments wore the SS runes in silver on their right collar patch, and ranking in the form of silver braid bars and white metal pips on their left patch. *Totenkopf* armoured personnel wore the silver death's-head embroidered on the right patch, and, in the case of Privates, on both patches. The tank battalion of the *Prinz Eugen* Division, which employed captured French Renault and Somua tanks against Tito's partisans, wore the divisional *Odalrune* insignia on the right patch. Personnel of the *Leibstandarte* wore an 'LAH' cypher on the shoulder straps, in pink embroidery, white metal and gold metal for enlisted men, NCOs and officers respectively. Enlisted men sometimes wore it on a slip-on loop of black cloth fixed over the shoulder strap instead.

The silver or silver-grey SS sleeve eagle was worn on the upper left arm. The black and silver cuff titles bearing the divisional name were worn on the left forearm of the black tank jacket; *Adolf Hitler* and *Hitlerjugend* in copperplate script, and the other divisions in block upper and lower case lettering. In the *Leibstandarte* only, the tank crew 'crossover' jacket bore silver *Tresse* round the upper lapels and collar for NCOs, although this does not seem to have been universal.

The black *Schutzmütze* bore a silver-grey embroidered SS death's-head, distinguished from the Army Panzer version by having a lower jaw, low on the front, with the SS version of the eagle and swastika above; this was the same shape as the arm eagle, with wings coming to a point. In 1940-41 the beret was replaced by a black version of the early SS sidecap; this had a centre gusset folded off-centre to the right, a skull-embossed silver grey button sewn to the front of the turn-up, a chevron of pink *Waffenfarbe* round the button, and a white SS eagle (silver for officers) on a black triangular backing sewn to the upper central part of the turn-up on the left side. Photos show this cap worn by armoured personnel of the '*LAH*' in Greece, 1941. Later in the year the normal Army-style black sidecap was issued, with an SS eagle high on the front of the crown and a skull on the turn-up beneath it, with or without a pink piping chevron. Officers' sidecaps were piped in silver in the Army fashion. In 1941/42 a black sidecap of distinctly SS shape appeared, and superseded the old Army pattern. This was of the same shape as the SS field grey sidecap, that is, it had a continuous turn-up with an unscooped front, exactly like the Luftwaffe sidecap. Badges were worn on it exactly as on the Army-style cap, and officers had the upper edge of the turn-up piped silver. Officers also wore either the *Schirmmütze* or the 'old style field cap'. These had field grey crowns piped pink or white*, black bands piped pink or white, and metal or woven silver SS eagle and skull insignia. Shirts were grey, and ties black.

In 1943 a black version of the *Einheitsfeldmütze* was issued, as to Army Panzer units. There seem to have been different versions; some were of Army two-button style, and some had only a single plastic button fastening the turn-up at the front. Officers' caps had silver crown seam piping. The death's-head was sometimes worn high on the front of the crown, with the SS eagle on the left side at the top centre of the turn-up. Others bore a single badge, woven on a black triangular backing, on the crown front; this comprised a small version of the eagle above a crude version of the death's-head with notably long crossbones, in white or silver-grey.

It was also in 1942-43 that a new version of the

black Panzer jacket began to appear in numbers in SS armoured units. This was a special SS version, identifiable by the collar shape. The upper and lower lapels became much smaller than on the Army jacket, and the corner of the upper lapel was rounded rather than pointed; the front closure became vertical, whereas on the Army jacket it slanted from top right to bottom left.

Waffen-SS self-propelled artillery units were not bedevilled by the changes of insignia to which Army units were subject. They wore the field grey version of the tank uniform, receiving it in 1940-41. Photos of the *Leibstandarte* in Greece in 1941 show it in use, complete with laced ankle boots and canvas web gaiters. On the other hand, a photo of a StuG III in Russia in the summer of that year shows a crew from *Das Reich* wearing the black Panzer uniform as a stop-gap. When the grey uniform was issued it bore the normal black and silver SS collar patches, and black shoulder-straps piped either red, for artillery, or pink, for *Panzerjäger* (with a 'P' cypher, as in the Army. In the élite *Leibstandarte*, NCO *Tresse* was sometimes worn round the collar by appropriate ranks. (It is believed that one SS assault gun battalion, the *Sturmgeschütz Abteilung* of the 11th SS Volunteer Panzer-Grenadier Division *Nordland*, which bore the honour title *Hermann von Salza*, wore collar patches with red-piped edges for enlisted ranks.) Headgear comprised field grey sidecaps, *Schirmmützen*, old style officer's field caps, and later *Einheitsfeldmützen*, with conven-

Waffen-SS armoured crewmen on a march near the Franco-Spanish border in summer 1940. They wear the black Panzer uniform complete with the Schutzmütze; *no cuff-titles or shoulder strap monograms identify the unit* (Brian L. Davis).

This is an obscure question. Originally Waffen-SS officers of all branches of service wore white-piped Schirmmützen. Late in 1940 an order changed this piping to the Waffenfarbe of the particular branch, eg, rose pink for armoured personnel. Shortly afterwards this order was rescinded, but photos show many officers retaining the pink-piped caps right up to the end of the war. The two styles were certainly seen side by side.

Two Waffen-SS *Panzer NCOs displaying regulation, and distinctly non-regulation uniforms. (Left) a young SS-Unterscharführer of 3rd SS-Panzer-Regiment 'Totenkopf' in the turret of his Panther. The division's skull collar patch can be seen on his right lapel, with a rank patch on the left. The throat-mike junction box is clearly shown here. (Right) is an SS-Rottenführer of 5th SS-Panzer-Regiment 'Wiking', with the chevrons of that rank, the SS arm eagle, and the divisional cuff-title. His jacket collar is piped pink, as are his collar patches – a regimental peculiarity.* Waffenfarbe *piping was only very occasionally seen on SS collar patches; the armoured car crews of the LSSAH wore it very early in the war; and the SP crews of the 'Nordland' Division's 11th SS-Panzer-Abteilung (Sturmgeschütz) 'Hermann von Salza' are reported to have worn red-piped patches* (Bundesarchiv).

tional insignia of service, rank and branch. Unit cuff titles and sleeve eagles were worn on the grey uniform, and black and silver-grey rank chevrons where appropriate. A special Waffen-SS version of the field grey 'crossover' jacket was issued, with the smaller rounded collar and vertical closure, and this had almost entirely replaced the older Army style by 1944.

Several different types of camouflage clothing were employed by SS armoured crews, apart from Army clothing occasionally pressed into service by individuals or during shortages. The baggy, collar-less SS camouflage smock with gathered cuffs and waist and a drawstring neck was sometimes observed. By summer 1943 a special one-piece camouflage overall was in widespread use by tank gun crews, in the standard SS spotted camouflage scheme. This had a small falling collar, two patch pockets on the chest with straight flaps and metal buttons, and two slash pockets conventionally placed in the 'trousers'; it fastened centrally from throat to crotch with five metal buttons. By 1944 a special two-piece tank camouflage uniform was quite widely observed, also in spotted SS pattern

material; like the overall it was of thin, shoddy material and non-reversible. This two-piece suit was cut almost identically to the black SS Panzer uniform, double-breasted, with a large falling collar and broad lapels, the dimensions being roughly the same as those of the reduced-collar black and grey uniforms of the SS. From 1943 a spotted camouflage material version of the peaked *Einheitsfeldmütze* was widely issued, and seems to have been popular with tank crews. Finally, officers not infrequently had privately ordered camouflage jackets made up in Army or SS-pattern material, varying in many details but often resembling the standard four-pocket service tunic in shape. On all these camouflage garments the question of insignia seems to have been a matter for the individual or the unit commander. Officially they should have been limited to the stylised black and green rank patch on the left upper sleeve. In practice, photos show shoulder straps, sleeve eagles, even cuff titles and collar patches in some cases. The former two items seem to have been common, and it is believed that sleeve eagles were actually applied at factory stage to at least some batches of the one-piece overalls, in dull green-on-black thread.

As in Army units, Waffen-SS crews displayed a motley variety of clothing in the front lines. The author has seen a typical photo of the Waffen-SS crew of a Tiger I tank in France in 1944. The NCO commander wears the black *Einheitsfeldmütze*, a grey shirt with shoulder straps attached, and black uniform trousers gathered over laced boots. A second crewman wears the black *Einheitsfeldmütze* with one-piece frontal insignia and the reed green two-piece denim uniform with attached shoulder straps and sleeve eagle. A third wears the black sidecap, and the two-piece camouflage uniform of Panzer cut and SS pattern, apparently without any insignia.

Winter clothing generally followed Army styles. In the winter of 1941-42 field grey greatcoats with dark green collars were worn, together with any improvised improvements the individual could manage: Russian quilted khaki uniforms, fur or sheepskin, etc. In the winter of 1942-43 the reversible padded winter uniform was issued, and photos show SS troops wearing both the white/mouse grey version and, less frequently, the white/splinter camouflage type. Later, perhaps in 1943-44, a definitive version reversed in white and SS spotted camouflage was issued. There was also a short-lived issue of a long parka in grey material, with a fur-lined hood and matching overtrousers; this had two breast pockets with pointed buttoned flaps, and two slanted skirt pockets. It was of pullover design, opening down to the breastbone only, with about four metal buttons. It was in use in 1943-44 but was later generally withdrawn.

In the 12th SS Panzer Division *Hitlerjugend* in France, late 1944, there seems to have been a limited issue of leather U-Boat clothing. This was in heavy black glossy leather, and comprised a crotch-length jacket with five metal buttons down the central closure, a vestigial standing collar over which the cloth jacket collar was folded, and a single concealed pocket on the left breast with a rectangular external flap closed by a concealed button. Straight leather trousers were worn with the jacket, and insignia seem to have been limited to shoulder straps. Photos show men of the 2nd Battalion, 12th SS Panzer Regiment, wearing this outfit; how widespread was its issue within the unit is uncertain.

Luftwaffe armoured units

The tank regiment raised during the enlargement of the Luftwaffe's *Hermann Göring* Brigade to divisional status in 1942, and supporting light armoured elements, were issued the Army-style black Panzer vehicle uniform with certain peculiarities of insignia. (This was first worn as early as 1938, with the formation of a Panzer-Späh-Zug in the Regiment *General Göring*.) The collar was piped white instead of pink, and some, at least, of the officers seem to have worn silver collar piping. The Luftwaffe's wavy-winged national eagle was worn on the right breast, in white or silver according to rank. The shoulder straps were black, with conventional ranking and lace, and with white piping or underlay for all ranks and branches prior to April 1943. From that month, individual arm-of-service *Waffenfarbe* appeared on the straps – pink for tank units, red for artillery, etc. The collar patches were

originally of Army shape: long black rectangles, slightly canted, with metal death's-heads, but with white edge piping. (Not infrequently, Army Panzer officers drafted into the Luftwaffe formation as cadres seem to have retained their pink-piped patches.) These white-piped black patches seem from photographs to have been widely retained even after orders of January 1943, April 1943 and January 1944 superseded them. In January 1943 the patches were officially replaced by smaller ones, of Luftwaffe lozenge shape, in white cloth, with pink piping round the edge and white metal death's-heads. In April the pink piping was removed. In January 1944 the white patches went altogether, and death's-heads were supposed to be pinned directly to the collar. In practice it appears that the original black patches, and the death's-heads worn without patches, were more commonly observed than either style of white patch, although

Panzer officers of the Luftwaffe's 'Hermann Göring' Division in 1943, wearing Luftwaffe officers' blue-grey Schirmmützen, *and black Panzer uniform with white or silver-piped collars, black patches piped white, white shoulder strap underlay, and Luftwaffe breast eagles. On the original print the centre man can be seen to wear an outdated style of divisional cuff-title with Gothic lettering (Bundesarchiv).*

a black patent leather chinstrap in place of cords, and both insignia in pressed silver-grey alloy with the cockade colours painted on. The black *Einheitsfeldmütze* was also issued in 1943-44, with Luftwaffe insignia.

A divisional cuff-title was worn on the right forearm, in several versions. The original 1936 type was widely retained by veterans. This was dark blue with the Gothic script legend *General Göring*; for officers, lettering and edging stripes top and bottom were silver. NCOs had light grey lettering and edges, and enlisted men, grey lettering and no edging. In May 1942 it was replaced by one reading *Hermann Göring* in Gothic script, in silver or grey according to rank, and with edging only for officers. Only a few months later this was in turn replaced by a block capitals version, with the same rank variations.

Self-propelled artillery of the *Hermann Göring* Division were issued the field grey version of the Panzer uniform; photos also exist of a version in Luftwaffe blue-grey. Conventional shoulder straps, breast eagles, and cuff titles were worn, but collar insignia seem to have been limited to the metal death's-head pinned directly to the collar by all ranks.

The author has been unable to confirm absolutely the uniform worn by SP artillery battalions of the

Captured 'Hermann Göring' officer arriving in Britain from Sicily, wearing the German Army's black tank officer's field cap, and Luftwaffe tropical uniform with a divisional cuff-title in the definitive version. Such mixtures of Army/Luftwaffe items were not uncommon in this formation, many of whose cadre were seconded from the Army.

Luftwaffe Hauptmann of a Marder III Panzerjäger unit photographed in Russia, 1943 or 1944. He wears an enlisted man's Einheitsfeldmütze without crown piping and the Fliegerbluse – note lack of breast pockets. The Waffenfarbe is hard to guess; anti-tank personnel of Luftwaffe Field Divisions would wear dark green collar patches and pink underlay to the shoulder straps, but the two items seem to be the same medium shade here. Possibly it is yellow – 2nd Fallschirm-Division fought in Russia in 1943 and up until April 1944 (Bundesarchiv).

all types crop up in photos.

Shirts were light or dark blue-grey, with black ties. Headgear comprised either the black Army side-cap, or a black version of the Luftwaffe's side-cap, with a smooth, un-scooped upper line to the turn-up. The top of the turn-up was piped silver all round for officers. A small Luftwaffe eagle and swastika was worn on the front of the crown, in white or silver depending on rank, and the national cockade, in the form of a raised boss, was sewn on the front of the turn-up. Officers also made widespread use of the Luftwaffe *Schirmmütze*. Of conventional German shape, this had a dark blue-grey crown, a ribbed black band, silver piping at crown seam and on both edges of the band, a stiff black peak, and silver chin-cords. The eagle and swastika was worn in silver wire on the front of the crown, and an ornate silver wire badge on the band represented a wreath surrounding a cockade, the whole supported by stylised wings. The NCO's version had a slightly smaller crown, white piping,

Luftwaffe Field Divisions which saw service on the Russian Front. In common with most units in these formations, it seems possible that the blue-grey *Fliegerbluse* was the normal front line dress, with matching trousers, ankle boots and blue-grey web gaiters. It is equally likely that the grey cross-over jacket and trousers of Army *Sturmartillerie* units were worn, with Luftwaffe shoulder straps and collar patches. (One of the figures in our colour plates displays the uniform of a Luftwaffe paratroop self-propelled assault gun commander of *Sturmge-schütz Brigade XII* on the French front in 1944 – the Army uniform with appropriate Luftwaffe in-signia.) Shoulder straps were in Luftwaffe blue-grey with normal rank distinctions, and red or pink piping and underlay for artillery or anti-tank units. The collar patches were of Luftwaffe lozenge shape, in dark green, and for enlisted men and NCOs were piped round the edge with *Waffenfarbe*, red or pink according to branch. Officers of all branches had silver cord edge piping on the patches. Luftwaffe ranking was worn on the patches in the usual sequence of stylised 'wings' in silver-grey metal, and for officers, in the form of silver embroidered wings and oakleaf sprays and wreathes. NCOs wore silver *Tresse* round the collar. Luftwaffe blue-grey sidecaps and, later, *Einheitsfeldmützen* were the normal headgear.

Like other arms of service in the division, the tank crews of the *Hermann Göring* Division were often seen wearing Waffen-SS pattern spotted and streaked camouflage smocks and helmet covers over their vehicle uniforms. In other Luftwaffe Field Divisions the angular splinter-pattern camou-flage scheme, as used by the Army, was favoured, usually in the form of a single-breasted field jacket reaching to the thighs, with a falling collar and shoulder straps of the same material. Rank shoulder straps seem often to have been applied to this, and the Luftwaffe eagle appears on the right breast. This field jacket was almost cer-tainly issued to Luftwaffe *Sturmgeschütz* crews.

In Sicily and Italy, where the *Hermann Goring* saw most of its service, there was widespread use of Luftwaffe tropical clothing in hot weather. This was quite different from the Army outfit. It was constructed of a sandy-yellow drill, very pale in shade, and comprised sidecap or peaked tropical field cap; a four-pocket tunic with an open collar, four blue-grey metal front buttons and pleated patch pockets with straight flaps and metal buttons; and baggy trousers with a large patch pocket on the front of the left thigh. Luftwaffe-style national eagles were worn on the caps and the right breast, and cockades beneath them on the caps. Shoulder straps were those of the Continental blue-grey

uniform, and no collar patches were worn. Decor-ations, cuff titles, etc, were worn in the conventional way. It was not unusual to observe headgear in black or blue-grey worn with tropical tunics and trousers. Shorts in the same pale sandy shade were also worn, and the lightweight blue 'sports' shorts are also evident in some photographs of artillery crews.

United States

The US Army pioneered the use of entirely separate combat and service dress uniforms; and for this reason only field clothing was normally to be seen among armoured crews in the front line.

When American tanks landed in French North Africa late in 1942 the standard uniform was the one-piece light grey-green overall and the 'tanker's jacket' windcheater described in Part 2; the definitive version of the leather crash helmet; brown laced ankle boots, and minimal personal webbing, if any. The overseas cap was seen in this theatre as out-of-the-line headgear, in both the brown 'olive drab' winter version and the light sandy drill 'khaki chino' summer version. It was still piped according to branch and rank, but the only applied insignia were officers' rankings; the enlisted men no longer wore the branch badge, and the coloured backing to the ranking was abandoned by officers. From some point in 1943 enlisted men's piping became mixed green and black for the armoured troops, but it is not clear

A view of the US tank crash helmet, displayed on a dummy head. The earphones are missing here – they would be inserted under the snap-fastened diamond of leather on the cheekpieces, protruding through the central hole (G. A. Embleton).

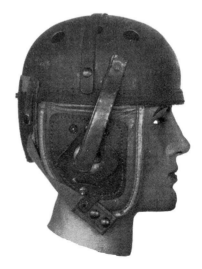

The officer's overseas cap, with Captain's rank bars; the tank windcheater, with patch pockets in this case; and the OD wool trousers (Philip Katcher).

how widely or how quickly this was seen, in practice.

The tank jacket had no shoulder straps, so officers usually pinned their metal ranking through a patch of leather and then to the points of the shoulders, to prevent tearing. Divisional patches were now worn on the top of the left sleeve by all ranks; they were often discarded in the front line, for security reasons. NCOs wore their chevrons on both arms of the jacket, and sometimes on the overalls.

The standard US Army shirt and trousers in brownish 'olive drab' were often seen among tank crews, as among the troops of all branches, in warm weather.

The crash helmet is illustrated in accompanying photos. Its pierced leather skull, riveted neck guard, and the centres of the cheek pieces were of leather painted olive green. The lining, which showed round the side and lower edges of neck and cheek pieces, was light tan leather. Two flat metal springs covered in tan leather projected down over the cheek pieces from swivels on the skull, to hold the earphones in the cheek pieces tight to the head — there was no chinstrap on the helmet. Snap-fastened lengths of narrow leather or elastic webbing connected the neck guard to each cheek piece, and held goggle straps and earphone leads in place — the latter usually led backwards horizontally from the housing in each cheek piece, united at one side or the other of the neck guard, and then fell in a single cable to about shoulder level, ending in a long cylindrical jack-plug.

In 1943-44, when colder campaigning rendered the overalls obviously deficient, a set of thickly padded overtrousers was issued to tank crews. In grey-green proofed material with thick blanket interlining which gave them a chunky appearance, these had a 'bib' front extending up to the mid-chest, where fabric braces over the shoulders engaged with metal clips. They may be seen in detail in an accompanying photo. Late in the war it seems that a version without the bib front became available.

The 'flyer's helmet' was still in use; in greenish olive drab padded cloth, with snap-fasteners for the chinstrap and no holes or housings for the earphones, it still had the deep neck flap for tucking into the collar. It is seen in photos worn for warmth under the crash helmet (a tight fit indeed, impossible without a large size of helmet) and under the standard steel helmet, which was increasingly worn when exposed in the turret by tank commanders during the latter part of the war. The knitted woollen 'beanie' skull cap, with its short knitted peak, was also as widely seen among tank crews as among other troops. So were the brownish olive sweater issued to US troops, with a low standing collar and buttons down to mid-chest; and rubber overboots with metal clip fasteners.

The crews of open-topped vehicles such as tank-destroyers at first wore the tank crash helmet, but quickly reverted to steel helmets for all but the driver and co-driver. Photos of this category of troops show a motley mixture of tank jackets and overalls with standard infantry uniforms, both 1941 and 1943 models; but armoured crew uniform items predominate.

In the Pacific theatre the normal dress was the standard darkish green OD two-piece fatigue suit worn by all US troops. Of herringbone twill, this

Left *A Priest SP howitzer crewman of the 274th Armored Field Artillery Battalion, 3rd US Armored Division, photographed near Bastogne early in January 1945. Interestingly, he wears complete 'tanker's' uniform, by no means universal among SP gun crews. The canvas 'flyer's helmet' is worn over a woollen 'beanie' cap. The tank windcheater is worn underneath the heavy bib-fronted winter over-trousers; and note rubber over-boots with metal snaps (US Army).*

unknown among tank crews. The crash helmet was the same as that worn in Europe. From 1943 a soft, peaked field cap in green OD began to be seen as casual headgear; and the steel helmet was often worn in a theatre known for its determined sniping. These remarks apply equally to both US Army and Marine Corps tank crews, although the latter also wore their distinctive soft fatigue cap with its eight-sided crown; the left breast pocket of their fatigues bore the black stencilled 'U.S.M.C.' and globe-and-anchor badge. In isolated cases tank crews seem to have worn the printed camouflage fatigues worn by some Marine units in 1943-44, but this seems to have depended on the practice in their parent divisions.

Soviet Union

When Germany invaded Russia in 1941, Soviet tank troops were still wearing the uniform, helmet and overall described in Part 2. Overalls were a mixture of black, dark blue, and khaki. It appears that from the outbreak of war or slightly before, overalls were made mainly in shades of khaki. Their basic design does not seem to have changed throughout the war, although details such as pocket number and type varied. The tank helmet appeared in 1941 in a more economical version made of black canvas rather than brown leather, and progressively, as old stocks were lost or used up, this combination of black canvas helmet and khaki overalls became more common until it was almost universal. Apart from the helmet, front-line headgear was unchanged; the khaki (or, occasionally, perhaps, grey) *pilotka*, the grey cloth and fleece *ushanka*, and the grey peaked *furashka*. During the war a cold-weather version of the tank helmet was produced, with a deep neck and ear piece lined with fur; this is illustrated in an accompanying photograph.

The 1943 uniform regulations altered the service dress of the Red Army. (It seems most unlikely that tank troops retained the steel grey version authorised in 1935 in any significant numbers after 1943.) The shirt-tunic now changed back to a more Tzarist appearance, with a standing collar, without insignia, fastened by two small buttons. The front fly now had three visible buttons, and the breast

Above *M18 Hellcat tank destroyer crewmen of the 306th Anti-Tank Company, US 77th Infantry Division, re-ammunition during a pause in the fighting on Okinawa, May 1945. They wear a mixture of tank and steel helmets, the latter with a stylised outline of the divisional insignia (left-hand man) on each side in white; two-piece light OD herringbone twill fatigue suits; and double-buckle combat boots (sitting man) (US Army).*

consisted of a straight-cut shirt worn outside the trousers and falling to hip level, with an open stepped collar, patch breast pockets with straight buttoned flaps, and five or six exposed green buttons down the front. The straight, loose trousers had large patch pockets on the outside face of each thigh, again with straight buttoned flaps. They were usually worn loose or rolled at the ankle over the laced boots; the long web gaiters were unpopular with even the infantry in this theatre, and almost pockets disappeared from the uniform of enlisted ranks. Officers retained pockets, but concealed ones, with only the pointed, buttoned flap visible. The piping disappeared from officers' shirt-tunics, and the only mark of rank was the stiff shoulder board, re-introduced for all ranks.

The field service shoulder boards of tank troops were khaki, with red piping round the long edges and the pointed inner end. Ranking for NCOs was in the form of cloth bars worn across the boards, with sometimes a metal tank badge worn just 'outboard' of the stripes. Corporals, Junior Sergeants, Sergeants and Senior Sergeants wore respectively from one to three narrow red stripes, and one broad stripe. Sergeant-Majors wore a T-shaped arrangement: a broad stripe across the board and a thin one extending from it down the centre to the outer end. Junior Lieutenants, Lieutenants, Senior Lieutenants and Captains wore a single thin red stripe down the centre of the board. Ranking was by small silver stars; one on the stripe, one each side, one on and one each side, and two on and one each side, respectively. Field officers had two red stripes lengthways, dividing the board into three equal strips. Majors, Lieutenant-Colonels and Colonels wore larger silver stars, respectively one between the stripes, one on each stripe, and one between and two on. A white metal tank motif was pinned to the shoulder board just 'outside' the brass button, and the ranking stars were worn at the outer end.

The young commander of a T-34/76 leans round the huge turret hatch of his vehicle; the photo was probably taken in 1941 or 1942. He wears the well-known padded tank helmet, probably in brown leather at this date, in its summer version. The overalls seem to be khaki, and he wears ranking pinned directly to the collar points, with no sign of the regulation backing patch of gold-piped black: the two red and gold squares of a Lieutenant are visible, with perhaps a 'tank' branch badge above them on the collar (Imperial War Museum).

The collar patches of the *kaftan* changed in 1943, all ranks now adopting a plain khaki patch in the same canted rectangle shape as that worn on the old fall-collar *rubaha*. A large brass button was worn at the outer end, and the patches of all ranks were piped red round the long and outer edges.

A new belt buckle appeared from 1943: a rectangular brass plate with clipped corners, and a raised star motif in the centre. It was seen in use alongside the old frame buckles.

Personnel of self-propelled artillery units wore exactly the same uniforms as tank troops apart from the small metal arm of service motifs on the collar patches prior to 1943, and the shoulder boards after 1943. This was a brass device in the shape of crossed cannon barrels. Steel helmets were worn in open-topped vehicles.

Medals were sometimes worn on the shirt-tunic, but not, as far as photographs suggest, on the tank overall. The enamelled Guards Unit badge, marking a unit citation, was often worn on the right breast of the shirt-tunic, above all other insignia. This was a gold wreath surrounding a red star, with a red banner with gold cyrillic lettering floating across the top of the wreath. Horizontal red or gold wound stripes, signifying light or heavy wounds, were sometimes sewn above the

Interesting group of Soviet Army officers wearing the deep, fleece-lined winter tank helmet, apparently in black fabric. The three in the foreground wear pre-1943 shirt-tunics in a very dark shade, with the characteristic breast pockets and fall collars of this garment. The colour contrasts sharply with the left rear man's uniform, which is khaki. Could these officers be wearing a dark steel-grey version, for the armoured branch? Various decorations can be made out, including the Guards Unit badge on the right breast in all cases. The front left officer has two wound stripes, apparently gold, above the inner edge of his right breast pocket. Collar patches are black piped in gold, and seem to bear the crossed hammer and wrench of technical troops (Imperial War Museum).

inner end of the right breast pocket after July 1942, and in a corresponding position after the removal of pockets in 1943.

Apart from the *kaftan*, armoured crews were sometimes issued in winter with reversed sheepskin coats of natural tan colour, with deep falling fleece collars. They reached nearly to the knee, and fastened on the right breast by loops and buttons or toggles. Khaki quilted winter uniforms and large felt boots were also issued, as to other types of troops. The former were usually collarless jackets, fastening by loops and toggles on the right breast, and matching trousers, of a thick, vertically quilted design. All kinds of captured Axis clothing and personal equipment were frequently observed. By 1945 a black leather $\frac{3}{4}$-length jacket was to be seen in some numbers, worn over the overalls.

Italy

When Italy entered the war in 1940 her armoured units were as follows:

An armoured corps of three armoured divisions: 131st Division *Centauro*, in Albania, with 5th *Bersaglieri* Regiment, 131st Tank Regiment, 131st Artillery Regiment, and services; 132nd Division *Ariete*, at Verona, with 8th *Bersaglieri* Regiment, 32nd Tank Regiment, 132nd Artillery Regiment, and services; 133rd Division *Littorio*, at Parma, with 12th *Bersaglieri* Regiment, 33rd Tank Regiment, 133rd Artillery Regiment, and services.

The home-based 1st, 2nd, 3rd and 4th Tank Regiments.

Italian tank crewmen board their M.13/40 in North Africa. One wears the light sandy-drill bustina cap, the rest the leather crash helmet. Left and centre foreground figures wear sandy-drill slacks, one with the regulation strapped cavalry gaiters to the knee, the other hanging loose. All wear the black leather coat. The right-hand man wears the blue one-piece overalls.

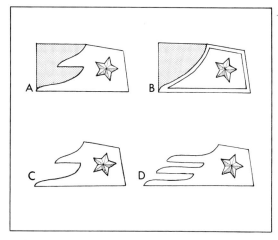

Italian collar insignia worn by armoured units: (A) tank troops – double scarlet 'flame' on blue patch; (B) armoured artillery – black 'pipe' outlined with yellow piping on blue patch; (C) Bersaglieri – double 'flames' in Burgundy red; (D) cavalry – triple 'flames'.

One tank battalion attached to each of the two motorised divisions, 101st Division *Trieste* and 102nd Division *Trento*.

Independent battalions of L-tanks attached to infantry divisions in Africa.

One battalion in the Aegean Islands.

Two medium tank companies in Italian East Africa.

Apart from these tank units, significant numbers of cavalry units were also equipped with light tanks L3 and L6. Often a cavalry regiment would have one group of squadrons armoured and serving in a different theatre to the horsed group or groups; the 3rd Group of the regiment *Lancieri di Novara* was armoured and serving in North Africa while the rest of the regiment served on horseback in Russia. *Bersaglieri* units were also equipped with L6 tanks and armoured cars in some cases. The full list of units outside the armoured Corps which were in fact equipped with armour is as follows, with notes on collar insignia where confirmed. Note that, eg, 'three black flames on red' means a black three-point 'flame' collar device on a red backing patch.

Cavalry Reconnaissance Regiment (R.E.Co.) *Cavalleggeri Lodi* – three black flames on red.

Cavalry Reconnaissance Regiment (R.E.Co.) *Lancieri di Montebello* – three green flames on black.

Motorised Regiment *Cavalleggeri di Lucca* – three apricot flames on black.

Mechanised Regiment *Vittorio Emanuele 2°* – three lemon yellow flames edged black.

Armoured Cavalry Groups

2nd Armoured Group *Cavalleggeri Guide* – three white flames on bright blue.

3rd Armoured Group *Lancieri di Novara* – three white flames.

3rd Armoured Car Group *Nizza Cavalleggeria* – three crimson flames.

3rd Armoured Car Group *Cavalleggeri di Monferrato* – three crimson flames on black.

4th Armoured Group *Nizza Cavalleria* – three crimson flames.

3rd Armoured Group *Lancieri di Aosta* – three scarlet flames.

3rd Armoured Group *Genova Cavalleria* – three lemon yellow flames.

3rd Armoured Group *Cavalleggeri di Alessandria* – three orange flames on black.

1st Group of Squadrons *San Marco*
2nd Group of Squadrons *San Giusto* } light tank and armoured car units detached from the tank corps –
3rd Group of Squadrons *San Giorgio* } two scarlet flames on bright blue.

184th Tank Detachment *Cavalleggeri di Sardegna* – ?

(All flames listed above have silver star at front end.)

Bersaglieri

18th Motorised/Armoured Regiment consisting of:
VIII Armoured Battalion (*Trieste* Division)   } two-point collar flame in burgundy red,
XXII Armoured Battalion (*Centauro* Division)   } unpiped and without a backing patch,
LXVII Armoured Battalion (3rd *Celere* Division)   } but with the usual star.

Arditi

103rd, 113th and 123rd Companies of 10th *Arditi* Regiment (an airborne commando regiment) – two-point light blue flame, no backing or piping; silver star.

Artillery

131st, 132nd 133rd and 235th Armoured
  Artillery Regiments   } single black 'pipe' edged yellow, on
3rd *Articelere* Regiment   } bright blue.

Below left *Italian tank Major's shoulder board, as worn on the tropical tunic: black cloth, with blue outer piping, gold lace inner edge, gold branch badge and star. The long point was worn at the rear of the shoulder.*

Below right *Italian AFV helmet in black leather, used from 1935 onwards. The soft leather neck-piece is turned up to show the broad chinstrap pierced over the ear.*

Below *1944: the crew of a light L.3 tank of the Guardia Nazionale Repubblicana, the gendarmerie force which replaced the Carabinieri during Mussolini's short-lived Italian Socialist Republic, 1943-45. German influence is apparent in the skull badges attached to their helmets. Pre-Armistice army uniforms are worn, with double black collar flames on which a wreath and gladius replaced the star of the Royal Army (Furio Lorenzetti).*

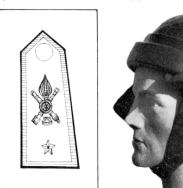

The uniforms worn in the field did not change significantly from those described under Part 2. The normal vehicle uniform was the domed crash-helmet or the *bustina* cap; the dark blue overalls and/or black leather coat; and, in Europe, the regulation baggy grey-green semi-breeches with knee-length black buckled leather gaiters or grey puttees, with laced black ankle boots. In Africa straight, loose khaki drill slacks were sometimes observed; shorts were also much used, but the long gaiters were also to be seen. The collar devices described above and in Part 2 were worn on both grey and khaki drill uniforms; ranking was worn on the tropical uniform exactly as on the grey uniform by NCOs, but officers – as mentioned earlier – wore ranking on the end of their black, blue-piped shoulder boards. A khaki *bustina* bore branch devices and ranking in the same way as on the grey version. Unofficial unit badges were sometimes pinned to the breast pockets of the tunic. Belts, holsters, and cavalry-type pouch bandoliers in grey leather remained the only equipment normally worn.

After the September 1943 armistice the Italian Liberation Corps fighting with the Allies in the south was not supplied with armour; but some units of Mussolini's Italian Social Republican forces, based in the north and trained and organised by the Germans, had a few armoured vehicles. There were not very many, because in the immediate aftermath of the defection of most Italian forces from the Axis, Germany grabbed such Italian armour as was potentially useful for her own forces. This amounted to little more than a few score of the reliable Semovente armoured assault guns. German armour was not, it seems, supplied to the army of the RSI, which had two main armoured units, weakly equipped: the Armoured Group *Leonessa* and the Group of Armoured Squadrons *Leoncello*. In addition, armoured vehicles were operated in small numbers by the *Lupo* Battalion of the 10th MAS Division (Marines); the 1st Recce Group, Alpine Division *Monterosa;* Recce Group, *Cacciatori degli Appennini;* the Group of Armoured Squadrons *San Giusto;* and the Montebello Battalion of the political police who replaced the *carabinieri*, the National Republican Guard. Tank crew uniforms were Italian-made but were clearly inspired by German styles; our front cover illustration shows a captain of the *Leonessa* Group in a costume obviously modelled on Germany's first Panzer uniform, down to the death's-head cap-badge. In action this uniform would doubtless have been supplemented by the black leather coat. The minimum changes made to pre-1943 uniforms by RSI troops would be the removal of the star from the collar devices, and its replacement by a wreathed Roman sword badge; collar flames were, in theory, always of the triple-pointed shape.

Japan

Japan made little use of tanks during the Second World War. In the island war they were encountered in small numbers, usually operating as detached companies and in the role of mobile pillboxes. In Malaya and Burma they were encountered in slightly larger numbers, but the clash of tank versus tank was virtually unknown, and the primary role remained that of infantry support — a role in which their crews showed little skill or appreciation of the special capabilities of armour, due to their domination by the infantry branch.

The uniforms described in Part 2 remained in use throughout the war. The Pacific campaigns seem to have been fought largely in standard Japanese Army tropical dress, and photos show tank crews in jungle green shirtsleeve order and field caps more often than in tank overalls and padded helmets. This tropical uniform was basically similar in cut to the 1938 temperate climate service dress. The field cap acquired, in many cases, a neck curtain made up of four separate strips of cloth covering ears and nape, and in its tropical form usually had a cloth rather than a leather chinstrap. The shirt varied widely; some had patch breast pockets, unpleated, and with either straight or pointed flaps. Others had a single pocket, usually on the left. The sleeves could be either long, short, or reaching to just below the elbow. The neck was worn open; sometimes rank patches appeared on both points of the collar, sometimes they were omitted altogether, and sometimes a single patch was worn above the left breast pocket. Half-breeches were worn with puttees and black canvas

Japanese tank crewman in summer overall and helmet. This photo was found inside an abandoned Type 95 tank by men of 146th Regiment, Royal Armoured Corps, in Burma (Bryan Perrett)

and rubber split-toed *tabi* boots; shorts are also to be seen, worn with *tabis*, and ankle socks in white. Japanese shorts were usually of generously wide cut, and rather long.

Officers had tropical tunics very similar to those of the temperate uniform, but some had four box-pleated patch pockets. The tunic was worn open at the neck, and the shirt collar — white or pale sandy or grey drill — was folded open over it. The rank patches were thus worn on the lower lapel of the open collar, so that the shirt would not hide them. Legwear varied from lightweight breeches and black jackboots to buckled leggings or puttees and ankle boots. The personal equipment such as holsters, map cases and binoculars was usually slung on narrow crossbelts of brown leather or green proofed canvas, with a green cloth waistbelt with prominent stitching worn overall to hold the various items down to the body. The cap was like that of the enlisted ranks, though in better material and better cut. All ranks wore tropical uniform of a wide range of shades, from deep green to light sandy drill, but green tones were the more common. Buttons were of plastic or horn. White scarfs and sweat-rags round the neck were common among all ranks.

Poland

Polish tank troops who escaped in 1939 went to France, and some fought there in spring 1940, wearing French uniforms with Polish insignia. They seem generally to have acquired the 1935 French tank crew helmet. Those who escaped to England, together with those who were released in 1942 from Russian internment and allowed to join the Free Polish forces abroad, were uniformed by the British. At first this amounted to the khaki field service cap, battledress and denims with a rather mixed bag of webbing and leather personal equipment and an equally mixed display of Polish insignia. A more uniform picture emerged in time, and in 1944-45 two complete Polish Armoured Divisions were fighting with the other Allies in north-west Europe and Italy. They wore entirely British uniforms — battledress, black RAC beret, denims, leather jerkins, rimless RAC helmets and, from winter 1944 in Europe, the 'zoot suit'. Their insignia were Polish, however, and were extremely attractive and colourful. Mr Gustav Krupa, a 1st Armoured Division veteran to whom the author is indebted for these notes, mentions that most insignia were worn even in the front line; this is typical of exile soldiers of all nations, of course, whose *ésprit de corps* tends to be much more fiercely nationalist than that of more fortunate units.

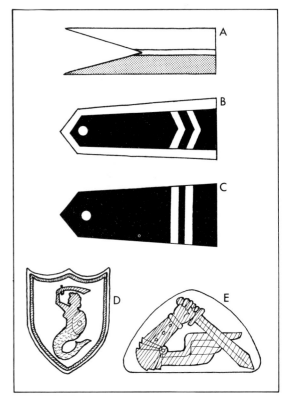

Battledress insignia worn by Free Polish armoured personnel. (A), (B) and (C) were worn by 10th Armoured Cavalry Brigade, 1st Armoured Division. (A) Collar pennant style – see text for regimental colours; (B) black left-hand shoulder board with Staff Sergeant's ranking, and (C) with Corporal's ranking. Silver stripes with fine red lines down both edges, in all positions. (D) Silver on crimson patch of II Polish Corps; (E) white on khaki patch of 2nd Armoured Division.

Some examples of the insignia worn by these crews follow, under regimental headings. It should be noted that generally the battledress and beret bore Polish ranking, as described in Part 2. British tropical KD was issued in the Italian summer campaigns.

1st Polish Armoured Division, north-west Europe
The armoured element was built on a core of numerous survivors of 10th Mechanised Cavalry Brigade, and in honour of their old formation all ranks wore, on battledress though not on denims, one left-hand black cloth shoulder board with Polish ranking. There are photos showing officers with British cloth ranking pips and crowns on the right-hand shoulder strap of the BD blouse; but generally, all-Polish ranking seems to have been the case.

10th Mounted Rifles The divisional armoured

Polish Lieutenant-Colonel of the Carpathian Lancers, 2nd Polish Armoured Division, on a recce near Pessaro, Italy. He wears a black RAC beret with the silver national badge above his ranking, obscured here; a khaki drill tropical service tunic; silver metal ranking on the shoulder strap; and regimental 'pennants' in dark blue and crimson, with silver palm-tree badges.

recce regiment, and not part of 10th Mechanised Cavalry Brigade — black strap not worn. Collar pennants were swallow-tailed, green over yellow with white central bar (see line illustration for detail). White/silver-on-crimson shoulder title 'PO-LAND' in arc shape just below shoulder seams.

1st Armoured Regiment Black left shoulder board; orange lanyard from left shoulder to breast pocket. Swallow-tail collar pennants, black over orange, crimson central bar. (NB, the front edge of these pennants was normally cut back in a slant to match line of BD collar edge. When repeated on beret, as in some cases listed below, the edge was left vertical.) White or silver lettering on crimson arc, 'POLAND', at top of both sleeves. Left sleeve: orange, black and white divisional patch above red/yellow halved RAC arm-of-service strip. Right sleeve: either divisional patch repeated, or, in 1945, arms of Belgian town of St Niklaas Waas,

which the unit liberated: a blue shield of 'sabre-tasche' shape, edged gold, with gold lily in top left corner, and gold central figure of robed bishop with mitre and crozier, right hand raised in blessing.

2nd Armoured Regiment Black left shoulder board; orange lanyard on left shoulder. Swallow-tail pennants on collar, black over orange, white central bar. Arm insignia as above except, 1945, arms of Beveren Waas worn upper right sleeve: 'sabretasche' shaped shield, with complex scene in natural colours of St Martin, mounted, parting red cloak with beggar.

24th Lancers Armoured Regiment Black left shoulder board; black lanyard on left shoulder. All white swallow-tail collar pennants with yellow central bar. National shoulder title, divisional shoulder patch and RAC strip worn on both sleeves.

10th Dragoons Black left shoulder board; black lanyard left shoulder. Swallow-tailed collar pennants, crimson above orange, green central bar. Left sleeve as above. Right sleeve, replacing divisional patch, St Andrew's cross with an escutcheon in centre bearing arms of Lanark.

2nd Polish Armoured Division, Italy

Generally all units wore the white/silver-on-crimson 'POLAND' shoulder title. On the left upper sleeve was worn II Polish Corps' insignia in the same colours: a crimson shield with three-point top line, a silver inner border, and a silver Warsaw mermaid with raised sabre and round shield. Immediately below this appeared the divisional patch: a semi-circle or 'rounded triangle' with curved top and straight bottom edges, bearing a silver armoured, winged crooked arm with a broadsword. Below this appeared a coloured felt strip like the RAC strip, but in different single colours according to regiment. On the right sleeve the insignia of British 8th Army appeared below the 'POLAND' title, and no other insignia or felt strips were worn below this. Ranking was all Polish. The usual national cap badge above ranking was worn centrally on the beret. Additional regimental insignia within this colourful formation were as follows:

4th Armoured Regiment 'Skorpion' On beret, on wearer's left of badge, a crimson cloth parallelogram (rhombus) about 40 mm on a side bearing a silver scorpion facing down and left as viewed. Swallow-tailed collar pennants, black over orange with central crimson bar; silver scorpions pinned through these, facing inwards on collar, about 15 mm long. Red felt strip on left arm.

6th Armoured Regiment 'Lwowski' On beret, left of badge, blue cloth rhombus with gold rampant lion, facing right as viewed. Collar pennant not swallow-tailed but single long triangle, like prewar tank units' patch, halved black over orange with mid-blue central bar. Blue left arm strip.

7th Armoured Regiment On beret, left of badge, black cloth rhombus with left and bottom edges piped orange, right and top edges piped dark blue; on this patch the silver 'winged arm' badge of the divisional insignia. This insignia repeated on swallow-tailed collar pennants, dark blue over crimson, no central bar.

10th Hussars Bright blue collar pennants charged with a gold 'knot', made from attached gold cord; the knot was repeated left of the beret badge.

1st Lancers Armoured Regiment 'Krechowiecki' On beret, left of badge, swallow-tailed pennant in crimson over white, no central bar. Same pennant on collar. Yellow felt strip on left arm.

Carpathian Lancers On beret, left of badge, swallow-tailed pennant in dark blue over crimson. On collar, same pennant with silver badge pinned to it — two palm trees from a crescent; see photo. No felt arm strip.

Miscellaneous

Belgium's small tank force, numbering about 200 vehicles locally developed from Renault and Carden-Loyd models, was wiped out in two weeks of May 1940. Information on tank crew uniforms is scanty, but the following notes are believed accurate as far as they go. Among the armoured cavalry regiments were the 1st Guides and the 2nd and 3rd Lancers.

When serving in the vehicles, officers and men seem to have worn the 1926 model French steel tank helmet painted khaki, with lion-mask front badge, comb, large neck-guard, and brown leather brow-pad and chinstrap. A crotch-length leather jacket in either black or very dark brown leather was worn. A troop of lancers photographed with French Berliet VUDB armoured cars in about 1932 display these jackets, single-breasted for enlisted men and double-breasted for officers; no other differences are apparent, but the photo is of poor quality for detailed examination. Officers have two rows of four silver buttons, set close together down the centre of the torso; enlisted men have one central row. A single button seems to be set centrally on the outer face of the cuff, about 'three fingers' up from the bottom edge. There are no breast pockets and no shoulder straps, and internal skirt pockets with large straight flaps without visible buttons.

Enlisted men wore khaki trousers, slightly flared at the thigh, with brown laced ankleboots and knee-length brown gaiters buckled at the front just below the top and above the anklebone — these were cut away sharply to accommodate the instep. Officers wore flared fawn riding breeches and black jack-boots. Enlisted men wore a brown leather belt with two-prong brass frame buckle, and officers a Sam Browne with cross-strap over the right shoulder. Holsters were worn on the belt.

Cloth headgear for enlisted men below the rank of Sergeant was a khaki sidecap of stiff and rather Spanish appearance, with a single central 'ridge' rather than a gusset. This front-to-back crest was piped in branch colour, and had a hanging tassel of the same colour from the front top corner — for Guides, amaranth red, and for Lancers, white. A branch badge was worn well forward on the left side of the cap turn-up, which was also piped in branch colour round its upper edge; the badges were a crown above crossed sabres above the unit number for Guides, and crossed lances above the unit number for Lancers.

Officers, Warrant Officers and Sergeants wore a khaki cloth peaked cap of British appearance, with a khaki-covered peak. A black-yellow-red tricolour cockade was worn on the front of the crown by all ranks. All officers had double silver chin-cords, as did Warrant Officers, and Sergeants had brown chinstraps. Company officers had plain khaki hat-bands, and field officers silver piping along the bottom edge. Branch badges were worn on the front of the band: crowned crossed sabres for Guides, crossed lances for Lancers, in silver. Field-grade officers had a silver vertical bar each side of the badge, the whole height of the band.

The author has been unable to confirm whether or not branch and rank patches were worn on the points of the fall collar of the leather coat in the front line. If they were, which seems possible for officers but unlikely for enlisted men, they would have been as follows: *Enlisted men* – Diamond shapes, bottom point elongated, in amaranth with green piping on upper two edges for Guides; white piped royal blue on upper edges for Lancers. *Officers* – Metal branch badges pinned directly to collar, above ranking pinned directly to collar. One, two and three six-point gold stars for company officers (in the case of Captains, two stars above one star); three stars below a short gold horizontal bar for Captain-Commandants; one, two and three stars above a thicker bar for field officers.

Hungary had a small tank arm, and contributed troops to Germany's Russian campaign. A known photograph showing cadets of the Ludowika Academy illustrates the early tank crew uniform: khaki overalls worn over khaki service dress, with the black leather Italian crash helmet. Later in the war, about 1942, a brown leather jacket and trousers were issued; the jacket was sometimes seen with the khaki service dress semi-breeches and either black German-style marching boots or puttees and ankle boots. The collar of the jacket was faced with khaki cloth. Pointed gorget patches worn on the khaki tunic were certainly repeated on the collar of the khaki overall, and possibly on that of the leather jacket; these were in dark blue for tank troops. A khaki sidecap and a peaked field cap both had a high 'peak' at the front of the crown. The sidecap was cut high, with a front flap fixed in the vertical position by two buttons. At the front of the

Below left *Wireless operator, Hungarian tank troops, 1943. The brown leather jacket and trousers described in the text are worn with a new type of helmet which appeared in 1942. A development of the Italian type, this had prominent earphone housings; at first issued to wireless operators only, it gradually became more widely available until whole crews wore them.* **Centre** *Rumanian tank NCO, Don campaign, Russia 1942. The large black beret and khaki overalls, as described in the text, are worn by this PzKpfw 38(t) commander. Note yellow ranking stripes around shoulder straps. He holds a red and white German traffic direction paddle.* **Right** *Finnish Lieutenant of a T-34 unit, 1944. He wears a captured Soviet tank helmet in brown leather; a leather jacket which appears to be black, with his black Sam Browne belt; grey breeches, and black riding boots. The only insignia worn are the two small gilt roses of his rank on the front edges of the stand-and-fall collar (Sketches courtesy Steven Zaloga).*

crown, placed high, was the circular red, white and green national cockade.

On the sidecaps of officers, ranking was in the form of inverted chevrons of gold metallic lace on the front of the crown, running up to the cockade: company officers were identified by one, two or three thin lace chevrons, field officers by narrow chevrons above a medium chevron. All ranks wore a triangular piece of cloth in arm of service colour on the left side of the sidecap, trimmed with three lengths of khaki braid. These insignia were all repeated on the field cap. NCOs wore one to three six-pointed stars on the gorget patch; officers had one to three stars and a thin gold lace patch edging for company grades, and one to three stars on a gold lace backing mounted on the edged patch for field grades. The German helmet was worn in open-topped armoured vehicles.

Rumania also contributed some tanks to the Eastern Front. Khaki overalls were worn over the khaki service dress uniform. Early in the war the French tank crew helmet was worn, painted khaki; by 1942 a floppy black beret seems to have replaced it, worn without insignia. Ranking was worn on the shoulder straps of the overall, in the form of yellow and gold stripes round the strap: one to three stripes in yellow for NCO grades, and one to three stripes in gold for company officers. Field officers

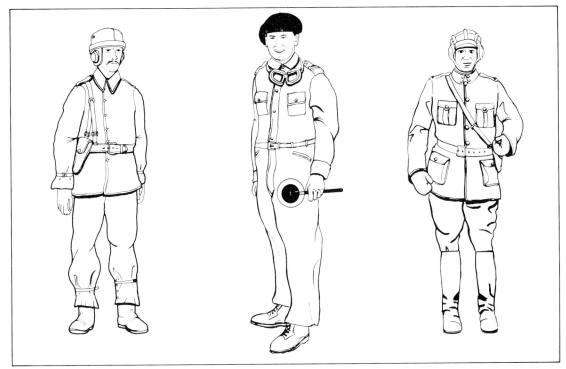

The crew of a colourfully painted Sherman of the 1st Chinese-American Provisional Tank Group wear fatigue caps and shirts and slacks in US light grey-green 'Olive Drab'. In the original print one appears to have a round blue and white Chinese sunburst badge on his cap. Lashio, March 1945 (US Army).

had a medium width gold stripe down the centre with one to three narrow stripes across the strap. Where the overall collar was worn open to reveal the tunic collar, this would have been of khaki cloth of a brownish shade, in the stand-and-fall style, with large bastion-ended gorget patches in the grey arm of service colour of the armoured troops.

Finland had some armoured units in action against Russia on the northern sector of the Eastern Front in 1942-44. The equipment was a mixture of German and captured Soviet vehicles. The normal field service uniform of mid-grey cloth was very plain. It consisted of a fieldcap of generally German appearance, or a sidecap; a single-breasted tunic with plain fall collar, plain shoulder straps, fly front, round cuffs with two buttons at the rear, and concealed breast pockets with pointed buttoned flaps; and straight trousers worn with black marching boots, in the German style. An accompanying line drawing shows a T-34 commander wearing a leather jacket and a captured Russian tank helmet.

Ranking was pinned directly to the collar of the combat tunic and the leather jacket, in the form of gilt roses vertically arranged up the front edge:

one to three for company officers, and one to three larger roses for field grades. NCOs wore their ranking in the form of yellow chevrons on the shoulder straps, point inwards: one to four narrow chevrons, and one very thick gold chevron for Sergeant-Majors. It seems likely, but the author cannot confirm from direct examination of photos, that these rankings would also have been worn on the leather jacket. The fieldcap was similar to the German *Bergmütze*, with cloth peak and turn-up. A circular cockade in white/blue/white was worn high on the front. The sidecap had a black chinstrap, and the same cockade. On fur winter caps the cockade was worn by officers above a silver rampant lion badge.

China had light armoured forces in the field in the late 1930s, but these had been virtually wiped out by the outbreak of the Second World War. Such as survived seem to have worn standard service dress: light khaki in summer, brownish khaki wool in temperate climates and bright blue wadded cotton in winter. Typically, the tunic was single-breasted with four patch pockets with pointed buttoned flaps; there was a stand-and-fall collar and five exposed front buttons. A soft, round field cap with a cloth peak was worn, with the national insignia – a white sunburst on a blue button – on the front of the crown. Long, tight puttees; shorts or semi-breeches; and ankle boots or sandals were worn. Various specialist headgears were occasionally seen, left over from the 1930s: notably Russian brown leather helmets supplied with Soviet BA-10 and T-26 vehicles, and German steel helmets.

Insignia appear sparse, although normal ranking would sometimes have been seen on the collar – one to three yellow metal three-point stars for junior NCOs, the same on a yellow stripe for senior NCOs; company officers had two silver and one gold stripes and one to three stars, and field officers two gold and one silver stripes and one to three stars. A rectangular patch of white cloth with black ideograph script was often seen above the left breast pocket. This was supposed to be edged in arm of service colour, and backing patches on the collar were also supposed to be differentiated in this way, but under actual field conditions it was probably most unusual. Tank units would presumably have worn cavalry yellow.

After major US aid began to reach Chiang Kai-Shek in 1943, a mixed Sino-American tank unit was formed and saw action in Burma in 1945 – the 1st Provisional Tank Group. Crews wore light grey-green American overalls and soft fatigue caps; insignia was probably at a minimum, but the cap cockade was commonly seen.

THE POSTWAR PERIOD

Great Britain

The vehicle uniform of the British tank crewman since 1945 has been based on a one-piece denim overall and a beret. The overalls have varied in details of design over the years, but not too much significance should be attached to use of different patterns by different units at different times. This is a utility garment, not a 'uniform' item as such, and it is a mistake to generalise from particular examples.

In the early 1950s a type with plentiful pockets was issued to some units, including the 17th/21st Lancers; it is illustrated in this chapter. It was

(Left) Corporal, 'C' Squadron, 7 RTR; Korea, 1950-51. This NCO of the Churchill tank unit which fought in the first winter of the Korean War wears the red/green shoulder tallies and lanyard of 7 RTR, the regimental tank arm badge, and the white 'frozen orifice' on a black square of the Commonwealth Brigade. (Right) from the sublime to the ridiculous . . . Trooper, 17th/21st Lancers, BAOR, 1955. This scruffy radio operator (the slung Sten identifies him – other crewmen wore revolvers) wears the mid-grey tank denims then issued to that regiment. They have two breast and two thigh pockets, and an integral cloth belt; a small field dressing pocket is visible on the front of the right hip. The rubber boots were non-regulation, but sensible on the North German Plain in winter (Mike Chappell).

unusual in being a darkish grey in shade, fading with use to light grey. Most denims issued have been in varying shades of greenish khaki, and, typically, have had a single left breast pocket and a single pocket outside the left thigh, with pointed flaps fastened by concealed buttons. A modern type has more numerous pockets, and is illustrated on Colour Plate 8.

One special case is the RTR, which since about 1950 has enjoyed the exclusive use of black tank denims. These varied in detail but normally seem to have been of the fairly light-weight style with single chest and thigh pockets; photos accompany this chapter. An extra pocket has sometimes been added in the form of a brassard-like over-sleeve fitting to the end of the shoulder strap. In some cases at least, khaki-green examples of this have been worn on black RTR suits. Some RTR suits have a pocket on the outside face of each lower leg. Coloured shoulder strap tallies in RTR regimental colours, and coloured lanyards on the left shoulder, have also been worn on the black overall at most times by most units. The tallies are sometimes a

4th RTR Saladin crew in Aden, 1964, wearing standard tropical khaki drill uniforms with large blue regimental shoulder strap tallies and blue lanyards (The Tank).

loop at the very outer end of the strap, sometimes a sleeve almost as long as the strap itself. Coloured scarves of regimental shades and usually in terry-towelling have normally been worn for exercises, parades, etc; some Colonels have disliked these, and the camouflage net veil widely worn as a scarf with combat dress by the Army as a whole has been substituted. Since about 1968 name tabs have been worn on the tank overall above the left breast pocket, in black lettering on white strips. Rank chevrons are normally in white tape and temporarily fixed, by snap fastener or brassard, on the right sleeve only. Webbing is normally limited to a belt (and holster for exercises) and is blackened. Old 1937 and 1944 pattern web belts are used in large numbers to this day. Sometimes the overall

Major, Royal Tank Regiment, 1970s. Black beret; black RTR-pattern tank denims with single pockets on left breast and thigh, and pockets on outside of each lower leg. Cloth rank crowns on black backing half overlap the narrow coloured regimental shoulder strap tallies; note lanyard round left shoulder. A set of pencil pockets on a khaki-green brassard fitting can be seen on the left upper arm (The Tank).

legs are gathered into or over the boot, sometimes into black web anklets or short brown ankle-puttees. The black beret has been exclusive to the RTR since about 1950.

The armoured cavalry regiments mainly wear the dark blue beret introduced for the Army as a whole in the late 1940s. Regimental cap badges are worn, often on coloured patches, and usually in gold or silver embroidered form by officers. Some units have special berets: the Royal Scots Greys wear a very pale grey beret with a black patch for the badge; the Royal Hussars wear a brown beret, with enlisted ranks wearing a red patch behind the badge. Enlisted ranks of the 14th/20th King's Hussars wear their black eagle cap badge on an oval patch of lemon yellow: the 4th/7th Royal Dragoon Guards have a red star-shaped patch behind the badge; and all ranks of the QRIH wear a green band round the beret – see Colour Plate 8.

Regimental – or even squadron – scarves in facing colours are common, but change with too much frequency according to the Colonel's taste for an up-to-date listing to be possible. The two regiments of the Household Cavalry both wear black polo-neck sweaters under the khaki-green tank overall.

Webbing, often of 1937 pattern, is usually black. Its use varies from unit to unit; some always wear rather complete webbing, including anklets and holsters – the 3rd Carabiniers continued their wartime tradition in this respect – and some wear an absolute minimum.

The 1960s saw the general introduction of name tabs on the left breast of the various khaki-green overalls worn by armoured cavalry units, in either black on white or black on green. Regiments also vary in their ranking practice. In some, officers wear simple cloth ranking on slip-overs; in others, metal ranking and shoulder-titles are worn on combat dress. NCOs' ranking is generally white, detachable, and on the right arm only.

The old 1943 'zoot suit' was often used in cold weather in the 1950s and 1960s; drivers seem to have had a priority in its issue. With the introduction of better cold-weather clothing – sweaters for use under overalls, and parkas for use over them – its use has almost ceased; but in the late 1960s RTR crews were still wearing it over the black overalls on winter exercises.

Regiments serving in the Mediterranean areas – when Britain still had local training facilities and defence commitments there – wore regulation khaki drill shirts and shorts or slacks; in the Far East tropical shirtsleeve uniform, of a lightish grey-green tone after a few washes, is universal. 'Tribal items' such as RTR white tank arm badges, regimental tallies and lanyards, etc, have normally been worn on these local uniforms, together with appropriate formation patches such as the black spitting cat on a yellow square of the Singapore garrison, or the Hong Kong garrison patch of a gold oriental dragon facing to the left on a rectangle horizontally divided red-black-red.

In some regiments officers have been allowed or encouraged to wear regimentally coloured sidecaps in the vehicle, but this is not common. One example is the 'tent hat' of the QRIH, which is sometimes seen in the turret of vehicles on exercise. A more modern headgear is the new glass fibre 'bone dome' helmet, with sophisticated communications equipment, which is worn by crews of Scorpions and, at the time of writing, was being introduced to the first Chieftain MBT regiments. It may be general RAC issue in time.

In the 1950s-60s one occasionally saw photos of tank crews wearing the khaki-green two-piece combat fatigue outfit then worn by the Army as a whole. Today, one sometimes sees photos of crews wearing the current combat suit of DPM camouflage. These cases are rare, and today usually occur when photos of the inside of a new vehicle are taken and a crew of nearby squaddies is shoved into it to give the internal arrangement and equipment some scale and meaning!

United States

The crews of the Chaffee, Sherman, Pershing and Patton tanks which fought in the Korean War of 1950-53 do not seem to have retained the tanker's windcheater in any significant numbers. The normal outfits were one- or two-piece herringbone twill fatigue overalls, in a grey-green tone of olive drab; the two-piece combat fatigues worn by the Army as a whole, with their four-pocket thigh-length jacket and plain trousers in greenish OD; and a range of special winter clothing. In summer the fatigues or overalls were worn alone; in winter, following the 'layering principle', they were still worn but with a range of sweaters, button-in pile liners, etc, underneath, and with a heavily lined three-quarter length parka with a fur-trimmed hood over the top. The Second World War pierced-skull tank crash helmet was still widely worn. Normal cloth headgear were the peaked OD fatigue cap in summer; and a pile-lined version with ear- and neck-piece folding down, or tying up over the crown, in winter. Insignia of rank were often pinned to the underside of the front peak, which was worn folded up vertically much of the time (see accompanying photos).

In the late 1950s and 1960s the standard GI combat fatigues, with seasonal additions, remained

Crewmen and fitters prepare M-26 Pershing tanks of the 73rd Medium Tank Battalion for action near Munsan-ni, Korea, March 1952. The crews wear wartime helmets, twill overalls (note large thigh pockets, not a feature of the normal green combat fatigues) and fur-trimmed parkas (US Army).

the normal crew dress when serving in the vehicle. The pierced-skull helmet was retained for many years with updated communications gear, such as the addition of a wire mike-boom to the right cheek flap.

In their next war, Vietnam, the tankers continued to wear GI fatigues, though of the special tropical variety. Still in a green shade of OD, these were designed for wear in humid climates and had, supposedly, a 'quick-drying' capability. The fatigue jacket now had pockets with slanted edges, designed to make access easier when wearing full web harness – an improvement enjoyed by US paratroops in the Second World War, but not granted to the infantryman and tanker for 20 years. Insignia of rank and formation patches were normally worn in cloth, in 'subdued' styles of black on green, on these fatigues. There were some exceptions – see the example on Colour Plate 7. Two other items of equipment were typical of the Vietnam War tanker: the 'flak jacket' or fragmentation vest, very widely worn by exposed commanders, and the new glass fibre tanker's 'bone dome' tank helmet, with built-in earphone shells

Flameproof Combat Vehicle Crew (CVC) suit, under development for the US Army by NARADCOM in November 1977; and the new commander's helmet (US Army).

and mike-boom, which was issued during the mid-1960s. The normal cloth headgear was a small-brimmed, floppy bush-hat in OD cloth.

(Some **Australian** tankers also served in Vietnam with Centurion tanks. Jungle green fatigues were worn, sometimes including the small bush-hat; shirts were of 'safari' type, and were worn either inside or outside the trousers. Black British-style berets with silver badges were normally worn in the front line. Boots were either black leather, or US canvas and leather jungle style; both were calf-length and laced high.)

American tankers today wear the general issue combat fatigues, with cold weather additions such as hooded parkas. There is a one-piece flame-resistant overall for vehicle crews under development, which may be general issue by the time this book is published; a photo accompanies this chapter. A new type of crash helmet has also been in use since the mid-1970s, and is shown in photos in this chapter; initially it seems to have been issued to commanders of vehicles only. Finally, it has been observed since about 1973 that some US tankers – apparently on a unit basis – have been wearing a black, British-style beret. This bit of 'flash' may have been authorised in the immediate aftermath of the change-over from a conscript to a volunteer

army: US paratroops in Germany adopted a maroon beret at about the same time. Photos show the black beret worn without insignia, and with officer's insignia of rank. Whether enamelled regimental crests are ever worn on it is unclear.

France

In the Indo-China War of 1946-54, French tank crews wore the same motley collection of French, British and US tropical combat fatigues as the rest of their army. By 1950 this was becoming a little more standardised, and the French fatigues were widely worn in the field – although not universally, as a photo in this chapter shows. The French fatigues were of a jungle green shade which washed and faded grey-green. The jacket was crotch-length, with a wide open, stepped collar with notably long upper points. There were four patch pockets with pointed flaps and concealed buttons, and plain shoulder straps. The jacket could be worn either over or tucked into the trousers, next to the skin or over a shirt. The trousers were baggy, and had two large patch pockets with 'bellows' sides on the outside of the thighs, the bottom edges just above the knee. They were often bloused and gathered at the ankle. Laced leather ankle boots of black or brown, US two-buckle combat boots, and olive canvas 'sneakers' with black rubber soles and welts were all worn.

Headgear comprised a mixture of cloth bush-hats of sandy drill or the same shade as the fatigues, with tapes to tie the sides of the brim up; large berets of a pale sandy drill shade, normally pulled down on the left, worn sometimes without insignia, sometimes with a variety of metal badges including the prewar helm and cannons device; and regimental sidecaps in various colours. Ranking practice remained as in the Free French forces in 1944-45 – officers usually wore rank stripes round the end of the shoulder straps, and NCOs wore short diagonals on tabs fixed to the front closure of the jacket or shirt.

In the Algerian War of 1954-61 this general picture continued, with the green fatigue suit being normal dress when in the vehicle. The bush-hat was rarely worn by armoured crews in this campaign. The tank and armoured car crews wore the regimental sidecaps; the sandy coloured beret; and, increasingly as the war continued, a beret of midnight blue pulled down on the left with a new silver cap badge for the whole branch – an open, pierced circle containing a new version of the helm and cannons badge, with the helm full face. A crash helmet illustrated during these years, in use by crews of both armoured cars and tanks, seems to have been derived from the US wartime model.

The ventilated skull was identical, but the cheek and neck pieces had gone. A very shallow leather strip protected the base of the skull, falling only as far as the level of the earlobe, and forked leather chinstraps replaced the cheek pieces.

In both these wars the armoured car crews of the Foreign Legion wore their white képis whenever practical. In Algeria a sandy drill cover was normally worn over the képi for operations in the field, those of officers being cut out at the front to show their gold grenade badge and a section of the rank stripes round the top edge. In the last years of the war the dark green beret, first introduced for Legion paratroopers, began to spread to all Legion units for field wear. Legion armoured car crews were photographed wearing this in Algeria, with a silver badge bearing their seven-flame grenade in an open circular rim. (In Indo-China it had not been unknown for Legion armour to wear a large beret, apparently of white cotton; a photo exists of the crew of an M8 75 mm self-propelled howitzer so dressed, but the Legion was always a law unto itself and this may have been a strictly local practice.) The dark green and blue *REC* side-cap certainly survived into the early 1950s.

The French armoured regiments of the 1970s still wear the same two-piece green fatigue uniform as the rest of the army. This is now a new

The M-24 Chaffee of Capitaine Darmane, OC 5th Squadron, 1ᵉ Chasseurs à cheval, photographed in Indo-China, 1952. The commander, with binoculars, wears three silver chevrons of rank on the front of his sidecap, which in this branch was light blue with a madder-red gusset. He wears the US field jacket M1941. The trooper second from left, in the US helmet, has the regimental badge on a fob from his breast pocket button. The rest of the crew (mixed French-Vietnamese: most regiments were forced to recruit some personnel locally by this date) wear a motley collection of khaki and green fatigue clothing, and webbing equipment of British and US origin (ECPA).

outfit, of superior material and cut. It is worn with the jacket outside the trousers, which are of much slimmer cut than in the 1950s. The stepped collar is still of notably broad outline, with long upper points. Pale khaki drill shirts, or olive pullovers with fall collars, are both worn under it, with their collars falling outside. The jacket, elasticated at the waist, has concealed breast pockets reached by two vertical zips down their inner edges. There is a fly front, and two internal skirt pockets with straight flaps, clipped at the corners, and with concealed fastenings. The trouser thigh pockets are still present but are of much slimmer outline. Knees and elbows are reinforced with doubling. Rank is still worn on shoulder loops for officers and frontal tabs for NCOs – the latter are now fixed with Velcro, as are the name tabs which are generally worn on the upper right chest, in black lettering on white. Photos of exercises in the 1970s show that coloured divisional patches are occasionally worn on the right shoulder of the fatigue jacket.

The helmet described above appears in photographs of both armoured car and AMX-30 tank crews in the 1960s, but has generally been replaced by a new type. This retains the plain 'bowl' shape, very similar to the British wartime RAC and paratroop helmets but more tightly fitting. The unventilated skull has a small cut-out in the rim on each side level with the ear, and into these fit the upper curves of large oval earphone shells, free-mounted on the strapping of the helmet and slanting forward and down at an angle. A small strip of extra plate is still fitted under the rear rim, extending down to cover the base of the skull. The helmet is made of a fibre compound, and painted khaki-green. A wire microphone boom extends forward from the right earphone shell. Large single-lens goggles, similar to US wartime models, are issued with a variety of clear or tinted lenses. A 'plastron' or plastic junction box for earphone and microphone jacks is worn on the centre of the chest on khaki fabric straps which pass from its upper corners back over each shoulder, down the back of the shoulder, forward under each arm, and join the lower corners of the box. Helmet and goggles have heavy khaki web straps; all cables and plugs are black, and the junction box is grey-green.

The midnight blue (in practice, black) beret, with the circular pierced silver helm-and-cannons badge over the right ear, is now standard among all French armoured regiments – except, of course, the Legion! The 1st Foreign Cavalry still wear their distinctive green berets with silver grenade badges, and exchange these for képis whenever possible, and for all parades in the vehicles.

French armour crews wear light brown leather belts and holsters, and MAT 49 magazine pouches in the same material – the MAT 49 is the standard crew weapon, and the automatic pistol is worn by the commander of the vehicle. The French holster has a very broad, deep rectangular flap held down by a strap.

Federal Germany

Three outfits may be observed among Bundeswehr tank and AFV crews when serving with the vehicle: the tank suit, the standard Army combat fatigues, and the shirtsleeve order in summer. With all these outfits the usual headgear for all ranks is a beret. Up until the end of the 1960s all crews wore a light brown beret with a national cockade above grey crossed sabres, embroidered on a brown cloth patch, as the badge. This is illustrated on Colour Plate 8. Since about 1970 battle tank crews have worn instead a black beret with a metal badge, similar in general appearance to the Second World War Panzer Assault badge, though with a modern tank going from right to left – a photo in this chapter shows this. The brown beret and cockade-and-sabres badge are retained by APC and SP gun crews.

The fatigue suit is in grey-green, of a greener shade than wartime *feldgrau*. It consists of a thigh-length single-breasted jacket, and narrowly cut trousers, with calf-length black boots – for tank men, usually laced paratrooper-style. (Some examples of the unlaced marching boot may be seen.) The jacket has shoulder straps, an open stepped collar over which the shirt collar is often folded, and pleated patch breast pockets with pointed flaps with concealed fastenings. The jacket has a fly front. The trousers have conventional slash side pockets; below these on both outer thighs, the tops level with the crotch, are two patch pockets. The trousers are issued in summer and winter weights. Photos from the 1960s show the winter trousers with pleated, pointed-flap thigh pockets; more recent photos of summer trousers show unpleated thigh pockets with straight flaps. Whether the difference is one of time, or season, or both, is obscure. The shirt worn in summer has an open stepped collar, shoulder straps, plain patch pockets with straight flaps clipped at the corners, and green plastic buttons down the front and on pocket and shoulder. Both jacket and shirt bear at the top of each sleeve a small black/red/yellow national flag.

This flash also appears on both sleeves of the tank suit. Of grey-green material, this has a fly-zip down the front, two horizontal zip fastenings for internal chest pockets high on each side, an elasticated waist, no shoulder straps, and a flap

Bundeswehr Leopard tank crewman making use of a means of communication of a rather earlier age of warfare, during Exercise 'Reforger', 1974. Note tank badge in dull white metal on the black beret; the Alpenjäger insignia is 'liberated' or traded from an Alpine unit which this tank brigade was operating during the exercise (Digby Smith).

across the back high on the shoulderblades concealing a handle for hauling casualties out of their turrets.

On the tank suit ranking is worn on printed cloth patches on both upper arms below the national flash by all ranks. On the shirt and fatigue jacket officers wear ranking on shoulder strap slip-overs, as do senior NCOs, and junior NCOs wear stripes on the upper arms. The emblems of officers' rank are in the form of grey diamond-shaped pips; one, two and three identify company officers, and one, two and three with the lower or outer pip in a horseshoe of oakleaves mark the three field ranks. Senior NCOs have shoulder strap *Tresse* in the wartime style but in 'old gold', or bronze. The *Unteroffizier* wears an open-ended shoulder strap shape; *Stabsunteroffizier* has a closed shape. *Feldwebel* and *Oberfeldwebel* have one and two small inward or upward-pointing chevrons at the lower or outer end of the strap. The *Hauptfeldwebel* has a squared loop shape with 'tails', like an *Odalrune*; this loop with one or two chevrons beneath it identifies *Stabsfeldwebel* and *Oberstabsfeldwebel*. Junior NCOs wear one, two and three yellow diagonals on the upper sleeves, high at the rear, to identify *Gefreiter*, *Obergefreiter* and *Hauptgefreiter*.

Pink is still the *Waffenfarbe* of tank troops, and red that of the artillery. A narrow loop of these shades appears round the outer end of the shoulder straps of fatigue jackets and shirts.

Colour Plate 8 illustrates the tank suit, with senior NCO ranking.

Holland

Dark olive green tank suits are worn by Dutch crews; see Colour Plate 8. The headgear is a black beret, with silver badge. This represents St George and the Dragon, superimposed on a stylised 'W' which in practice looks like a pointed figure '8' on its side. The badge is pinned through a rectangular cloth patch in regimental colours. The 'Hussars van Boreel' have a light blue patch with dark blue side stripes; the 'Hussars of Prince Alexander' have a light blue patch with *ponceau*-red side stripes; and the 'Hussars van Sytzama' have a light blue patch with white side stripes. Light blue cravats are often worn. Ranking is worn on chocolate brown slip-overs on the shoulders. Junior NCOs wear small inward-pointing chevrons – one and two thick yellow chevrons for two classes of Corporal. Sergeants and Sergeant-Majors have gold chevrons – one thick, one thick and one thin, and two thick. Warrant Officers have a gold button-shape. Company officers wear one, two and three silver six-pointed stars, twos and threes arranged side by side and in a triangle point outwards. Field officers wear the same beneath a short gold bar.

Belgium

Photos show olive green tank suits, and also in some cases a two-piece camouflage uniform in green, yellow, black and red-brown, with a hood. Officers seem to wear shoulder strap slip-overs with ranking very similar to Dutch practice. The slip-overs are usually black. Company officers wear one, two and three six-point gold stars, Lieutenants having two side by side, and Captains 'two inside one'. Field officers have a short gold bar below or outside the stars, contrasting with Dutch practice. NCOs seem to wear diagonals, high at the rear, on the upper arms – two, three, four divided into pairs, and three above two, identifying Corporal, Sergeant, First Sergeant and Sergeant-Major. Headgear is a black beret, with regimental badges in silver pinned through coloured patches of heater shield shape.

The badges are of individual regimental design and too varied to describe in detail. The armour is drawn from the traditional branches of service – Guides, Lancers and Chasseurs. The beret patches of these units are respectively amaranth red, white, and a rather orange shade of yellow. Chasseurs wear badges based on crossed sabres points up, a crown, a bugle-horn and a number, with or without scrolls. Lancer badges have crowned crossed lances, wreaths and/or scrolls, numbers and a variety of extra motifs. Guides badges are generally pear-shaped in outline, with side scrolls swelling out and down from a crown and enclosing numbers, crossed swords, thistles, etc.

Italy

The 1st Tank Regiment was reformed on July 10 1948, and renamed 132nd on April 1 1949. Septem-

ber 1948 saw the reformation of the *Ariete* Division, incorporating this regiment; equipment included the Sherman and Firefly, M5 Stuart, and a few old M15/42 tanks. Italy entered NATO in spring 1949 and began receiving newer American equipment including large numbers of M24 Chaffees. *Centauro* was reformed in 1951, incorporating the reborn 31st Tank Regiment; and between 1953 and 1967 there was a third armoured division, *Pozzuolo del Friuli*, subsequently disbanded, the name passing to a cavalry brigade. In 1975 regimental identity was abandoned, and the basic unit became the battalion; these are assembled into tactical brigades and divisions as required.

Apart from the tank battalions in the named divisions, which operate a mixture of M47, M60A1 and Leopard tanks, there are tank units with traditional cavalry identities which are supposedly equipped with Leopards throughout, although this may not yet be entirely true. Collar patches for the *carristi* are still the double scarlet flames on bright blue, currently in the form of small enamelled metal flames pinned to a cloth patch. Cavalry units are listed as follows, with service dress collar insignia: 1st Tank Group *Nizza Cavalleria* – three crimson flames; 2nd Mechanised Group *Piemonte Cavalleria* – three scarlet flames, edged black; 3rd Armoured Group *Savoia Cavalleria* – three black flames; 4th Mechanised Group *Genova Cavalleria* – three lemon yellow flames; 5th Tank Group *Lancieri di Novara* – three white flames; 6th Tank Group *Lancieri di Aosta* – three scarlet flames; 7th Recce Group *Lancieri di Milano* – three crimson flames, edged black; 8th Armoured Group *Lancieri di Montebello* – three green flames edged black; 9th Tank Group *Lancieri di Firenze* – three orange flames, edged black; 12th Recce Group *Cavallegeri di Saluzzo* – three black flames on yellow field; 14th Recce Squadron *Cavalleggeri di Alessandria* – three orange flames on black field; 15th Recce Group *Cavalleggeri di Lodi* – three black flames on red field; 19th Recce Group *Cavalleggeri Guide* – three white flames on bright blue field; 28th Tank Group *Cavalleggeri di Treviso* – three scarlet flames on bright blue field; ('Group' is the battalion-sized unit of cavalry or artillery).

The post-war Italian service uniform is a khaki-brown battledress with an open collar, virtually identical to British 1949 BD, worn with a light khaki shirt and tie, high laced black combat boots (initially, US double-buckle flap type) and pale khaki British-style webbing equipment. In the 1950s the sleeveless brown leather British 'trench jerkin' was often worn in winter. From the early 1960s up to 1977, combat dress was a two-piece suit in camouflage material (illustrated on Colour Plate 8) but in that year a new two-piece suit in a brownish olive shade was introduced. This has a jacket with skirts to crotch length, a fly front with simple fall collar worn open over a shirt or crew-necked sweater, and four large bellows pockets. Those on the chest, tilted out at the top, have a pointed flap with a central snap; the skirt pockets are set vertically, and have straight flaps with snaps at each corner. The waist is noticeably elasticated, and there are plain shoulder straps on which ranking is worn in the form of lighter khaki slip-overs. A small white five-point star is always worn on the collar points by all ranks – both on the camouflage and olive-coloured combat dress. Headgear is a black beret with hanging tapes, or the US wartime leather tank crash helmet with new communications fittings including a microphone mouthpiece on a wire 'spring' from the right side. The black leather coat is still worn in cold weather over combat dress.

Prior to 1975 the branch cap badge (of wartime pattern apart from the removal of the Royal crown) was worn centrally, and a ranking insignia was worn over the left eye by officers and warrant officers; at about that time the ranking disappeared

Italian Leopard tank commander of 19th Recce Group 'Cavalleggeri Guide', June 1977. The US wartime tank helmet has an added mike-boom. The brownish-olive combat jacket has white stars on each collar point, obscured here. The regimental scarf, worn bandana-style, is halved light blue and white (Furio Lorenzetti).

and the branch badge, now surrounded by a ring instead of being in cut-out silhouette, moved to the left. Ranking remained as in the Second World War until the early 1970s. In about 1973-75 the lengthways bars of the grades of *maresciallo* and the senior Warrant Officer grade of *aiutante* became gold bars worn across the butt of the shoulder strap – gold edged black for the three grades of *maresciallo*, and three gold bars and a star edged red for an *aiutante*. Field officers lost the gold edging to their shoulder straps and acquired instead a gold 'mural crown' device at the end – eg, Lieutenant-Colonels wear a crown and two stars. NCO chevrons remain as in the Second World War, in yellow and black. Divisional insignia would sometimes be seen on the left upper arm of the service dress of crews parading in their vehicles in the 1950s, and on summer shirtsleeve order since then, under the same conditions – they have not generally been displayed on the camouflage or olive combat suits. They take the form of 'heater' shields, divided diagonally with blue at top right, red at bottom left. Edged in gold, they bear a gold centaur pulling a bow and prancing to the left (*Centauro*) and a gold ram's head in left profile (*Ariete*).

The different units listed above, and the tank regiments of the *carristi* proper, wear coloured scarves with combat dress. These are in the colour of the collar flames. When a unit has flames edged in a second colour, or on a field of a second colour, then the scarf is halved. Sometimes – probably according to unit tradition or commander's taste – these scarves are worn tied at the back, with an unbroken triangle of material showing at the throat, like a cowpuncher's bandana; the colour division then shows straight down the centre of the cloth, with the main (flame) colour always on the wearer's right. Sometimes a more normal 'ascot' folding is used, the rolled and tied scarf giving the front 'tail' an unbroken area of main flame colour.

Units of many types include some armour on their establishment, including marines, border police and infantry; in these cases only that part of the unit actually equipped with armour wear the black beret, with their own cap badge. The Armoured Artillery Regiment wear tank crew combat dress in their SP guns, including the black coat, with the Second World War pattern steel helmet.

The Warsaw Pact

The following notes are inevitably fairly general; the available photographs are posed and released and captioned entirely according to the requirements of propaganda, and interpretation is therefore a little hit-and-miss.

The Soviet Union

Shortly after 1945 a dark tank overall began to return, gradually replacing the various khaki wartime models. It seems to have appeared in both dark blue and black, and to have been very similar to the prewar pattern: a one-piece suit with a fly front, and single left breast and right front thigh pockets. The leather coat which had appeared in 1944-45 remained in service until about the early 1960s.

The black canvas tank helmet now has earphones in all cases, and throat microphones whose strap yoke may often be seen in photos hanging loose on the soldier's chest. The fleece-lined version with deeper cheek and neck-flaps continues to be issued in winter. In recent years it has become common to see the turret number of the tank painted, during exercises at least, along the front horizontal pad of the helmet in white or coloured digits.

During the late 1960s or early 1970s a new two-piece tank uniform appeared, and is now almost universal to judge from photos. In heavy black (or occasionally, dark grey) cloth, it has a straight-cut blouse which falls to just below the hips, and baggy trousers gathered at the ankle over the usual soft black leather boots. The jacket has a plain fall collar, a fly front, a deep hem, buttoned wrist-bands, and three pockets: an internal left breast pocket with a flap slanting up and outwards, and two internal rib pockets at waist level, with vertical openings level with the front of the arms. The trousers seem to have thigh pockets with straight flaps on the outside of each leg, the flap just visible below the blouse hem. A winter version of the suit is warmly and bulkily lined, and has a fall collar faced with pile or fleece, in black or dark grey.

Photos do not show any field ranking on the black suit. For parades and posed exercise photos, everyday shoulder boards in branch colours and lace are attached. For tank troops and armoured artillery these are basically black, with gold 'CA' cyphers for Privates; one, two and three thin gold stripes, one thick gold stripe, and one thick gold lengthways stripe, for NCOs. Warrant Officers have boards of black glazed thread with a checkered effect, and one or two gold stars. Officers have the usual gold lace and red cloth boards, with stars in ranking sequence, as described under the 1943 regulations; only the shape has changed, losing the button and acquiring a wedge-ended shape at the neck end, the long point at the back.

The upper left arm patch identifying the branch is sometimes seen on the suit, taken from the everyday uniform. This is a black shield with a broad gold rim, with a gold three-quarter-front

A Red Army field officer of tank troops leading a parade in the early 1950s. The black three-quarter length leather coat worn from the 1940s to 1960s has been 'badged up' for the occasion with parade shoulder boards in gold lace and red, and black greatcoat collar tabs piped red. The star of a Hero of the Soviet Union is worn on the left breast (Zdenek Bryna).

view of a tank at the bottom and a red star above this. Shield-shaped enamelled proficiency badges may also be seen on parade, with ornate outlines; they are basically gold, with a gold hammer and sickle on a red disc in a white ring in the upper part, above a gold stylised tank in profile.

Crews of SP guns and APCs also wear tank clothing and helmets, and may wear parade additions as described above. Colour Plate 8 shows an APC commander with the Motor Rifle branch parade straps and patch.

Officers sometimes wear Sam Brownes and holsters. Men often wear no belts; sometimes, a broad leather belt with a rectangular brass plate bearing a star badge.

Grey pile caps may be worn in winter when away from the vehicle.

Poland

All the European satellite countries received black or brown Soviet tank helmets and the cast-off wartime Soviet khaki tank suits, or manufactured their own copies, in the 1950s. In the last decade national differences have appeared. The suit currently worn by Polish tank units is the most striking of these.

It consists of a black leather two-piece uniform: a bulky waist-length jacket, and trousers baggy in the thigh but tapered to the ankle. The jacket appears in summer and lined winter weights, the latter having a brown fleece collar facing, and the former having a plain fall collar. There is a fly front, and a broad waist-band with a short integral belt in the style of British battledress, fastened with a steel frame buckle just to the right of the front closure. There are prominent horizontal seams across the chest and back midway down the shoulder, and a vertical central seam at the back from the horizontal seam down to the waist-band. There are two internal chest pockets, the left having an external flap slanted up and out, the right having a straight flap. There is a large pocket on the outside of the right thigh, its straight flap fastened, like those on the chest, with snaps at both corners. The boots are brown, reaching the top of the ankle, laced on the instep and with a buckled flap at the ankle, rather similar to US wartime combat boots. The jacket has shoulder straps in black, on which stylised ranking is worn. Junior NCOs have two to four thin silver transverse stripes. Senior NCOs and Warrant Officers have silver edging round the pointed shoulder straps, except across the butt end, and outward-pointing chevrons on the face of the strap. Representative examples are: two chevrons; two chevrons inside one stripe; one chevron outside a star; four stars. Company officers have straps without edging, with one to four stars. Field officers have two stripes across the outer end of the strap, and one to four stars.

Czechoslovakia

In the 1950s-1960s, a grey-brown drab overall was extensively photographed. This had a fall collar, a buttoned front, and four patch pockets with or without flaps on both sides of the chest and both thigh fronts. Boots were as for Polish crews, described above. Belts were brown leather with a rectangular brass plate. Helmets, in the 1950s and early 1960s, seem to have been of obsolete Soviet brown leather style, in summer and lined winter weights.

In the 1970s Czech crews have acquired a black suit very similar to that worn by Soviet tank troops, and the black helmet. A small black rectangular patch is worn on the right breast, with ranking attached. One, two and three dull silver buttons, arranged vertically, identify junior NCOs. Senior NCOs have one to three stars, in the latter case arranged two in a vertical row and one centrally to the right. 'Ensigns' wear top and bottom edging to the patch, in grey braid, and one to three grey stars arranged horizontally. Company officers wear one to four gold stars; Captains, for instance, have two arranged one above the other and two arranged in a line, centrally on the right of the

vertical pair. Field officers have yellow braid top and bottom, and one to three gold stars arranged horizontally.

East Germany

In summer, DDR tank crews seem to wear the camouflage suit worn as combat fatigues by the rest of their army. This is a two-piece outfit in a grey-green shade with a vertical 'rain' pattern in dark brown. It has an open stepped collar, internal breast pockets with straight flaps, and a straight flap with two corner snaps on each upper arm. Ranking shoulder straps are attached to this suit. They are of field grey for enlisted ranks, with drab greenish piping round the edge, and for senior NCOs an inner edging of *Tresse* in grey glazed braid. This *Tresse*, and the grey pips of ranks from Sergeant-Major upwards, follow Second World War styles very closely. Officers have drab silver-grey copies of wartime shoulder straps, identical apart from the field grey and drab green underlay and piping. In all cases ranks with two pips have them arranged side by side across the outer end of the strap. The black Soviet-style helmet is worn.

Hungary

Today Hungarian crews wear a two-piece uniform in drab khaki-green. The jacket reaches below the hips, and has four internal pockets; the breast pockets have zipped openings slanted slightly down and inwards, the rib pockets have openings at an angle of about 50 degrees. The jacket has plain shoulder straps to which ranking is added. NCOs have one, two and three bronze stars, the threes arranged in a triangle. Senior NCOs have one, two and three stars inside a gold stripe. Warrant Officers wear one thin inside one thick gold stripe. Sub-lieutenants have a single star on a lengthways strip of gold braid, centrally. Other company grades have one to three stars arranged vertically, and field officers one to three stars on a wide lengthways strip of gold braid with a pointed inner end reaching the button. Winter jackets have grey fleece collar facing and thick lining. The helmet is the black Soviet type; boots are the lace-and-double-buckle Polish type, in brown.

Rumania

Current dress is a very plain dark grey one-piece overall with fly front, fall collar, no visible pockets, and rank shoulder boards at least in the case of officers. These are of Russian style, but with squared inner ends with rounded corners. They are of gold lace, with black piping, and stripes and gold stars of rank in the Soviet sequence; a silver tank symbol is worn between button and ranking.

Bulgaria

Crews of tanks and other armoured fighting vehicles apparently wear a grey two-piece suit. The jacket, hip-length, has about six exposed front buttons and two patch breast pockets with straight buttoned flaps. The cuffs and waist have doubled bands; and there are shoulder straps on which Soviet-style ranking is worn. Representative examples are three red stripes across the outer end, for a Senior Sergeant; one central lengthways stripe with three silver stars in a triangle, for a Lieutenant; and two thinner lengthways stripes with a star on the outer end of each, for Lieutenant-Colonel. The winter suit has a brown fleece collar facing; the helmet is black, Soviet-style. Some locally made helmets seem to differ in having only the padded rolls which run from front to back, without the cross-wise brown pad.

The Middle East
Israel

The rag-tag of British, French and Russian equipment used in very small numbers by the Israelis in their 1948 War of Independence was crewed by an equally motley collection of soldiers. Shirt-sleeve order and loose slacks were the normal wear, in many shades of pale khaki drill, British khaki, and olive green. Headgear included black berets without insignia, US steel helmets, British RAC steel helmets, and Russian tank helmets.

By the 1967 War the Armoured Corps had become a properly disciplined force. Normal combat dress

Cheerful Israeli AMX-13 crew photographed in 1967 wearing a mixture of French camouflage jackets and light khaki drill shirts, with the US wartime tank helmet.

was a shirt and trousers of olive green (similar to British 'jungle green'), a black beret pulled down on the right, and black boots laced high. The shirt had an open, stepped collar, shoulder straps, and patch breast pockets with straight flaps. Sleeves were invariably worn rolled above the elbow. The tight-cut trousers were tucked into the boots; they had two pockets at the front of the hips expanded by 'bellows' gussets. In the vehicle the US Second World War tank helmet was worn, with a wire microphone boom extending round to the face from the right cheek piece. An olive green peaked field cap was quite widely worn in the desert; of soft cloth, it was basically similar to the US fatigue cap but sloped down from back to front rather markedly, and had a peak-binding in lighter, browner khaki tape. No badge was worn on this cap. The beret badge is of dull bronze, and shows the left profile of a tank, above a scroll, superimposed on an open, circular wreath; it is worn pinned through a patch of scarlet cloth.

Insignia was, and is, limited to ranking. NCOs wear white tape bars on the upper arm, sloping diagonally from high at the front to low at the back. One, two, three, and three with a superimposed bronze fig-leaf are worn by Senior Privates, Corporals, Sergeants and Staff Sergeants respectively. On combat dress officers wear ranking in the form of grass-green cloth shapes on a pale khaki drill slip-over on both shoulder straps. Company officers wear one, two and three transverse bars; field officers wear one, two and three fig-leaves.

Webbing is of mixed origin; tank troops rarely wear more than a British, French or US belt and a British or Belgian webbing holster, and a US canteen. The normal crew weapon is the Uzi sub-machine-gun, carried by all personnel, who fight as infantry if 'dismounted'.

A few photos show a minority of tank crews in 1967 wearing an olive green one-piece tank suit with a very low standing collar closing from left to right with a small tab. It had a central zip from throat to crotch, horizontal zips closing two internal chest pockets, zipped thigh pockets on the front of each leg, and a flap across the shoulderblades covering a strap for hauling casualties out of the tank. There were cloth shoulder straps on which officers wore ranking slip-overs.

By the 1973 Yom Kippur War Israeli tank crews seem to have been universally issued with another tank suit, possibly of US manufacture. This was also olive green, but had a fall collar; most noticeable differences from the first type were zipped chest pockets slanting downwards and inwards. The US 'bone dome' tank helmet was also general issue by 1973; of light greenish khaki fibreglass, it has black rubber edging, and wire and plastic microphone equipment. Suit and helmet are both illustrated in the accompanying photos and colour paintings. The beret, peaked field cap, and insignia are unchanged from those described above.

A final comment on general appearance: while yielding to nobody in his admiration of the professional excellence of the Israeli army, the author must point out that the Israeli soldiers he saw in considerable numbers in 1968, from frontier positions in Kuneitra to the cafes of Dizengoff Street, were quite the most aggressively sloppy looking articles that ever gave a Sergeant-Major nightmares!

Egypt

The combat dress of Egypt's weak armoured units in the 1948 War of Israeli Independence seems to have comprised a one-piece denim overall in sandy-coloured khaki drill, a green beret worn without a badge, and British 1937 webbing belts and gaiters scrubbed off-white. NCO chevrons were British in design, and were supposed to be in branch colour – yellow for the armoured cavalry – but may have been plain white on combat overalls. The author has found no pictorial evidence for this uniform, which is taken entirely from written descriptions, and cannot vouch for its accuracy.

Since the 1952 revolution which brought Egypt under Soviet influence the black canvas tank helmet of Russian design and manufacture has been worn by all armoured crews. Combat dress is the same for all branches except certain élite commando units. Since 1955 it has comprised a shirt worn hanging loose outside trousers, both in a very pale sandy drill material. A soft peaked field cap in the same material, shaped like a US Army fatigue cap but rather lower in the crown and sloping slightly from back to front at the top, is also virtually universal in the field. The shirt is straight at the bottom and has an open, stepped collar, two patch breast pockets with straight flaps, and shoulder straps. The trousers are worn straight and loose to the instep and in some, but not all, cases have a large pocket with a straight flap on the front of the right thigh. Officers have better quality uniforms and stiffened caps – see Colour Plate 7 – but are otherwise hard to distinguish from their men. Study of a significant number of photos has failed to turn up a single example of NCO chevrons worn on combat dress, but this is of course inconclusive. Officers wear ranking on the shoulder straps: gilt five-point stars and gilt eagles with folded wings, in the British sequence – one, two and three stars for company officers, an eagle for Majors, an eagle with one or two stars for Lieutenant-Colonels and Colonels. No cap insignia are normally worn in the field. Webbing is minimal, and usually takes the form of British 1937-pattern belts, possibly with Russian pouches and holsters. Personal kit is carried in Russian olive green webbing haversacks. The traditional *djellabah* or desert robe, of generously loose cut and in a variety of combinations of brown and grey striped thinly with black and white, is often carried in the field in place of a greatcoat for wear on cold nights. Drab khaki wool sweaters are worn in cool weather, usually beneath the loose shirt. Copies of the US water canteen are widely carried on the belt.

Photos recently published of a Cairo parade in October 1978 show T-54 crews in a dark olive green shirtsleeve uniform, with black Soviet tank helmets, black 'paratrooper' boots, dark olive web belts of US style and pale sandy web holsters on the left hip.

Syria

Photos of Syrian troops are even rarer than those of Egyptians, and the author can only offer a few general notes. In the 1967 and 1973 wars and the Lebanon intervention, Syrian tank crews seem to have worn the Russian black canvas tank helmet almost exclusively. The cloth headgear for the whole army since the early 1970s is a soft olive green field cap with a peak, much like the Egyptian and Cuban style. The use of black tank suits of Russian manufacture in the 1967 war is suggested by one Israeli description of combat on the Golan Heights. Colour photos of T-55s and T-62s since then have shown both black overalls and khaki ones in use; the latter are a greyish-brown drab and may perhaps be of Czech manufacture, given that country's role as chief exporter for the Warsaw Pact? Poor photos suggest that the khaki and black overalls may both be worn even within a single crew. The normal combat uniform is olive green, consisting of a two-pocket shirt with open collar and shoulder straps and a pair of straight slacks falling unconfined over black boots. Ranking for officers is virtually indistinguishable from Egyptian styles, and is worn on the shoulder straps. NCO ranking is in the form of large British-type chevrons in white. Senior ranks wear three, and three with a star beneath, point upwards. Junior ranks wear two, point up; two, point down, and one, point down. Written regulations specify grey backing for armoured units, but it is very unlikely this appears on combat clothing. The same applies to a cloth shoulder title for armoured troops illustrated in the 1960s – a black arc with white Arabic lettering, worn at the top of the sleeve.

Jordan

The Arab Legion, raised and led by British officers, became the Jordan Arab Army in 1956. Its units still retain a generally British appearance, being much smarter, cleaner, and more 'regimental'-looking than other Arab armies. This superiority is reflected in its performance in combat: it has always been the most formidable of Israel's enemies.

Prior to the mid-1960s the uniform for all branches was a battledress blouse and trousers, worn with sand-coloured British 1937 webbing belts, holsters and gaiters and black ankle boots by armoured units. Winter uniform was in mustard-khaki serge: the blouse had a closed collar, unpleated pockets, and visible buttons, and the trousers lacked the large left thigh pocket of British BD. The summer uniform was identical in cut but of a lighter cloth of pale khaki drill. The tank corps wore, and still wear, a black British-style beret pulled on the right, with the national cap badge in silver – a pierced insignia showing crossed scimitars beneath a Hashemite crown, in a wreath, with script across the centre. For formal parades curved silver script shoulder strap titles were worn. Ranking was British in style; company officers wore one, two and three gold eight-point stars of rather rounded overall shape on the shoulder straps, and field officers wore a gold Hashemite crown, a crown and one star, and a crown and two stars. NCOs wore one, two and three white chevrons of British size and shape. Sometimes these were mounted on brassards, sometimes they were sewn to the uniform.

The three tank regiments wore a yellow cloth patch at the top of each arm; this was square, bearing a green wreath below a red or black crown, and regimental motifs were carried in the centre of the wreath. The 1st Regiment wore crossed lances, the 2nd a hawk, and the 3rd a scorpion.

During the 1960s the uniform changed slowly from khaki to olive green shirtsleeve style, but this process was incomplete by the 1967 War. Both styles were seen in action, and sometimes mixtures – eg, green shirts with khaki drill trousers. The change-over is now virtually complete; but Colour Plate 7 shows a khaki drill shirtsleeve uniform taken from a photo of the early 1970s, so it is probably a mistake to assume complete consistency. Insignia and webbing are unchanged.

Southern Africa

South of the Sahara there are only two significant armoured organisations in Africa: the Cuban expeditionary forces which have installed and/or maintained in power the various black African dictatorships, and the South African Armoured Corps. This, like the rest of the Republic's forces, is largely composed of national servicemen around a hard core cadre of regulars and instructors. The 1st Special Service Battalion is the only armoured unit currently active, and other units have been absorbed into it: eg, the Pretoria Regiment became 'A' Squadron, 1 SSB. The unit's actual strength and equipment is classified at the time of writing. It had, in 1973, five lettered squadrons apart from its headquarters element. Three were based at the Bloemfontein base, one at

(Left) Korporaal, 1 Spesiale Diens-Bataljon, South African army, 1974. (Centre left) South African 1st Lieutenant in bush hat. Both wear the 'neutria' tank suit, and insignia, described in the text. (Centre right and right) Trooper and Major, Rhodesian Armoured Corps, 1978. Both wear the black tank suit worn by regulars, and the black beret with insignia as described in the text (Mike Chappell).

Zeerust ('C' Squadron) and one at Walvis Bay in South-West Africa ('D' Squadron). At that time the author believes that 'A' and 'B' operated the Centurion tank, 'C' the Eland (Panhard) armoured car. There is a strong suggestion that the Eland force has been greatly strengthened in the last five years, as this vehicle is made under licence in the Republic. The distinction between full-time regular units and the very large and active Citizen Force reserve is hard to nail down, especially as the CF provided combat units for the Angolan fighting in 1975/76. The Armoured Corps also includes an APC element; in 1973 this was a squadron of 1 SSB, but again, with the expansion of the APC force and the planned introduction of mechanised infantry units this deployment may have changed. It is worth recording that the links of military co-operation between South Africa and that other beleagured pioneer state, Israel, are close; this may well prove significant in the field of armour procurement.

The South African soldier's combat dress is of a shade known as 'neutria', a sort of light chocolate brown. The SSB wear a tank suit, illustrated in line drawings accompanying this chapter, in this shade. The headgear is the black British-style beret with the regiment's traditional 'protea' cap-badge in silver. Ranking is worn on light khaki drill shoulder strap slip-overs by officers, and on brassards looped over the end of them by NCOs. Junior officers wear one, two and three five-pointed stars, in brass or cloth. Majors wear a pentagonal shape, echoing the shape of Cape Town's 17th century castle. Lieutenant-Colonels and Colonels wear the castle inside one and two stars. Lance-Corporals, Corporals and Sergeants wear large German-style triangular chevrons in white tape on brown; Staff-Sergeants wear three chevrons below a castle. Unit insignia are not worn on combat dress. A short-brimmed, floppy bush-hat similar to current British issue but in 'neutria' is worn by commanders when necessary (ie, when the heat of the veldt and desert starts to cook them alive in the turret).

Rhodesia also has a small Armoured Corps, but little is known about its exact size or equipment. It is currently organised in four sabre squadrons and one headquarters squadron. 1, 2 and 3 Squadrons are composed of national servicemen with a regular cadre; 4 Squadron is entirely regular and is led by the Corps commander, an American Major named Darrell Winkler. Equipment includes some Ferret armoured scout cars; a local development of the Ferret mounting a new and more heavily-armed turret is planned to come into service soon. There are other and heavier armoured fighting vehicles on the inventory, but details

are classified. Several locally-produced APC types and light patrol vehicles, armoured against mines, are being put into series manufacture soon, based on Land Rovers and various other light trucks.

The regulars, at least, wear a black tank suit illustrated herewith; other personnel wear Rhodesian camouflaged shirts and trousers. The headgear is the black British beret; the insignia for all ranks is a badge apparently slightly modified from the buck's-head-and-scroll of the old wartime Southern Rhodesian Armoured Car Company, worn over a strip of red/yellow halved ribbon. Officer's ranking is worn on light KD shoulder strap slip-overs with black capitals 'RHODESIA' across the end; junior officers wear a four-pointed device similar to the British 'pip', and field officers a motif in an open-ended oval wreath; all these are black cut-out silhouettes. Uzi sub-machine-guns are carried as crew weapons. A stable belt is sometimes worn with the camouflage uniform; it has buckles at the front, and is coloured in bands, top to bottom: broad red, broad yellow, thin red, broad yellow, broad red.

Asia

Indian and Pakistani tank crews appear to wear jungle-green shirtsleeve order uniforms, with ranking in British style on the sleeves and on shoulder strap slip-overs. The gold and red stripes illustrated on Colour Plate 4 were retained after independence, into the 1960s at least. Black berets, and green turbans for Sikhs, are still worn; Indian crews use black canvas Russian-style tank helmets in significant numbers.

South-East Asian armies have little armour, apart from the forces of Vietnam. The close of the Vietnam War brought a windfall of US equipment to the Communists, who use it alongside their Russian armour. Olive green shirtsleeve order with black Russian-style tank helmets are normal, but some US tank helmets may have been taken over from ARVN stocks.

Chinese tank crews have used Russian-style clothing since the civil war of the late 1940s. A photo of Communist Chinese tank crews parading with captured Japanese Type 97 tanks in 1952 shows what appear to be brown leather Russian helmets, and black or dark blue Russian overalls tucked into brown knee-boots. More recent photos show Russian helmets in several slightly differing styles, and overalls of a range of khaki shades – a colour photo of today's tank crews shows a wide variety of colour tones within a single company. In cold weather, such as they faced in the Korean War, two-piece drab khaki quilted uniforms were worn with the Russian helmet.